Golfwatching

A Viewer's Guide to the World of Golf

Golfwatching

A Viewer's Guide to the World of Golf

By George Peper
Editor-in-Chief, *GOLF Magazine*

Photographs by the PGA Tour Staff Photographers,
John Johnson, and Others

Instructional Tips and Drawings by Jim McQueen
Drawings of Course Holes By Ron Ramsey
Computer-generated Art by Trevor Johnston
Statistics Compiled by David Barrett

HARRY N ABRAMS INC PUBLISHERS

Table of Contents

Project Director: Margaret L. Kaplan

Designer: Larry Hasak

Photo Editor: John K. Crowley

Library of Congress Cataloging-in-Publication Data
Peper, George. Golfwatching: a viewer's guide to the world of golf / by George Peper. p. cm.

Includes index. ISBN 0-8109-3385-3
1. Golf —Tournaments.   I. Title.
GV970.p37 1995
796.352'6 — dc20   94-42152

Published in 1995 by
Harry N. Abrams, Incorporated, New York A Times Mirror Company

ENDPAPERS:
18th Hole at Atlanta Country Club

HALF TITLE:
18th hole at Olympic Country Club

TITLE:
The Ryder Cup

CONTENTS PAGE:
Greg Norman tees off during the PGA Grand Slam at Poipu Golf Resort, 1994

THIS PAGE:
15th hole at TPC at River Highlands

Introduction

DURING THE PAST DECADE OR SO, THE GAME OF GOLF has grown and expanded more quickly than at any time since the emergence of Arnold Palmer. And nowhere has this growth been more dramatic or visible than in the arena of professional competition.

In the United States alone, three men's professional tours now crisscross the country with combined schedules of more than 120 tournaments. The main circuit—the PGA Tour—begins in the first week of January and continues without interruption through the end of October. The Senior PGA Tour, which started in 1980 with just two tournaments, has become the biggest success story in modern professional sports, with a year-long schedule of over 40 events. And the Nike Tour, founded in 1990 as the Ben Hogan Tour, a stepping-stone for professionals aspiring to the PGA Tour, today brings a full schedule of competitive golf to dozens of smaller cities across America. Whereas in 1975 the PGA Tour played for prize money of less than $8 million, today the total purse for the three tours is nearly $100 million.

On the women's side, the growth has been equally dramatic. The LPGA Tour, which tottered on the brink of bankruptcy during the mid-1970s, has become the most successful franchise in women's sports, with a current schedule of 40 events and prize money in excess of $20 million.

Concurrent with the growth in America has come a burgeoning of professional golf overseas—in Great Britain and Ireland, Europe and Scandinavia, South Africa, Australia, and the Far East. And whereas the age of expansion in America has failed to produce a single dominant player (our last bona fide superstar was Jack Nicklaus), the foreign tours have spawned a succession of charismatic heroes who have not only conquered their home circuits but also dominated the major events on the world stage. Players such as Seve Ballesteros, Nick Faldo, Greg Norman, and Nick Price have fueled interest in men's golf worldwide, as have the likes of Laura Davies, Helen Alfredsson, and Liselotte Neumann on the ladies' side.

This foreign challenge to the tradition of American supremacy has been witnessed most vividly in the Ryder Cup Matches, the biennial competition between the United States and Europe. For the first half-century's worth of these matches, the foreign team was limited to players from Great Britain & Ireland, with the result that, through 1985, America had dominated the matches with 21 victories, 3 losses, and 1 tie. Since 1985, however, the score stands at 2-2-1.

The result of this challenge has been a rekindling of American interest in international competition. Today, the hottest ticket in golf is the Ryder Cup. Moreover, the last decade has produced a spate of similar events—notably the Dunhill Cup and the Presidents Cup on the men's Tour and the Solheim Cup on the LPGA Tour—that match teams of Americans against teams from other areas of the globe.

However, at the same time that it has expanded, the world of competitive golf has become smaller—through television. And whereas a decade ago golf events were broadcast only by the three major networks—ABC, CBS, and NBC—today the game appears on a plethora of cable stations as well, with coverage over all four days of the competition.

It's little wonder that most of the recent additions to golf's calendar were developed with Nielsen Ratings in mind. Events such as The Skins Game, the Franklin Funds Shark Shootout, and the Wendy's 3-Tour Challenge are examples of that quintessentially American genre, the made-for-television event. In all, the American TV golf schedule now totals just under 1000 hours each year. And that does *not* count The Golf Channel, the cable service that debuted in early 1995, beaming the game into American homes seven days a week, 24 hours a day.

It is thus that a book entitled *Golfwatching* became inevitable. The 81 chapters that follow—on the most significant golf events around the world—are intended as a companion for TV viewers as well as a guide for anyone planning to attend a tournament in person or play golf on one of the tournament courses.

I hope you'll enjoy the book, and find it useful.

George Peper
Grandview, New York
January, 1995

EXPLANATION OF RATING SYSTEMS

"Course Difficulty" and "Prestige" ratings have been computed for each of the 44 tournaments on the PGA Tour (including the four major championships), with all tournaments rated relative to the others. Here is how those numbers were arrived at:

Course Difficulty was calculated using two elements:
- *Average winning score:* Covers the period 1985-94 (or the number of years the current course has been used if less than 10).
- *USGA course rating:* The USGA rating system is based on the score a scratch player is expected to shoot.
- *Overall rating:* A tournament's rank in average winning score counts ⅔, USGA course rating rank counts ⅓.

Prestige was calculated according to field strength and winner quality, and adjusted, when appropriate, by certain plus factors:
- *Field strength:* For PGA Tour events, the average number of players in that year's top 20 on the money list in the field (1985-94). For the major championships and Players Championship, which draw international fields, the average number of players in the current top 30 on the Sony Ranking in the field (1990-94). (The majors and the Players Championship are rated ahead of the rest of the tournaments.)
- *Winner quality:* Based on the period 1970-94. Awards one point each time a tournament is won by a player with one major title, 1½ points for a win by a player with two majors, two points for a win by a player with three or more majors. Total points are divided by 25 (or the number of years a tournament has been held, if less than 25), giving an average per year. For the four majors, a player must have won a different major, or the same major in another year, to get credit.
- *Plus factors:* Additional considerations (such as tradition, course prestige, invitational field) add to a tournament's prestige.

Overall rating: A tournament's rank in field strength counts 50 percent, the winner quality rank counts 35 percent, and the course difficulty rank counts 15 percent. Small adjustments to the overall rating (from one to four places) have been made based on plus factors.

The Mercedes Championship

LA COSTA COUNTRY CLUB

American professional golf gets an elegant kickoff each January when the Tour's royalty convenes at the glitzy La Costa Country Club and Spa in Carlsbad, California. The week begins with a formal dinner and awards ceremony where the previous season's top performers are honored. After that, an exclusive field of players—only those who have won a tournament in the year past—go at each other for four rounds to determine their champion of champions. Indeed, from its inception in 1953 until 1994, this event was known as The Tournament of Champions. Now, with an upscale new sponsor in place, it is the Mercedes Championship.

Since La Costa is a resort, tee times are open to anyone who books into the hotel and spa. Just don't expect to play the course the pros play. The venue for the Mercedes Championship is a "composite"

THE TV HOLES

Expect birdies:
12

Expect bogeys:
Nowhere

Preceding pages:
18th hole at
Muirfield Village
Above: 10th hole
Right: 18th hole

What to Watch For . . .

BEARDS

Since this is the first event after a spell of hibernation, a smattering of players show up sporting the effects of two months without shaving. You'll also notice a few guys packing an inch or two of holiday indulgence around the waistline.

JACKETS AND TIES

This is the only event of the year at which the Tour pros are expected to dress up—well, for one night at least. The PGA Tour hands out its major awards for the previous season at a banquet at La Costa: Leading Money Winner, Rookie of the Year, Player of the Year, and a raft of winners in statistical categories. Originally, it was a black-tie affair; these days, the Tour's happy if no player shows up in jeans.

HAPPY LADIES

For the players' wives, this is the best tournament of the year, because they are given free run of the famed La Costa Spa. This means a hedonistic week of mud packs, massages, saunas, and herbal wraps.

A BIG GAP BETWEEN FIRST AND LAST

Typically at this tournament, last place is 25–30 strokes out of first. Why? There's no cut, so if a player shoots two bad rounds on Thursday and Friday, he can't go away and hide, and if he shoots two more on Saturday and Sunday, his embarrassing total is there for all to see. Also, since this is the first event after the winter layoff, a lot of players are rusty—particularly the ones who qualified by winning tournaments in early months of the previous year and struggled the remainder of the season.

Not Much Metal on the Mantle

It's impossible for a player to make the Mercedes Championship his only career win, but Bobby Mitchell and Mac O'Grady came close. They won only the Mercedes (then called the Tournament of Champions) and the event which qualified them for it.

La Costa Country Club

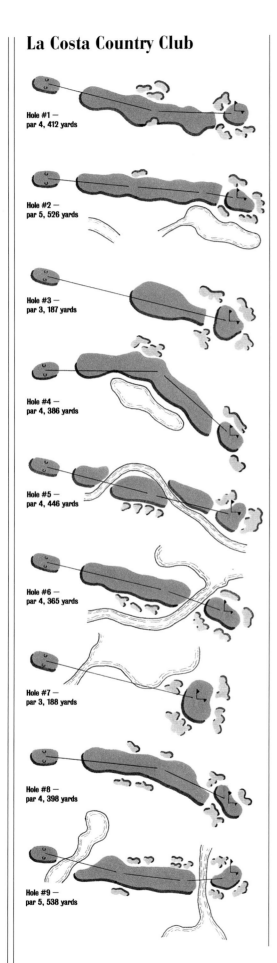

Hole #1 —
par 4, 412 yards

Hole #2 —
par 5, 526 yards

Hole #3 —
par 3, 187 yards

Hole #4 —
par 4, 386 yards

Hole #5 —
par 4, 446 yards

Hole #6 —
par 4, 365 yards

Hole #7 —
par 3, 188 yards

Hole #8 —
par 4, 398 yards

Hole #9 —
par 5, 538 yards

14th hole

course. As at The Country Club near Boston and Australia's famed Royal Melbourne, La Costa's tournament course is made up of the best holes from two contiguous 18–hole layouts. The front nine of the tournament course is comprised of the first three holes and last six holes of La Costa's North Course, while the back nine is the back nine of the South Course.

The tournament invariably comes down to a question of who can prevail over holes 15–18, a finishing stretch known as The Last Mile. The holes are not dauntingly long—three par fours averaging a little more than 400 yards, plus a medium-length par five—but they call for careful shot-

making, and when the pros catch them into the prevailing north wind, this mile can feel like ten miles.

Practical Matters

FOR TICKET INFORMATION
The Mercedes Championship
La Costa Country Club
2100 La Costa Del Mar Road
Carlsbad, CA 92009

COURSE
La Costa Country Club

ACCESS
Two resort courses, open to all hotel guests and La Costa members; all outside play is at the discretion of the Director of Golf.

COURSE RATING

Tees	Pro	Member
Yardage	7022	6257
Rating	75.4	70.3
Slope	142	127

GREEN FEES
$80, including cart
For more information:
(619) 438-9111 ext. 4243

PRO–AM
Spots open to the public? Yes
Handicap: Maximum of 21
Format: Best ball of team
Entry fee: $2500
For more information:
(619) 438-9111 ext. 4612

TOURNAMENT RATINGS

COURSE DIFFICULTY

Avg. winning score: 13.6 under par	21st on Tour
USGA course rating: 75.4 (3.4 over par)	10th on Tour
Overall rating: Moderate	16th on Tour

PRESTIGE

Field strength (9.0)	28th on Tour
Winner quality (.962)	8th on Tour
Course difficulty (above)	16th on Tour
Plus factors: Season opener, winners-only field	
Overall rating	18th on Tour

Local Knowledge

TACTICS FOR OPENING DAY

Whether your season begins in January or June, your first round of the year is a unique challenge. Do yourself a favor, and be ready for it.

The most important preparation is mental: Don't expect much. Remember, your muscle memory has been stretched out on the sofa for a while, so you can't count on your rhythm or coordination to be very sharp—and you should expect a particularly thick layer of rust on your short game and putting. So, if you must have a goal, make it a nonambitious one like "hit some solid shots." Don't aim for a specific score.

Physically, assuming you've been inactive over the winter, you can expect to give your muscles a rude awakening. So lessen the jolt by doing some loosening and stretching—ideally, every day for a week before you play, but minimally a few moments before you tee off.

Once on the course, your best game plan for round one is to keep your swing slow and smooth. On your tee shots, just try to make good contact and put the ball in the fairway; on your approaches, take a club more than you think you need, and swing well within yourself. If you can keep that kind of discipline, you may surprise yourself with a strong debut.

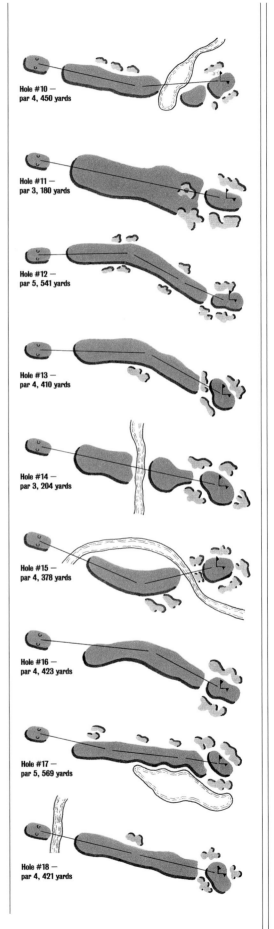

Hole #10 —
par 4, 450 yards

Hole #11 —
par 3, 180 yards

Hole #12 —
par 5, 541 yards

Hole #13 —
par 4, 410 yards

Hole #14 —
par 3, 204 yards

Hole #15 —
par 4, 378 yards

Hole #16 —
par 4, 423 yards

Hole #17 —
par 5, 569 yards

Hole #18 —
par 4, 421 yards

United Airlines Hawaiian Open

WAIALAE COUNTRY CLUB

When big-time tournament golf came to Hawaii in 1965, it came to the Waialae Country Club, Seth Raynor's gem on Oahu, just a few miles down the road from the beach at Waikiki. Thirty years later, scores of courses have sprung up in Paradise, but for the PGA Tour, Waialae is still the place to be.

The telecast of this event beams to more than 20 different countries, and those far-flung viewers are advised not to click off early, no matter what time zone they inhabit, because at Waialae's final hole anything is likely to happen. Named Kilou Loa (Hawaiian for Long Hook), it is a 552-yarder that doglegs left at nearly a right angle. Aggressive tee shots must avoid a clutch of bunkers at the inside of the turn, but after that it's usually straight downwind to the green. The scoring average here is about 4.5, eagles are not uncommon, and the leader often has to finish with a birdie to earn his victory.

Recently, an attempt has been made to stiffen the challenge at Waialae. Fairway bunkers have been added, and grass mounds have been sculpted along the edges of several fairways to improve definition, increase the penalty for errant tee shots, and enhance viewing for the gallery. Fundamentally, however, the biggest threat on this golf course is the northeast tradewinds, which in January can

THE TV HOLES

Expect birdies:

13, 18

Expect bogeys:

Nowhere

16th hole

What to Watch For . . .

EAGLES
With four reachable, relatively unprotected par fives, at least one of them downwind, even the shorter hitters get a few chances at 3. In most years, this tournament yields more eagles than any two events on the mainland.

BAREFOOT BEARERS
Even some of the regular Tour caddies go native in Paradise. Shorts are okay for the lads this week, too.

HOT PUTTING
At tournament time, Waialae's Tifdwarf greens are at pool-table smoothness and roll at about 11 on the Stimpmeter—this is one event where 40-footers find the hole with regularity.

EDIBLE TEE MARKERS
The tournament symbol is the pineapple, and at each hole two succulent specimens define the teeing ground.

EASTERN EXPOSURE
Since this is the closest Tour event to the Far East, the field invariably includes several Japanese players, and they usually acquit themselves well. In 1983, Isao Aoki became the first Japanese player to win an American Tour event when he holed out a 126-yard wedge for eagle on the last hole to edge Jack Renner by a stroke.

The Not-So-Rare Hawaiian Eagle

From 1991-93, Waialae CC yielded 185 eagles during the United Airlines Hawaiian Open. The next highest eagle total was at the TPC at Southwind (Federal Express St. Jude Classic), with 101; followed by TPC of Scottsdale (Phoenix Open), 96; and Oakwood CC (Quad Cities Open), 95.

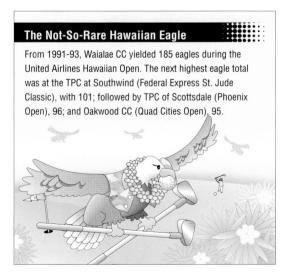

Waialae Country Club

Hole #1 —
par 5, 539 yards

Hole #2 —
par 4, 362 yards

Hole #3 —
par 4, 410 yards

Hole #4 —
par 3, 196 yards

Hole #5 —
par 4, 478 yards

Hole #6 —
par 4, 435 yards

Hole #7 —
par 3, 182 yards

Hole #8 —
par 4, 402 yards

Hole #9 —
par 5, 513 yards

4th hole

Practical Matters

FOR TICKET INFORMATION
The United Airlines
Hawaiian Open
677 Ala Moana Blvd.
Suite 207
Honolulu, HI 96813

COURSE
Waialae Country Club

ACCESS
Private — you must play with
a member

COURSE RATING

Tees	Pro	Member
Yardage	7012	6651
Rating	73.2	71.7
Slope	133	130

GREEN FEES
$50
For more information:
(808) 732-1457

PRO-AM
Spots open to the public? Yes
Handicap: Maximum of 21
Format: Best ball of team
Entry fee: $2800
For more information:
(808) 526-1232

swirl up to 40 miles per hour. But when the wind goes down, so do the scores. In 1994, Davis Love III blazed through his second round in 60 strokes —12 under par.

Hawaii is a long way to travel for four rounds of golf—two rounds for those who miss the cut—and a week in Honolulu is not inexpensive, but for the winner it's well worth the trip: In addition to the big first-prize check goes a $5000 golden pineapple and a card entitling the bearer to a year of free air travel anywhere in the world that United Airlines flies.

TOURNAMENT RATINGS

COURSE DIFFICULTY

Avg. winning score: 17.9 under par	39th on Tour
USGA course rating: 73.2 (1.2 over par)	38th on Tour
Overall rating: Vulnerable	43rd on Tour

PRESTIGE

Field strength (10.1)	20th on Tour
Winner quality (.417)	36th on Tour
Course difficulty (above)	43rd on Tour
Plus factors: Exotic setting	
Overall rating	31st on Tour

Local Knowledge

HITTING YOUR DRIVER OFF THE DECK

On a course such as Waialae, with a constant breeze and a collection of short par fives, you'll probably have at least one chance per round of getting home in two, even if you're only a medium-length hitter. But to pull it off, you'll likely have to hit both your tee shot and your second shot with a driver.

Don't be afraid to try this shot; it's a lot easier than it used to be, thanks to today's metal woods, most of which have a shallow face and a relatively low center of gravity, two design features that make it easy to get a ball airborne.

Nonetheless, you should try this shot only when you have a lie where the ball is sitting up a bit, with at least some part of it higher than the top of your clubface at address. The swing is basically the same as for a driver off the tee, but to give yourself an extra margin for error, widen your stance. This lowers your own center of gravity and facilitates the shallow, sweeping impact you want.

Try to keep your swing patient—remember that's a driver in your hands, so there's no need to lunge at the ball. As an added safeguard against a topped shot, put a little extra flex in your knees, and use "keep the flex" as your thought throughout the swing.

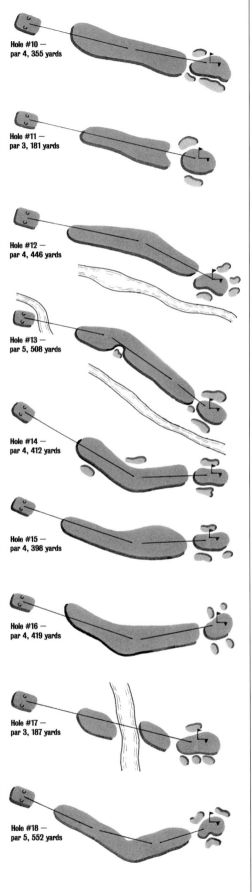

Hole #10 —
par 4, 355 yards

Hole #11 —
par 3, 181 yards

Hole #12 —
par 4, 446 yards

Hole #13 —
par 5, 508 yards

Hole #14 —
par 4, 412 yards

Hole #15 —
par 4, 398 yards

Hole #16 —
par 4, 419 yards

Hole #17 —
par 3, 187 yards

Hole #18 —
par 5, 552 yards

Northern Telecom Open

TUCSON NATIONAL GOLF CLUB

STARR PASS GOLF CLUB

Schizophrenic golfers of the world, rejoice. We have just the tournament for you. Out in Tucson, there's an event that takes place on two courses simultaneously, and the two layouts, despite being only a few miles from each other, are so dissimilar in their appearance and demands, they could have been designed by Dr. Jekyll and Mr. Hyde.

The course at the Tucson National Golf Club is one of the dowagers of the desert. Designed in the days before water restrictions, it is a traditional resort course, its broad, treelined fairways unfurling from the front lawn of the Tucson National Golf & Conference Resort. Six lakes dot the layout—and that's about five more than at most courses in this part of the world. Tucson National is one desert course where you won't have to do battle with the prickly saguaro, the jumping cholla, or any other botanical bullies—everything in play is lush, green, and manicured.

That is not to say this is an easy course. At 7148 yards from the back tees, TNGC gives even the Tour pros plenty to tackle, including mammoth number 15, at 663 yards the longest hole on the PGA Tour. And if the tournament should come down to number 18, anything might happen, because this is the most demanding hole on the course, a 465-yard uphill par four with lakes on both sides. Bogeys outnumber birdies here by about five to one.

In complete contrast is the other venue for the Northern Telecom Open, Starr Pass Golf Club. The work of Bob Cupp with play-

THE TV HOLES

Expect birdies:

11, 15
at Tucson National

11
at Starr Pass

Expect bogeys:

10, 18
at Tucson National

12
at Starr Pass

What to Watch For . . .

TWO-TONED TURF
Those who see these courses for the first time—whether on television or in person—may validly assume that half the grass has succumbed to some sort of arboreal plague. Throughout the winter, much of the rough and greenside area is the color of straw. This is intentional, the result of sowing those areas with bermudagrass and a native plant called six-weeks grass, both of which turn yellow when dormant.

HEROIC HEADGEAR
The civic group that helps run this event is The Conquistadors, a non-profit organization of 135 Tucson businessmen. Each Conquistador is the proud owner of a gleaming golden helmet, the likes of which Francisco Coronado sported, and a similar crown is presented to each Tucson champion. Originally, the helmets were made in Toledo, Spain, of black steel in a rather crude design. Now a local Tucson firm produces them, properly gold-plated and engraved. The winners usually don the helmet for the obligatory trophy photo; after that they're rarely seen in it.

DEPRESSED GALLERIES
Since Starr Pass was originally a TPC layout, it was designed to accommodate large tournament galleries. But there's a difference here: The areas surrounding many greens are contoured with big dips so that spectators in the first few rows are actually below the playing surface. Players approaching these greens see rows of faces instead of full bodies.

**14th hole at
Starr Pass Golf Club**

Green Giants		
Longest Holes on the PGA Tour:		
Hole	**Course**	**Yards**
15	**Tucson National GC**	**663**
1	Castle Pines GC	644
16	Firestone CC (South)	625
2	TPC at Avenel	622
14	Walt Disney World (Magnolia)	614
13	TPC at Summerlin	606
5	Pleasant Valley CC	606
5	Oak Hills CC	604
1	Spyglass Hill GC	600

Tucson National Golf Club

Hole #1 —
par 4, 410 yards

Hole #2 —
par 5, 495 yards

Hole #3 —
par 4, 377 yards

Hole #4 —
par 3, 170 yards

Hole #5 —
par 4, 395 yards

Hole #6 —
par 4, 426 yards

Hole #7 —
par 3, 202 yards

Hole #8 —
par 5, 528 yards

Hole #9 —
par 4, 430 yards

er-consultant Craig Stadler, Starr Pass was opened in 1986 as part of the PGA Tour's network of Tournament Players Clubs, but in 1991 it converted to a semiprivate facility.

This one is a tightrope walk through the desert, its ribbons of fairway snaking across broad tracts of no-man's-land. Each tee is an island of manicured grass, and each tee shot must be launched over the scrub to another island of fairway. On many holes, the approach also must fly across desert wasteland to the green. At number 14, for instance, a par five of just 489 yards, anyone who wants to reach the narrow green in two will have to execute a death-defying leap over a chasm. There are no lakes or ponds to contend with on this course. Nonetheless, four different types of hazards come into play—bunkers, desert washes, grassy hollows, and the desert itself —and if you hit your ball in some of these places, you may wish you were in water.

When Starr Pass was designed, the Northern Telecom Open was known as the Seiko/Tucson Match Play Championship, and this course was intended to hold the Tour's only match play event. As such, the architects tried to route the course so that

18th hole at Tucson National

the hardest holes would fall at the end of the round, where things are usually decided. As it worked out, however, the difficulty is spread evenly throughout each nine. No matter what the hole, a steep penalty is exacted for inaccuracy.

Once on the dance floor, there is some fancy stepping to do. Both Cupp and Stadler believe the true challenge of a course is in its greens, and that credo is reflected in every putting surface. Many feature multiple tiers, and all are fiercely contoured and fast.

Local Knowledge

CLUBS FOR SCRUB

Many desert courses have a local Rule that allows you to lift your ball out of the waste and place it on the edge of the fairway, adding a one-stroke penalty. At other clubs, you must play the ball as it lies, or choose one of the options under the Rule covering an unplayable lie.

If you're the intrepid type and you're planning a golf vacation in a desert area, consider this bit of practical advice: Designate one club as your desert weapon. The desert floor is as abrasive as sandpaper—it can really destroy the soles of your clubs—so do yourself a favor and limit the damage to one iron. You might even want to bring along an old club for this dirty work. Most of your shots will be recoveries—short pitches back into play—so any middle iron should do.

If you find yourself in a desert area near the green, don't reach automatically for a wedge. From a tight, sandy lie, even the best players have a good chance of scuffing or blading the ball. Instead, give some thought to banging the ball out with a putter. You'll almost always hit this shot squarely, and if the area between you and the green is open and closely mowed, a firmly struck putt is the smartest ploy.

Practical Matters

FOR TICKET INFORMATION

The Tucson Conquistadors
10 N. Norton
Tucson, AZ 85719

COURSES

Tucson National Golf Club, Starr Pass Golf Club

ACCESS

Tucson National Golf Club: Resort course with a small membership; open to the public, but priorities are given to hotel guests and members.
Starr Pass Golf Club: Semiprivate course—you must call two weeks ahead for tee time

COURSE RATING

TUCSON NATIONAL GOLF CLUB

Tees	Pro	Member
Yardage	7083/72	6549/73
Rating	74.8	71.0
Slope	136	122

STARR PASS GOLF CLUB

Tees	Pro	Member
Yardage	7010	6383
Rating	74.6	71.3
Slope	139	127

GREEN FEES

TUCSON NATIONAL GOLF CLUB
Winter: $85 for hotel guests, $99 outside play
Summer: $45 for hotel guests, $52 outside play
For more information: (602) 528-4856

STARR PASS GOLF CLUB
Winter: $89
Summer: $65
For more information: (602) 622-6060

PRO-AM

Spots open to the public? Yes
Handicap: Maximum of 21
Format: Best ball of team

Entry fee: Two tiers: $995 and $5000
For more information: (602) 624-GOLF

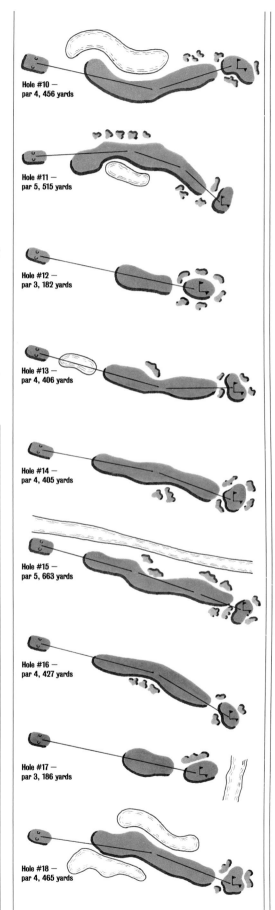

Hole #10 —
par 4, 456 yards

Hole #11 —
par 5, 515 yards

Hole #12 —
par 3, 182 yards

Hole #13 —
par 4, 406 yards

Hole #14 —
par 4, 405 yards

Hole #15 —
par 5, 663 yards

Hole #16 —
par 4, 427 yards

Hole #17 —
par 3, 186 yards

Hole #18 —
par 4, 465 yards

Phoenix Open

TPC OF SCOTTSDALE

Tour pros have a tendency to be harsh critics of golf courses, and the irony is that the ones they hate most are their own—the courses in the network of Tournament Players Clubs, owned and operated by the PGA Tour. The first of these, the TPC at Sawgrass, had to suffer through a firestorm of criticism before evolving into its present admired form, and virtually every one of its offspring has met with a similar blast from the pros.

Except for one: the TPC of Scottsdale. From the day it opened in 1986, this course has put smiles on the players' faces, and in one recent survey they voted the Phoenix Open the most popular tournament on Tour. The reason? This design by Jay Morrish and Tom Weiskopf (with player-consultants Howard Twitty and Jim Colbert) was the first municipal TPC course, and therefore the first one open to the public. As such, the architects had a special challenge—to design a course that would test the pros one week per year while pleasing the residents of Scottsdale the rest of the time. So the TPC of Scottsdale lacks the severe features of its progenitors. There are few forced carries, the greens have gentle rolls rather than wicked slopes, and large, shouldering mounds

THE TV HOLES

Expect birdies:
13, 15

Expect bogeys:
12, 14

15th hole

What to Watch For . . .

POWER PLAY
With broad fairways, large greens, and a lack of treacherous trouble, this is a course that encourages big hitters to hit big. It's more than a coincidence that the list of recent winners includes Paul Azinger, Sandy Lyle, and Mark Calcavecchia twice.

RUNAWAYS
On seven occasions, the margin of victory has been more than five strokes, and three times it was a dozen or more.

A PACKED HOUSE
This is one of the few tournaments on the PGA Tour that has consistently resisted the temptation to take on a corporate sponsor. As such it depends heavily on the loyalty and support of the local fans—and they do turn out, both as tournament volunteers and as spectators. On the weekend, it can seem as if most of Phoenix is here around the 18th green.

FREE CALLS
One of the tournament's corporate supporters is U.S. West Communications, and each year the company sets up a network of on-course telephones that won't accept a dime from you.

THE BIRD'S NEST
Each year the Thunderbirds, a civic group that runs the tournament, converts a hospitality tent into a pulsating disco that becomes for one week the hottest spot in Arizona. The Bird's Nest rocks into the wee hours from Wednesday through Saturday nights.

Left in the Dust

Widest Margins of Victory:

Margin	Player	Tournament
16 strokes	Bobby Locke	1948 Chicago Victory National Championships
14 strokes	Ben Hogan	1945 Portland Invitational
	Johnny Miller	**1975 Phoenix Open**
13 strokes	Byron Nelson	1945 Seattle Open
12 strokes	**Byron Nelson**	**1939 Phoenix Open**
	Arnold Palmer	**1962 Phoenix Open**
	José Maria Olazabal	1990 NEC World Series of Golf

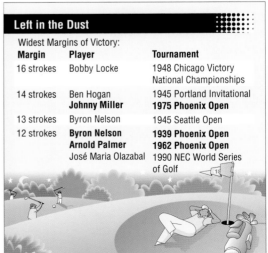

23

TPC of Scottsdale

Hole #1 —
par 4, 410 yards

Hole #2 —
par 4, 416 yards

Hole #3 —
par 5, 554 yards

Hole #4 —
par 3, 150 yards

Hole #5 —
par 4, 453 yards

Hole #6 —
par 4, 389 yards

Hole #7 —
par 3, 215 yards

Hole #8 —
par 4, 470 yards

Hole #9 —
par 4, 415 yards

provide definition while funneling errant shots back into play.

The site for this course was flat, barren desert, so the architects excavated, moved, and sculpted over a million cubic yards of dirt. Tracts of sandy waste remain within the layout, but most of these areas are out of play for the pros and serve as buffer zones between the action and the gallery.

If you want to see the men truly separated from the boys, hang out at either the 15th or 17th hole—depending on how sadistic you are. If you watch tournaments for the same reason that some people watch auto races—to see a dramatic crash—then 15 is your hole. Anyone who wants to reach this 501-yard par five in two shots will have to play a long-iron or fairway-wood shot across a lake to an island green. About one out of three guys finds the drink. But if you enjoy seeing the pros at their superhuman best, hang around the par-four 17th and watch the long-ballers try to drive the green. There are several drivable par fours on the Tour, but few are as inviting as this dead-flat 332-yarder that allows a rolling approach.

12th hole

This is a course where the pros can play boldly and expect to reap the rewards, and that's the way it's always been at Phoenix. It was at this event that Jack Nicklaus first shot 29 for nine holes (1964), that Arnold Palmer charged to victory three years in a row (1961–63), and that Johnny Miller once completed 72 holes in 260 strokes—24 under par, an average of one birdie every three holes.

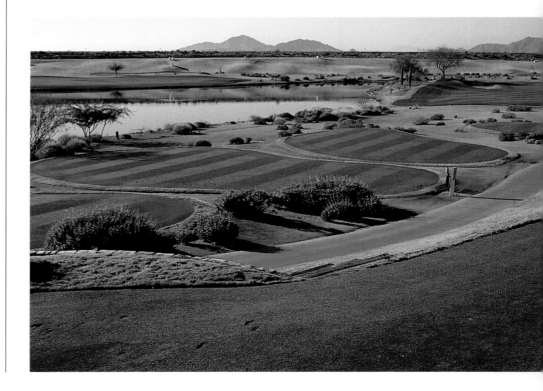

Local Knowledge

DON'T DO WHAT COMES NATURALLY

The wide-open spaces of a course like the TPC of Scottsdale invite every red-blooded golfer to let out the shaft a bit. The trick is to avoid doing what comes naturally, because what feels right is wrong.

Number one: Don't widen your stance— this may feel very stable and powerful, but if your feet are more than shoulder-width apart you'll be restricting your ability to make a full backswing turn. If anything, place your feet a bit closer together than normal.

Number two: Don't tighten your grip pressure. Again, this feels powerful, but a tight grip makes your arms tense and restricts a free-flowing armswing. Instead, grip the club a bit more lightly than usual.

Number three: Don't move your hands forward. This move, which delofts the club, looks and feels aggressive and strong, but it encourages a weak, wristy pickup of the club which reduces the arc of your swing and robs you of power. You're wiser to stand so that your hands are slightly behind. This position will set you up for a one-piece takeaway of the club and a full, powerful backswing.

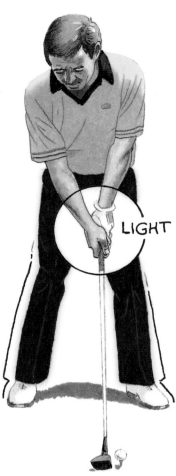

LIGHT

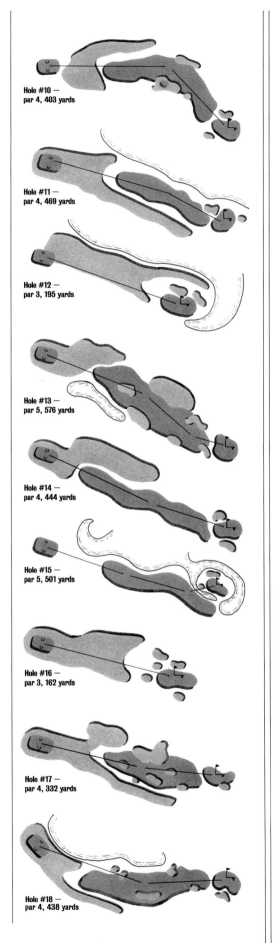

Hole #10 —
par 4, 403 yards

Hole #11 —
par 4, 469 yards

Hole #12 —
par 3, 195 yards

Hole #13 —
par 5, 576 yards

Hole #14 —
par 4, 444 yards

Hole #15 —
par 5, 501 yards

Hole #16 —
par 3, 162 yards

Hole #17 —
par 4, 332 yards

Hole #18 —
par 4, 438 yards

Practical Matters

FOR TICKET INFORMATION
The Phoenix Thunderbirds
7226 North Street #100
Phoenix, AZ 85020

COURSE
TPC of Scottsdale

ACCESS
Open to the public

COURSE RATING

Tees	Pro	Member
Yardage	6992	6508
Rating	73.9	71.0
Slope	131	124

GREEN FEES
In season: $81.09
Off season: $51.21
(rates include cart and tax)
For more information: (602) 585-4334

PRO–AM
Spots open to the public? Yes
Handicap: Must have a legitimate, registered handicap
Format: Best ball of team
Entry fee: Three pro-ams: $1650, $1950, $3950
For more information: (602) 870-0163

AT&T Pebble Beach National Pro-Am

PEBBLE BEACH GOLF LINKS

SPYGLASS HILL GOLF COURSE

POPPY HILLS GOLF COURSE

Welcome to the Greatest Show in Golf. For one week each year, a hundred or so of the game's best players pair up with a hundred or so celebrities from the worlds of entertainment, sports, business, and politics and do battle on three menacing courses, against a backdrop that Robert Louis Stevenson called "the most felicitous meeting of land and sea in Creation." The AT&T Pebble Beach National Pro-Am (originally the Bing Crosby Clambake) is the Tour's winter carnival, part U.S. Open, part Circus of the Stars.

For most of the pros, it's a love-hate thing. They love the beauty of the Monterey Peninsula but hate the prospect of "Crosby weather," which in late January can be better suited to duck hunting than golf. They love rubbing elbows with the movie stars, superathletes, and tycoons, but hate partnering them for a week of five-hour-plus rounds. Most of all, however, they love Pebble Beach but hate the two other courses.

The Pebble Beach Golf Links is, plain and simple, the most spectacular test of golf in the world. It would be a strong and memorable layout if its holes were stamped on an Iowa cornfield. Set as it is along the cliffs of the Pacific, it is utterly without peer. Although the opening stretch is maligned, those five holes suffer only because they are prelude to the grandeur of the next five, which run along the edge of the crashing Pacific—a par five that plays dramatically up the face of a headland, a tiny par three aimed straight at the sea, and then three nerve-shattering par fours along the cliffs.

Jack Neville and Douglas Grant—two fine amateur golfers who had never designed a course—plotted the holes at Pebble Beach, and their design has stood the test for over

THE TV HOLES

Expect birdies:

Nowhere
at Pebble Beach

12
at Spyglass Hill

10, 18
at Poppy Hills

Expect bogeys:

10
at Pebble Beach

18
at Spyglass Hill

16
at Poppy Hills

What to Watch For . . .

SILLINESS
In any year that Bill Murray plays, you can follow his group and get a free five-hour performance by a comic genius. Murray never uses the same line twice and interacts constantly with the crowd. Wear a crazy hat, and he'll probably steal it from you—at the very least, he'll ask you some loud questions about it.

SHUTTERBUGGERY
This is one of the few events that lets spectators bring cameras. Just don't snap when someone's in his backswing.

FINE-FEATHERED FELONS
The seagulls that fly near the cliff holes at Pebble are the world's most brazen birds. If you stop at the snack bar in this area, don't leave your goodies unattended, because the birds think nothing of diving in for a ham sandwich or a Twinkie. They're especially attracted to shiny objects, and more than one golfer has watched a gull swoop down, pluck his gold Rolex out of the cart, fly away, and, upon realizing it's inedible, drop it into the sea.

CONFUSION
Unless you attend this tournament on Sunday, prepare for a challenge, as play is spread over three different courses. For the same reason, the telecasts on Thursday, Friday, and Saturday are less than satisfying, as cameras cover only the action at Pebble, relying on remote reports from the two other courses. We see more bad shots from amateurs than good shots from pros, and when a leaderboard appears on the screen, there's a PB, SH, or PH next to each player's score, denoting the course he's playing that day. On Sunday, when the cut-survivors return to Pebble, things get sorted out.

6th hole at Pebble Beach Golf Links

Mean Greens			
Hardest Courses on the PGA Tour:			Avg.
Course	Par	Avg. Score	Over Par
Spyglass Hill GC	**72**	**73.962**	**1.962**
Firestone CC	70	71.940	1.940
Westchester CC	71	72.880	1.880
English Turn G & CC	72	73.638	1.638
TPC at River Highlands	70	71.547	1.547
Glen Abbey GC	72	73.412	1.412
Bay Hill Club	72	73.113	1.113
Poppy Hills GC	**72**	**73.066**	**1.066**

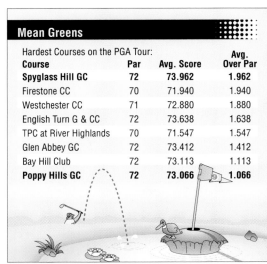

Pebble Beach Golf Links

Hole #1 —
par 4, 373 yards

Hole #2 —
par 5, 502 yards

Hole #3 —
par 4, 388 yards

Hole #4 —
par 4, 327 yards

Hole #5 —
par 3, 166 yards

Hole #6 —
par 5, 516 yards

Hole #7 —
par 3, 107 yards

Hole #8 —
par 4, 431 yards

Hole #9 —
par 4, 464 yards

80 years with only one major change. Prior to the 1929 U.S. Amateur, H. Chandler Egan converted the 379-yard 18th hole to a magnificent beast of a par five that curls 548 yards in a counterclockwise crescent along the rocky shore.

Why do the pros hate Spyglass Hill? Simple. It's the hardest of the 51 courses on the PGA Tour, taxing the players for an average score of 73.96, two over par. *Los Angeles Times* columnist Jim Murray called it a 300-acre unplayable lie, and Jack Nicklaus once said, "Spyglass is the kind of golf course that makes you want to go fishing." Designed in 1966 by Robert Trent Jones, Spyglass gets a player's attention at the very first hole, which tumbles 600 yards down toward the sea. The next four play through a series of natural sand dunes clad with patches of grasping ice plant. After number five, the course climbs up into the tall timber of the Del Monte Forest, where a collection of backbreakingly difficult par fours prey upon the legs and the soul. Two of these—numbers 8 and 16—rank as the second- and third-hardest holes on the Tour.

Poppy Hills had an impossibly tough act to follow when in 1991 it joined the AT&T rotation as a replacement for Cypress Point, the Alister Mackenzie jewel that has been called the Sistine Chapel of Golf. And in defense of architect

TOURNAMENT RATINGS

COURSE DIFFICULTY

Avg. winning score: 9.8 under par	8th on Tour
USGA course rating: 75.1 (3.1 over par)*	15th on Tour
Overall rating: Severe	11th on Tour

PRESTIGE

Field strength (13.5)	12th on Tour
Winner quality (.740)	18th on Tour
Course difficulty (above)	11th on Tour
Plus factors: Course rated 3rd in U.S., celebrity field, history (same site since 1947)	
Overall rating	9th on Tour

*Composite of two rounds at Pebble Beach, one each at Spyglass Hill and Poppy Hills

Robert Trent Jones, Jr., he gave his clients what they wanted, a big course that would test the world's best players but also accommodate heavy play by the members of the Northern California Golf Association.

Jones the younger created huge greens, to allow for multiple pin placements, and in those huge greens he made huge slopes. Indeed, the entire course is characterized by emphatic movement—up and down and right and left. Half are doglegs, and rarely does a plyer draw a completely level lie with a straightforward shot to a completely level landing area.

4th hole at Spyglass Hill Golf Course

Local Knowledge

FIGHTING THE FIERCEST FLORA

Mercifully, Monterey is one of the few places where you're likely to encounter *Mesembryanthemum crystallinium,* better known as ice plant. A member of the carpet-weed family, ice plant is a succulent that clings to the dunes and rocks along the Monterey Peninsula, snagging anything that comes near its fleshy fingers.

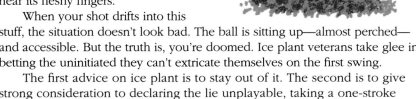

When your shot drifts into this stuff, the situation doesn't look bad. The ball is sitting up—almost perched—and accessible. But the truth is, you're doomed. Ice plant veterans take glee in betting the uninitiated they can't extricate themselves on the first swing.

The first advice on ice plant is to stay out of it. The second is to give strong consideration to declaring the lie unplayable, taking a one-stroke penalty, and dropping free of the stuff. However, if you must play, select a wedge—and only a wedge, play the ball well back in your stance, and chop down and through with all your might. If you move the ball, consider it an achievement, if you get it back into play, a miracle, and if you approximate your target, an accident.

Practical Matters

FOR TICKET INFORMATION
AT&T Pebble Beach National Pro-Am
200 East Franklin Street, Box 869
Monterey, CA 93942

ACCESS
All courses are public, but priority is given to guests of The Lodge at Pebble Beach and The Inn at Spanish Bay, as well as to local residents.

COURSES
Pebble Beach, Spyglass Hill, Poppy Hills

COURSE RATING

PEBBLE BEACH			SPYGLASS HILL			POPPY HILLS		
Tees	Pro	Member	Tees	Pro	Member	Tees	Pro	Member
Yardage	6799	6357	Yardage	6859	6346	Yardage	6865	6288
Rating	75.0	72.7	Rating	75.9	73.0	Rating	64.6	71.7
Slope	144	139	Slope	143	138	Slope	141	134

GREEN FEES

PEBBLE BEACH	SPYGLASS HILL	POPPY HILLS
$225 for nonguests; $175 for guests	$175 for outside guests; $125 for members of Northern California Golf Association	$95 for outside guests; $45 for members of Northern California Golf Association

For more information: (800) 654-9300 for Pebble Beach and Spyglass Hill; (408) 625-2144 for Poppy Hills.

PRO-AM
Spots open to the public? No
Handicap: Maximum of 21
Format: Best ball of amateur and his pro partner; same two are partners for three days on the three courses; after the third round the low 25 teams make the cut and return to Pebble Beach for the final round.
Entry fee: $3500
For more information: (408) 649-1533

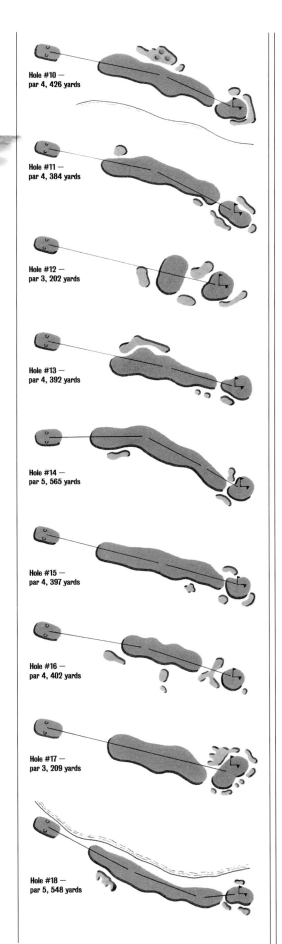

Hole #10 — par 4, 426 yards

Hole #11 — par 4, 384 yards

Hole #12 — par 3, 202 yards

Hole #13 — par 4, 392 yards

Hole #14 — par 5, 565 yards

Hole #15 — par 4, 397 yards

Hole #16 — par 4, 402 yards

Hole #17 — par 3, 209 yards

Hole #18 — par 5, 548 yards

Buick Invitational of California

TORREY PINES GOLF CLUB
[NORTH & SOUTH COURSES]

For the past decade or so, the PGA Tour has wanted to bring a Tournament Players Course to San Diego. A site has been selected and a design is in place. However, the maze of necessary environmental and zoning approvals has stalled the project.

That's not all bad, because until the pros get their own course, they have no complaints against the North and South courses at Torrey Pines—no complaints, despite the fact that they share these two courses with a few thousand golf-crazy San Diegans.

Torrey Pines is one of the very few public facilities to host the PGA Tour, and it may be the busiest, its two courses hosting more than 100,000 rounds of golf per year.

Pros and amateurs alike are spoiled by panoramic views of the Pacific Ocean and challenged by doglegging fairways lined with the namesake Torrey pines, an endangered species common only to this area and the Channel Islands off Santa Barbara.

Both courses are the work of Billy Bell, whose designs throughout California are known for their cleverly sloped, inscrutable greens. The surfaces at Torrey Pines aren't particularly fast, but they're

THE TV HOLES

Expect birdies:

14, 18
at North Course

13, 18
at South Course

Expect bogeys:

11
at North Course

11, 12
at South Course

13th hole,
South Course

What to Watch For . . .

CLIFFHANGERS
This course is perched on the edge of a canyon that drops 300 feet to the Pacific, and the edges of a few holes hug the precipice. It's not uncommon to see a player make like a mountain goat in order to get his ball back into play.

MORE CLIFFHANGERS
Thanks to a reachable but pond-guarded par five at the 18th hole, this event is as capable as any on the Tour at producing dramatic, down-to-the wire finishes.

DEVLIN'S BILLABONG
Hard by the 18th green is a pond that brought disaster to Australian Bruce Devlin in 1975. Three strokes off the lead as he came to the hole on Sunday, Devlin plummeted to a tie for 30th place after wading into the pond and taking six swipes in an attempt to water-blast his ball to the green. A plaque marks his watery grave.

FOG DELAYS
San Diego is famed for its perfect climate, but Torrey Pines, being a seaside course, is particularly sensitive to the vicissitudes of the weather. One morning, the fog was so thick, Tour officials canceled play for the day.

CRAIG STADLER JOKES
The Walrus, a local boy who lives in nearby La Jolla, will never live down the year he spread a towel on the ground and knelt on it to play a ball from under a tree. This was witnessed by a nationwide TV audience, and within moments viewers called in, noting that Stadler had violated the Rule that prohibits "building a stance." Stadler, who would have finished in second place, instead was disqualified.

Throwing in the Towel

Craig Stadler is remembered for being disqualified for kneeling on a towel (therefore "building a stance") in 1987, but he also tied the tournament record of 62 that year. Of the four players who have shot 62, none has won the tournament.

Player	Year	Final Standing
Gene Littler	1965	T9
Craig Stadler	1987	DQ
Andy Bean	1987	T23
Gil Morgan	1988	T3

Torrey Pines Golf Club– South Course

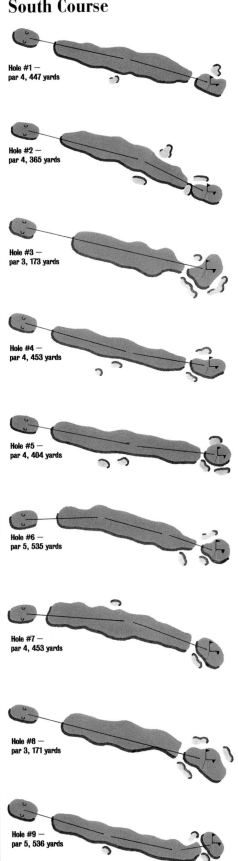

Hole #1 —
par 4, 447 yards

Hole #2 —
par 4, 365 yards

Hole #3 —
par 3, 173 yards

Hole #4 —
par 4, 453 yards

Hole #5 —
par 4, 404 yards

Hole #6 —
par 5, 535 yards

Hole #7 —
par 4, 453 yards

Hole #8 —
par 3, 171 yards

Hole #9 —
par 5, 536 yards

3rd hole, South Course

full of subtle breaks that confound the pros. Generally, the ball will move toward the ocean, but there are enough exceptions to keep everyone guessing. Ray Floyd, who twice lost this tournament in playoffs, claims both his losses came when he missed the same mystifying 10-footer at the 15th hole.

Both courses are used on Thursday and Friday, but once the cut is made, all play is on the South Course, which is 400 yards longer and plays about a stroke and a half tougher than the North.

The key coming down the stretch is to survive number 17, a lengthy par four that stretches along the edge of a canyon, and then get home in two for a birdie, maybe an eagle, at the docile finishing par five.

TOURNAMENT RATINGS

COURSE DIFFICULTY

Avg. winning score: 16.8 under par	35th on Tour
USGA course rating: 74.0 (2.0 over par)*	28th on Tour
Overall rating: Vulnerable	37th on Tour

PRESTIGE

Field strength (9.3)	25th on Tour
Winner quality (.400)	37th on Tour
Course difficulty (above)	37th on Tour
Plus factors: None	
Overall rating	33rd on Tour

*Composite of three rounds at South Course, one round at North Course

Practical Matters

FOR TICKET INFORMATION
Century Club of San Diego
9449 Friar's Rd.
Gate P
San Diego, CA 92108

COURSE RATING

SOUTH COURSE

Tees	Pro	Member
Yardage	7055	6705
Rating	74.6	72.6
Slope	136	130

NORTH COURSE

Tees	Pro	Member
Yardage	6647	6326
Rating	72.1	70.0
Slope	129	119

ACCESS
Municipal course, open to the public

COURSE
Torrey Pines, North and South

GREEN FEES
$40 weekdays,
$47 weekends and holidays
For more information:
(619) 552-1784

PRO-AM
Spots open to the public? Yes
Handicap: Maximum of 21
Format: Best ball of team
Entry fee: $2750
For more information: (619) 281-4653

Local Knowledge

DEALING WITH DIVOTS

On a heavily played public course such as those at Torrey Pines, you're apt to encounter fairways that are less than pristine, and once in a while you'll find that an otherwise fine tee shot has come to rest in another player's divot.

That's a bad break, but in most cases you should be able to extricate yourself without losing any ground on the hole. The key is to minimize the impedance of the divot by attacking the ball on a sharply downward angle. To do this, position the ball farther back in your stance than normal—about two inches to the rear of its usual position. As you swing, focus your attention on the front half of the ball. These adjustments will help you to hit down steeply and trap the ball. The result will be a low-flying shot, similar to a punch shot.

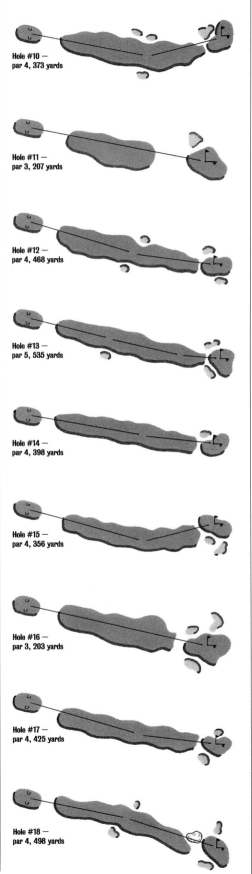

Hole #10 —
par 4, 373 yards

Hole #11 —
par 3, 207 yards

Hole #12 —
par 4, 468 yards

Hole #13 —
par 5, 535 yards

Hole #14 —
par 4, 398 yards

Hole #15 —
par 4, 356 yards

Hole #16 —
par 3, 203 yards

Hole #17 —
par 4, 425 yards

Hole #18 —
par 4, 498 yards

Bob Hope Chrysler Classic

BERMUDA DUNES

INDIAN RIDGE

INDIAN WELLS

LA QUINTA

TAMARISK

I t's the Bob Hope Just-After-Christmas Show, a star-studded golfathon featuring 384 deliriously wealthy amateurs in four rounds of frenzied competition, with special guest appearances by the top professionals from around the world. Sponsored by the Chrysler Corporation and brought to you live and in living color on NBC.

Before the average Tour pro tees off in this event, he takes a deep breath, tells himself to have fun, and prays for an extra helping of patience. The Hope is the PGA Tour's annual Operation Desert Storm, a four-course, five-day, 90-hole extravaganza.

There are actually five courses that host this event, but two of them—La Quinta Country Club and Tamarisk Country Club—take turns, serving in alternate years. The three other sites—Bermuda Dunes Country Club, Indian Wells Country Club, and Indian Ridge Country Club—rotate as the host club and venue for the final round.

None of these courses is a bear, and typically this event turns into a showcase of the Tour players' ability to make birdies. In 1993, Tom Kite posted a record total of 325, 35 under par for 90 holes.

The toughest of the five is the Indian Ridge course, which joined the rotation in 1994. Set in the heart of Palm Desert, within a mile of a half dozen other courses, this Arnold Palmer–designed par 72 measures 7067

16th hole at Indian Ridge Country Club

THE TV HOLES

Expect birdies:

13, 18
at Bermuda Dunes

17
at Indian Ridge

12, 14, 16, 18
at Indian Wells

11, 13, 18
at La Quinta

12, 13, 17, 18
at Tamarisk

Expect bogeys:

12, 16
at Indian Ridge

10
at Indian Wells

Nowhere
at the other three courses

What to Watch For . . .

MID-WEEK COMPETITION

Since this is a 90-hole event, it begins on Wednesday. Look for cable coverage that evening and for the first-round report in Thursday's paper.

SILVER & GOLD

If you've forgotten that Palm Springs is a mecca for rich retirees, the makeup of this gallery will quickly remind you. Most of the men have gray hair, most of the women sport enough bangles to start a jewelry store, and everyone has skin that looks like belting leather.

FINAL-ROUND THEATRICS

Maybe it's the proximity to Hollywood, maybe it's a function of the 90-hole format, or maybe it's just the legendary Hope sense of timing. Whatever the reason, no event on the Tour can match this one for Sunday drama: Playoffs occur about two years out of three, and in 1992 five players finished in a deadlock. The shootout was finally won by local boy John Cook, who birdied three playoff holes and then chipped-in at the fourth for an eagle. (Two other players—Rick Fehr and Gene Sauers—birdied all four sudden-death holes, only to lose.)

FEMININE PULCHRITUDE

An institution at this tournament are The Classic Girls—a trio of well-endowed lasses whose role is to greet the competitors, pose for photos, and generally burst out of their tops, one of which is emblazoned with "Hope," one with "Chrysler," and one with "Classic."

REPUBLICANS

Hope's most frequent partner? Gerald Ford. The featured amateur of recent years? Dan Quayle. If a ballot were taken of the gallery—or for that matter, the pro field—Reagan would be back in office. And let's not forget the tournament's flagship charity: The Eisenhower Medical Center.

No Heavy Lifting

The five courses used for the Bob Hope Chrysler Classic (four of them are played in a given year) all ranked among the nine easiest on Tour from 1991 to 93, including the three easiest.

Course	Avg. Score	Rank (out of 49)
Tamarisk CC	68.905	49
Indian Wells CC	69.075	48
Bermuda Dunes CC	69.531	47
La Quinta CC	70.109	44
PGA West (Palmer Course)	70.457	41

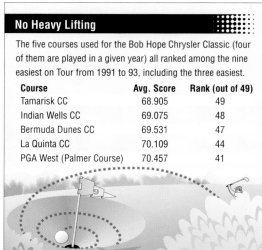

Indian Wells Country Club

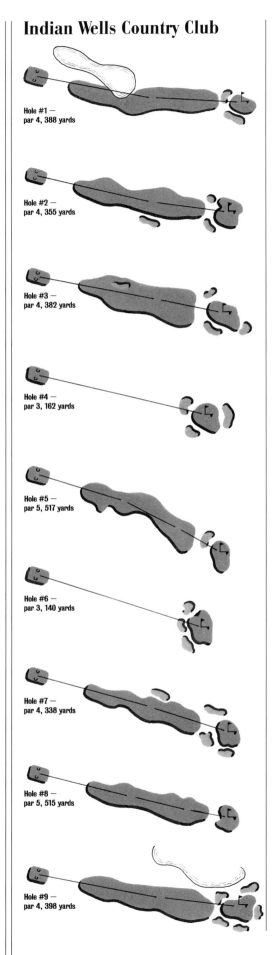

Hole #1 —
par 4, 388 yards

Hole #2 —
par 4, 355 yards

Hole #3 —
par 4, 382 yards

Hole #4 —
par 3, 162 yards

Hole #5 —
par 5, 517 yards

Hole #6 —
par 3, 140 yards

Hole #7 —
par 4, 338 yards

Hole #8 —
par 5, 515 yards

Hole #9 —
par 4, 398 yards

yards. Rated at 74.9, it is followed in lessening difficulty by the country clubs at La Quinta, Bermuda Dunes, Indian Wells (at 6478 yards the shortest course on the Tour), and finally Tamarisk, where the pros average 68.9.

One asset shared by each of the three co-host courses is a drama-producing final hole. The finish at Indian Wells runs along the rocky base of a mountain to a green menaced on the left by a five-tiered waterfall. Bermuda Dunes culminates in a hole of 513 yards with out of bounds to the left and a palm-lined lake that will catch any approach that is pushed or sliced to the right of the narrow green. And Indian Ridge ends with a 420-yard par five where the lengthy approach must find a green fronted by a lake.

Local Knowledge

THINK BEFORE YOU GAMBLE

Four of the five Bob Hope courses conclude with a reachable par-five hole, the longest of them only 532 yards—and that's from the pro tees. From the members' blocks, even a player of moderate strength has a chance of getting home in two. But with water guarding these greens, you need to weigh the risks against the rewards.

It's foolish to ruin a good round of golf with a big number at the last hole. But then again, if you know a birdie will enable you to shoot your career score or win a bet with your friends, you may want to give it a try. However, when you're in a match where you're one up at the 18th tee, it's usually wise to play safely and leave the pressure on your opponent.

You should also be honest in assessing your ability. Maybe you can hit a 3-wood 230 yards, but remember that the last 20 yards or so is roll. Don't expect to carry the ball 230, especially if there's water in front of the green. And if you're a slicer, your tendency is to miss your long shots to the right, so when water or other big trouble is on that side, think twice about taking a gamble—vice versa if you tend to hook the ball.

But when an honest self-appraisal tells you that your worst shot won't hurt you too severely, that's your signal to give it a go.

Practical Matters

FOR TICKET INFORMATION

Bob Hope Chrysler Classic
P.O. Box 865
Rancho Mirage, CA 92270

COURSES

Bermuda Dunes Country Club

Indian Ridge Country Club

Indian Wells Country Club

La Quinta Country Club

Tamarisk Country Club

ACCESS

Bermuda Dunes Country Club: Open to the public? No. Guests must play with a member.

Indian Ridge Country Club: Open to the Public? No. Guests must be introduced by or play with a member.

Indian Wells Country Club: Open to the public? Yes (summer only). Guests must be introduced by a member or play with a member.

La Quinta Country Club: Open to the public? No. Guests must play with a member.

Tamarisk Country Club: Open to the public? No. Guests must play with a member.

COURSE RATING

BERMUDA DUNES

Tees	Pro	Member
Yardage	6927	6542
Rating	73.5	70.8
Slope	126	118

INDIAN RIDGE

Tees	Pro	Member
Yardage	7067	6240
Rating	74.9	69.6
Slope	137	123

INDIAN WELLS

Tees	Pro	Member
Yardage	6478	6095
Rating	71.6	69.4
Slope	126	117

LA QUINTA

Yardage	6852	6532
Rating	74.0	72.0
Slope	133	129

TAMARISK

Tees	Pro	Member
Yardage	6881	6555
Rating	73.7	71.4
Slope	132	123

GREEN FEES

BERMUDA DUNES
Guest fee: $65
($50 off-season)

INDIAN RIDGE
Guest fee: $65 with member,
$100 without

INDIAN WELLS
Guest fee: $75 with member,
$150 without

LA QUINTA
Guest fee: $60

TAMARISK
Guest fee: $50
($35 off-season)

For more information: (619) 772-7222 for Indian Ridge, (619) 345-2561 for Indian Wells, (619) 345-2771 for Bermuda Dunes, (619) 564-4151 for La Quinta, and (619) 328-2141 for Tamarisk.

PRO-AM

Spots open to the public? No

Handicap: Maximum of 21

Format: Best ball of four (including pro). Four days of play, starting Wednesday and ending Saturday. Teams of three amateurs get a new pro partner each of the four days.

Entry fee: Varies between $3000 and $9500

For more information: (619) 346-8184

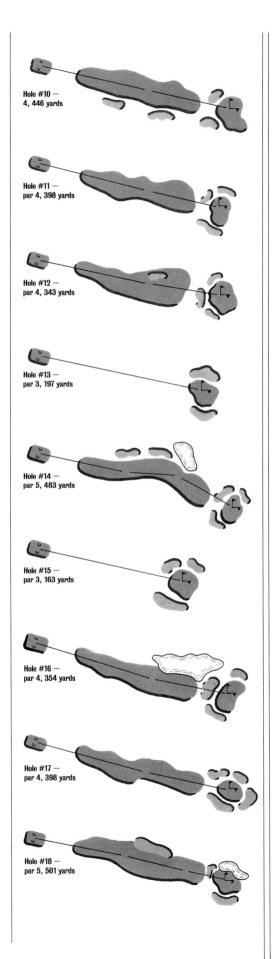

Hole #10 —
4, 446 yards

Hole #11 —
par 4, 398 yards

Hole #12 —
par 4, 343 yards

Hole #13 —
par 3, 197 yards

Hole #14 —
par 5, 483 yards

Hole #15 —
par 3, 163 yards

Hole #16 —
par 4, 354 yards

Hole #17 —
par 4, 398 yards

Hole #18 —
par 5, 501 yards

Nissan Los Angeles Open

RIVIERA COUNTRY CLUB

Over the past decade or so it has become fashionable among golf's cognoscenti to deprecate the efforts of the leading golf course architects—most notably Pete Dye and Jack Nicklaus—while worshiping the traditional "old-style courses" that were designed and built in the early part of this century. Architects such as Donald Ross, Alister Mackenzie, and A. W. Tillinghast have an almost mythical stature today and command more respect than they did back in the 1920s when they were in their designing prime.

Slightly less known—but only because he was less prolific—is another practitioner from this golden age of golf course architecture, George C. Thomas, a Philadelphia aristocrat who migrated west in 1919 and designed two dozen courses in southern California, most of them for no fee. The best known is the course at the Riviera Country Club.

But anyone who calls Riviera "traditional" has never seen it. In his design for the members of the Los Angeles Athletic Club, Thomas unveiled a collection of gambits that grabbed the golf fraternity by its knickers. One hole offered a split fairway with alternate routes, another featured a green half-barricaded by a grass mound the size of a locomotive. One par three called for a tee shot of nearly 240 yards and another had a pot bunker smack in the middle of its green. At Riviera, George Thomas broke a lot of rules, and triumphed.

THE TV HOLES

Expect birdies:
10

Expect bogeys:
15, 18

18th hole

What to Watch For . . .

SLIPPERY SYCAMORES

Back in 1950, as Sam Snead stood over a putt at the 18th hole to tie Ben Hogan and force a playoff, he was disrupted when a fan suddenly fell out of a tree. Snead backed off, then sank the putt and went on to beat Hogan. Forty-two years later, the same thing happened to Fred Couples as he prepared to hit a four-foot putt in a sudden-death playoff with Davis Love III. As Snead had, Couples stepped away for a moment, then sank the putt and went on to win.

GLITTERATI

Early Riviera members included Mary Pickford, Basil Rathbone, W.C. Fields, Spencer Tracy, Katharine Hepburn, Johnny Weissmuller, Burt Lancaster, Gregory Peck, Dean Martin, and Jerry Lewis, and it was as a young equestrian member here that Liz Taylor learned to ride a horse for her starring role in *National Velvet*. Scenes from numerous movies have been filmed at Riviera, including *Follow the Sun*, with Glenn Ford starring as Ben Hogan. More recently, the cast at Riviera has included Glen Campbell, Peter Falk, Peter Graves, Don Rickles, and Robert Wagner.

BARRANCA

For one week a year, the TV announcers toss around this word that sounds as if it came off the menu of a Mexican restaurant. According to *Webster's Intercollegiate*, it's derived from the Spanish and refers to the "deep ravine or gorge" which snakes through about half the holes at Riviera. Since there's rarely any water in it, it does not give the pros much trouble, but spectators should watch their step.

HOGAN TALK

In a span of 18 months, Ben Hogan won two Los Angeles Opens and a U.S. Open here.

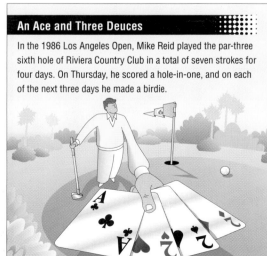

An Ace and Three Deuces

In the 1986 Los Angeles Open, Mike Reid played the par-three sixth hole of Riviera Country Club in a total of seven strokes for four days. On Thursday, he scored a hole-in-one, and on each of the next three days he made a birdie.

Riviera Country Club

Hole #1 —
par 5, 501 yards

Hole #2 —
par 4, 460 yards

Hole #3 —
par 4, 434 yards

Hole #4 —
par 3, 238 yards

Hole #5 —
par 4, 426 yards

Hole #6 —
par 3, 170 yards

Hole #7 —
par 4, 406 yards

Hole #8 —
par 4, 368 yards

Hole #9 —
par 4, 418 yards

When it opened in June of 1927, no one broke or equaled par. In fact, it was six months before anyone could do the deed, and Riviera has continued to confound and challenge generations of golfers ever since. Virtually no changes have been made in the course, but in 1993, Ben Crenshaw and his architectural partner Bill Coore plowed up, rebuilt, and restored all 18 of the greens, duplicating exactly the contours created by George Thomas.

In addition to the L.A. Open, the course has hosted the U.S. Open and two PGA Championships.

18th hole

TOURNAMENT RATINGS

COURSE DIFFICULTY

Avg. winning score: 13.7 under par	22nd on Tour
USGA course rating: 74.9 (3.9 over par)	3rd on Tour
Overall rating: Moderate	16th on Tour

PRESTIGE

Field strength (13.0)	15th on Tour
Winner quality (.680)	24th on Tour
Course difficulty (above)	16th on Tour
Plus factors: Course rated 20th in U.S., history (event began in 1926)	
Overall rating	17th on Tour

Local Knowledge

THE SOFT CHIP

Check the bags of the pros at Riviera, and you'll find that several players carry three wedges. One reason is the kikuyu grass in the greenside fringe. Balls do not bounce through this grass—they are snagged by it. As a result, the preferred shot is not a chip and run but a short, lofted pitch that flies over the fringe and stops quickly on the green.

You play this shot similarly to a standard pitch shot. Select your favorite pitching club—be that a pitching wedge, a sand wedge, or a third (60-degree) wedge—and address the ball in an open stance, your feet close together and your toes, knees, hips, and shoulders aligned to the left of the hole. If you have a very short shot and you want to make the ball climb fast and drop softly, build a little more loft into your setup by turning the face of your club open a few degrees and at the same time opening your stance a bit more.

The swing should be short back and short through. You can get good results from either a wristy motion that chops at the ball (for tight lies) or a stiff-wristed action that glides the club under the ball (for fluffy lies). Practice both methods and you'll be able to handle anything.

Practical Matters

FOR TICKET INFORMATION

Los Angeles Junior Chamber of Commerce
404 South Bixel St.
Los Angeles, CA 90017

COURSE

Riviera Country Club

ACCESS

Private course—you must play with a member, be introduced by a member, or be a member of a club with which Riviera has reciprocity.

COURSE RATING

Tees	Pro	Member
Yardage	6946/71	6513/72
Rating	74.9	72.4
Slope	142	135

GREEN FEES

Guest fee: $75 if play with a member; $150 unaccompanied
For more information: (310) 454-6591 ext. 259

PRO-AM

Spots open to the public? Yes
Handicap: Maximum of 21
Format: Best ball of team

Entry fee: Two tiers, $1750 and $3500
For more information: (213) 482-1311

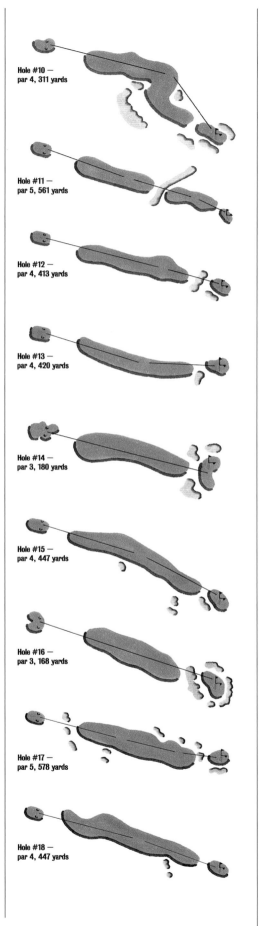

Hole #10 — par 4, 311 yards

Hole #11 — par 5, 561 yards

Hole #12 — par 4, 413 yards

Hole #13 — par 4, 420 yards

Hole #14 — par 3, 180 yards

Hole #15 — par 4, 447 yards

Hole #16 — par 3, 168 yards

Hole #17 — par 5, 578 yards

Hole #18 — par 4, 447 yards

Doral-Ryder Open

DORAL COUNTRY CLUB

J ack Nicklaus plays here—still. Ray Floyd has perfect attendance. Nick Faldo has made it his first victory of the year. Couples, Crenshaw, and Kite wouldn't miss it, and Greg Norman not only plays, he plays like the Great White Shark.

The Tour season may start in January at La Costa, but not until the Doral-Ryder Open does the competition get stiff and serious. Part of the reason is that this tournament is the first event of the year played on the East Coast, the start of the "Florida swing" that leads up to the Players Championship and ultimately The Masters. The other reason is the golf course.

Designed in 1962 by Dick Wilson, the Blue Course at the Doral Country Cub is the flagship of a five-course complex at this, the most famed of the golf resorts of southern Florida. Like most courses in the area, its fairways are dead flat and lined by big white bunkers, bermuda rough, and swaying palms. But this course is true blue— Wilson incorporated eight water hazards in his design—and when the wind kicks up, as it does almost every afternoon,

THE TV HOLES

Expect birdies:

Nowhere

Expect bogeys:

13, 18

18th hole

What to Watch For . . .

GRAND ENTRANCES
Miami International Airport is only a few miles away, and the course is smack on one of the approach routes.

HOME BOYS
Residents of southern Florida seem to respond well to a short commute. Ray Floyd and Andy Bean each have won Doral three times, and Jack Nicklaus and Greg Norman have two victories apiece.

CART TRAFFIC
Doral is a busy resort with five golf courses, and it's not about to shut down even for a PGA Tour event. As the pros ply their trade on the Blue Course, legions of the less talented putter around the other tracks.

CASTING ABOUT
The three favorite hobbies of PGA Tour pros are fishing, fishing, and fishing. Many of them travel with bass rods in their golf bags, and since the Doral property has almost as much water as turf, it's not uncommon to come upon a pro casting at the edge of a water hazard. Early in the week, there's even a fishing contest for the pros.

HIDING STARS
The practice ground at Doral is unusual in that it can be attacked from either end—two groups of players actually hit at each other. While most of the pros (and hotel guests) hit from the area near the hotel, many of the better-known players seek the comparative quiet of the opposite end, where there is a golf school operated by noted teacher Jim McLean. So if you want to watch some serious practice by Nick Faldo or Tom Kite, don't go to the place where most of the balls are being hit—go down to the end where they're rolling to a stop.

The Shark Strikes Twice
The course record of 62 has been shot twice — both by Greg "The Shark" Norman. The first time (1990) it gave him the tournament record for best final-round comeback (seven strokes). The second time (1993) it gave him the tournament record for the largest 54-hole lead (six strokes).

Doral Country Club

Hole #1 —
par 5, 514 yards

Hole #2 —
par 4, 355 yards

Hole #3 —
par 4, 398 yards

Hole #4 —
par 3, 237 yards

Hole #5 —
par 4, 371 yards

Hole #6 —
par 4, 427 yards

Hole #7 —
par 4, 415 yards

Hole #8 —
par 5, 528 yards

Hole #9 —
par 3, 163 yards

16th hole

playing through this 6939 yards can be like trying to negotiate a labyrinth.

Length is a big factor on several holes. Two of the par threes weigh in at 246 yards and 237 yards, and the 12th hole is a par five of 591 yards, often into the wind. But Wilson saved his best hole for last, a 425-yard par four that meanders along the edge of a lake to a long, narrow green. Ray Floyd calls it "the hardest par four in the world."

TOURNAMENT RATINGS

COURSE DIFFICULTY

Avg. winning score: 13.5 under par	20th on Tour
USGA course rating: 73.2 (1.2 over par)	38th on Tour
Overall rating: Moderate	27th on Tour

PRESTIGE

Field strength (14.3)	11th on Tour
Winner quality (.780)	16th on Tour
Course difficulty (above)	27th on Tour
Plus factors: Course rated 71st in U.S.	
Overall rating	13th on Tour

Practical Matters

FOR TICKET INFORMATION
Doral Country Club
P.O. Box 522927
Miami, FL 33152

COURSE
Doral Country Club

ACCESS
Resort course, open to all—
Doral hotel guests get priority
For more information:
(305) 592-2030

COURSE RATING

Tees	Pro	Member
Yardage	6939	6597
Rating	73.2	71.6
Slope	127	122

GREEN FEES
Guest fee: $150 for outside guests, $110 for hotel guests
For more information:
(305) 592-2030

PRO-AM
Spots open to the public? Yes
Handicap: Maximum of 21
Format: Best ball of team
Entry fee: Three-tiered pro-am
$1200, $1700, $3600
For more information:
(305) 477-GOLF

Local Knowledge

BEATING GREENSIDE BERMUDA

The rough that grows on most southeastern courses is thicker and more tangly than that of courses in the north. As a result, it confounds many visitors, particularly around the green, where too soft a swing leaves the ball in the grass and too aggressive a hit produces a jumper that flies well past its target.

Up north, the answer might be to open the face of a wedge and play the shot like a sand explosion. That doesn't work down south—in fact, the most useful tactic is just the opposite.

When you're faced with a greenside shot from bermuda rough, close the face of your club—turn the toe of the club about 30 degrees toward the ball. Now, when you make your swing, your club will be less likely to get caught in the grass. You'll produce a low shot that jumps quickly out of the grass and runs most of the way to the hole. It's a very simple shot—practice it for just a few minutes, and it will be a permanent part of your short-game arsenal.

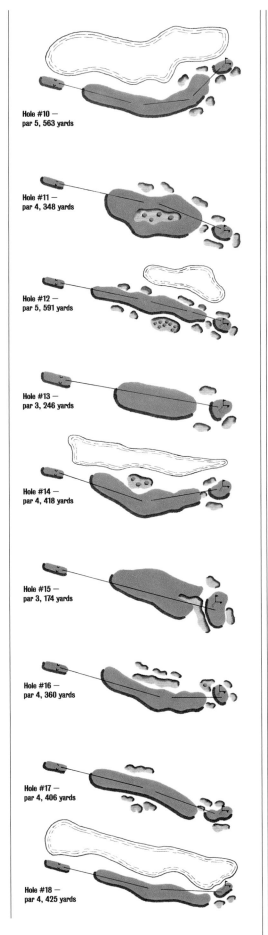

Hole #10 —
par 5, 563 yards

Hole #11 —
par 4, 348 yards

Hole #12 —
par 5, 591 yards

Hole #13 —
par 3, 246 yards

Hole #14 —
par 4, 418 yards

Hole #15 —
par 3, 174 yards

Hole #16 —
par 4, 360 yards

Hole #17 —
par 4, 406 yards

Hole #18 —
par 4, 425 yards

Honda Classic

TPC AT HERON BAY

The youngest golf course on the PGA Tour is the TPC at Heron Bay, in Coral Springs, Florida, which opens late in 1995 for a debut as host of the Honda Classic in the spring of 1996. It replaced the course at nearby Weston Hills, which four years earlier had replaced the TPC at Eagle Trace.

Heron Bay is in fact just a few minutes from Eagle Trace, but course architect Mark McCumber took pains to distinguish his design from that of its neighbor, which was a disaster during its days as Honda host. The routing of the course did not make sufficient allowance for the prevailing winds. Water was in play almost constantly, and when a strong crosswind combined with a narrow fairway or an all-carry approach to a lakeside green, the results were embarrassing for the pros, who complained immediately and loudly. That's what led to the interim stay at Weston Hills and the eventual move to Heron Bay. Heron Bay has less water: It comes into play for the pros on only three holes—most dramatically at the 18th, a 445-yard dogleg right

THE TV HOLES

Expect birdies:
13, 16
Expect bogeys:
18

18th hole at Weston Hills

What to Watch For . . .

HOMAGE TO THE MONSTER
McCumber has won two Doral-Ryder Opens, loves the course, and has consciously imitated it at Heron Bay. His design team made several visits to the Blue Monster, paced off the width of each fairway, made copies of the yardage book, and took photos of every hole.

FAST FINISHES
This event has a knack for producing grand finales. It was here that Corey Pavin holed out an 8-iron for eagle on the 72nd hole to tie Fred Couples, whom he then beat in a playoff, and it was here that the Golden Bear had his most golden finish.

FADERS
McCumber's trademark is a high, left-to-right ball, so it's no surprise that several holes at Heron Bay favor that sort of shot. Don't be surprised if the Tour's ultimate fader, Bruce Lietzke, does well here. He has won this tournament in the past and is usually a contender on TPC courses.

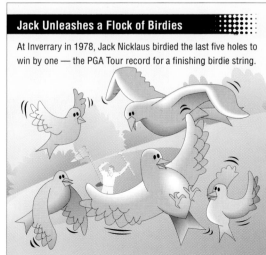

Jack Unleashes a Flock of Birdies

At Inverrary in 1978, Jack Nicklaus birdied the last five holes to win by one — the PGA Tour record for a finishing birdie string.

TPC at Heron Bay

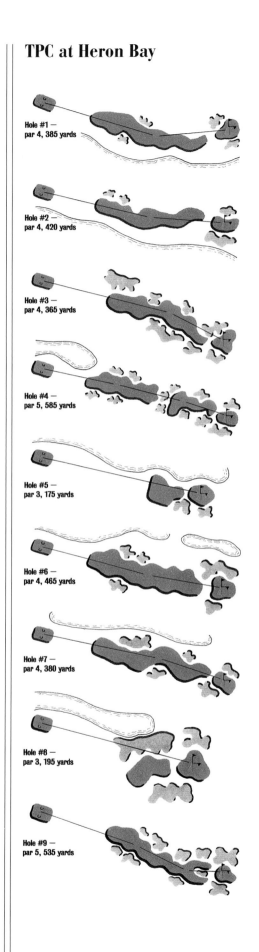

Hole #1 —
par 4, 385 yards

Hole #2 —
par 4, 420 yards

Hole #3 —
par 4, 365 yards

Hole #4 —
par 5, 585 yards

Hole #5 —
par 3, 175 yards

Hole #6 —
par 4, 465 yards

Hole #7 —
par 4, 380 yards

Hole #8 —
par 3, 195 yards

Hole #9 —
par 5, 535 yards

An artist's rendering of the new course at TPC at Heron Bay

with a lake running down the entire right side of the fairway. There is also less interference from cross-winds. Most of the holes run in a north-south direction and thus play either downwind or upwind in the prevailing breeze.

In fact, minimalism is the key at Heron Bay. The site McCumber and his associates were given was completely flat, barren, and featureless, and they didn't do much contriving with it. The broad fairways are contoured with humps and hollows and dotted with a hundred bunkers, and the last few greens are surrounded by the trademark TPC spectator mounds. But the course remains relatively treeless—the few trees that were brought in are used mostly for screening and as backdrops to the greens, which are large, to accommodate daily-fee play, but basically flat. It's not a pretty golf course, but it's the type of honest, straightforward layout that should please daily-fee players 51 weeks a year, yet test the PGA Tour for seven days in March.

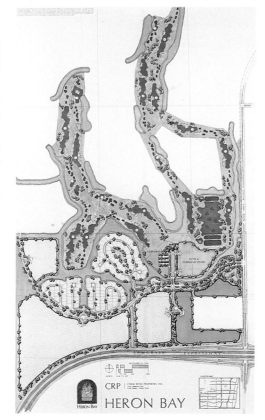

CRP

HERON BAY

Local Knowledge

THE HARDEST PUTT TO MAKE

Like many public courses, the TPC at Heron Bay has large greens. This moves play along, by minimizing the time spent on chip and pitch shots, and also reduces wear and tear from spikes, by allowing several pin positions which draw the traffic to different sectors of the green.

But in contrast to many large-green courses, those at Heron Bay are also relatively flat. The result is that one often faces the most difficult of all putts—a lengthy one that must be hit straight.

Why is it difficult? There's no opportunity to fiddle with the break and speed of the putt—you can't allow break with less speed, or play less break with a firmer hit. You *must* hit the ball on line and with the proper pace.

If you have trouble with such putts, it's probably because you tend to pull or push the ball off line, or allow your wrists to become too active in the stroke. Take a tip from the Tour pros, most of whom use a pure arm-and-shoulder stroke, with no wrist action. By letting the arms and shoulders determine the length and pace of your stroke, you have better control of the distance of the putt than you do by involving the more sudden and volatile movements of the wrists. And by keeping the wrists stiff you also improve your accuracy: Set the back of your left hand straight at your target, and keep it facing that way throughout the stroke, and you'll insure that the ball starts straight at the hole.

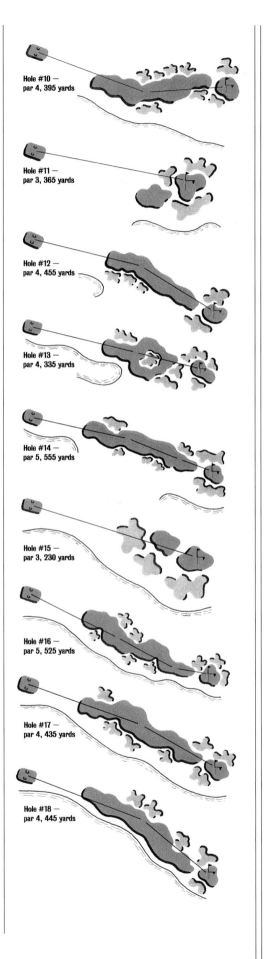

Hole #10 —
par 4, 395 yards

Hole #11 —
par 3, 365 yards

Hole #12 —
par 4, 455 yards

Hole #13 —
par 4, 335 yards

Hole #14 —
par 5, 555 yards

Hole #15 —
par 3, 230 yards

Hole #16 —
par 5, 525 yards

Hole #17 —
par 4, 435 yards

Hole #18 —
par 4, 445 yards

Bay Hill Invitational

BAY HILL CLUB

t begins with one impossible par four and ends with another. In between, there are no breathers. Beyond a doubt, Bay Hill is the toughest test of golf on the southeastern swing of the PGA Tour.

But the pros respect it and love it — just as they do the man who owns the Bay Hill Club—Arnold Palmer. Back in 1965, Palmer played an exhibition with Jack Nicklaus on this Dick Wilson course, and he liked the place so much he bought it. Then the game's ultimate tinkerer spent a quarter century refashioning the course in his own image. Today's Bay Hill is a course that rewards long, strong, straight tee shots — the kind Palmer made famous —

T H E
TV
H O L E S

Expect birdies:

16

Expect bogeys:

17, 18

and with six water hazards and over a hundred bunkers, it also encourages Arnie's brand of scrambling, gambling, go-for-broke golf.

At the very first tee you sense that it will be a challenging day. For years, Bay Hill's opener was a pansy of a par five, but in 1990 Arnie shortened it just a few yards and made it into a bull of a par four. In its first year in play it ranked as the hardest opening hole on the Tour.

Eagles are possible at 16, a 481-yard par five, but anyone who wants to putt for a 3 will have to show some Palmer aggressiveness, since a stream crosses in front of the green. After that, even birdies will be scarce, for Bay

What to Watch For . . .

LOYALTY TO THE KING

Today's generation of Tour players may respect Nicklaus the player, but they love Palmer the man. If the field here is strong, it is partly a reflection of their devotion to Arnold. When the TV commentators corral players for interviews at the 18th green, expect to see more than one heartfelt salute to the one they call The King.

TEAM ORLANDO

We're not talking about Shaquille O'Neal and The Magic. Team Orlando refers to the galaxy of international golfers living within a short radius of the Bay Hill Club: Fulton Allem, Ian Baker-Finch, Brad Bryant, Wayne Grady, Donnie Hammond, Scott Hoch, Mike Hulbert, Lee Janzen, Bob Lohr, Bret Ogle, Corey Pavin, Mark O'Meara, Craig Parry, Steve Pate, David Peebles, Denis Watson, and Payne Stewart.

LAYUPS

Again, we don't mean basketball. It's rare that you see a Tour player intentionally leave his second shot well short of a par-four green. But when a tee shot finds rough at Bay Hill's 18th, the ensuing assignment is a bit forbidding even for the pros. Rather than risk a half-hit shot that plops into the drink, the boys will wedge to the fairway, then wedge to the green, hoping for a one-putt par and accepting the probability of a bogey rather than risk a really big number.

MACHO MEMENTO

Fittingly for a tournament hosted by the game's most macho legend, the permanent trophy is a four-foot-long sword. Manufactured in the United Kingdom by Wilkinson Sword Ltd., it is hand-crafted with an etched steel blade and a silver and rosewood handle.

17th hole

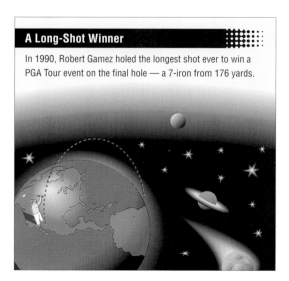

A Long-Shot Winner

In 1990, Robert Gamez holed the longest shot ever to win a PGA Tour event on the final hole — a 7-iron from 176 yards.

Bay Hill Club

Hole #1 —
par 4, 441 yards

Hole #2 —
par 3, 218 yards

Hole #3 —
par 4, 395 yards

Hole #4 —
par 5, 530 yards

Hole #5 —
par 4, 365 yards

Hole #6 —
par 5, 543 yards

Hole #7 —
par 3, 197 yards

Hole #8 —
par 4, 424 yards

Hole #9 —
par 4, 467 yards

14th hole

Hill finishes with a staggering one-two punch. The 219-yard 17th plays almost entirely over water to a shallow green.

And number 18 is where every player will have to hitch up his pants—441 yards up and over a hill to a boomerang-shaped green that hugs a rock-bound lake. It is the type of hole that looms large in one's mind throughout the day, but in 1990, 21-year-old Tour rookie Robert Gamez conquered it with the shot of the year, a 176-yard 7-iron that found the cup for an eagle. He edged Greg Norman by a stroke.

TOURNAMENT RATINGS

COURSE DIFFICULTY

Avg. winning score: 12.6 under par	16th on Tour
USGA course rating: 74.6 (2.6 over par)	21st on Tour
Overall rating: Moderate	21st on Tour

PRESTIGE

Field strength (15.5)	8th on Tour
Winner quality (.560)	28th on Tour
Course difficulty (above)	21st on Tour

Plus factors: Invitational, hosted by Arnold Palmer, international field, course rated 95th in U.S.

Overall rating	12th on Tour

Practical Matters

FOR TICKET INFORMATION
The Bay Hill Invitational
Bay Hill Club & Lodge
9000 Bay Blvd.
Orlando, FL 32819
(407) 876-2888

COURSE
Bay Hill Club

ACCESS
Private club—you must be introduced by a member.

COURSE RATING

Tees	Pro	Member
Yardage	7114	6547
Rating	74.6	71.8
Slope	141	127

GREEN FEES
$125, includes cart
For more information:
(407) 876-2429

PRO-AM
Spots open to the public?
Yes, but priority is given to participants from prior years
Handicap: Maximum of 21
Format: Best ball of four amateurs and pro
Entry fee: $3000
For more information:
(407) 876-2888

Local Knowledge

A SMOOTH MOVE FOR HARD CLUBS

The four par-threes at Bay Hill measure 218, 197, 206, and 219 yards. That's a total of 840 yards—and an average of 210—the longest quartet of short holes on the U.S Tour. What it means is that those who play Bay Hill should be prepared to exercise their long irons.

For most golfers, the long irons are the most difficult clubs in the bag to hit. But they needn't be so daunting, especially when you get to play them for a tee. The key to hitting them properly is in two words: smooth sweep. You don't hit these clubs—you wait for impact to happen.

Long iron play requires both practice and discipline, but you'll give yourself a head start if you address the ball so that your hands are even with it or just behind it. This probably means positioning the ball at a point roughly opposite your left instep, a bit forward of its usual position in your stance. To insure a smooth, long sweep through impact, take the club away the same way—draw it slowly back from the ball. Your takeaway should be a unified movement of the hands, arms, and shoulders, with not a hint of flippiness in the wrists. After that, just stay patient—wait for the club to finish its trip to the top of your swing, and then just allow the coil you've created to unwind. Don't try to hit at the ball or scoop it up. Remember, a 3-iron has more loft than a 4-wood, so there's no need to help the ball—just let yourself, and your club, make a smooth sweep.

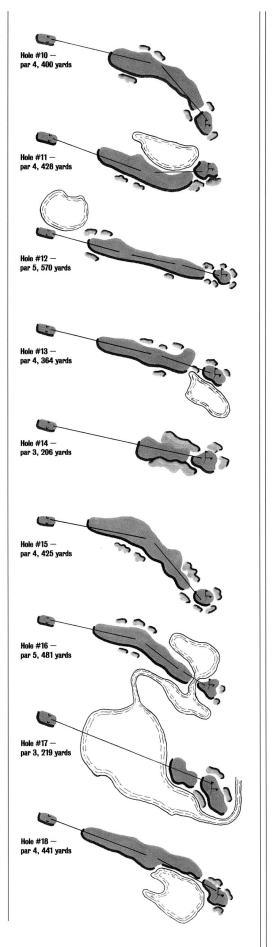

Hole #10 —
par 4, 400 yards

Hole #11 —
par 4, 428 yards

Hole #12 —
par 5, 570 yards

Hole #13 —
par 4, 364 yards

Hole #14 —
par 3, 206 yards

Hole #15 —
par 4, 425 yards

Hole #16 —
par 5, 481 yards

Hole #17 —
par 3, 219 yards

Hole #18 —
par 4, 441 yards

THE PLAYERS Championship

TPC AT SAWGRASS

I f you want to combine a family vacation with a chance to watch the pros, this is your tournament. About 45 minutes from the Jacksonville Airport—and one mile from a gorgeous white sand beach—is the Tournament Players Club (TPC) at Sawgrass. Here THE PLAYERS Championship unfolds each March—about the same time as your kids' spring break.

You'll get to watch a field that includes most of the top players in the world—guaranteed—and watch them on a course that makes spectating a pleasure. If the big boys inspire you to try your own hand, a half dozen superb and visitor-friendly layouts are within easy reach. And when the rest of the family gets bored, take heart—Walt Disney World is just a day trip away.

Tim Finchem wouldn't like the notion of lumping his tournament with Mickey and Goofy, but the Commissioner realizes better than most that his players are essentially entertainers, and in the TPC at Sawgrass he has given them a grand stage.

Finchem's predecessor, Deane Beman, was the co-designer of this course, along with architect Pete Dye, back in 1980, and the initial reviews from his own Tour players were less than enthusiastic. The most caustic remark came from the notoriously vituperative J.C. Snead, who characterized it as "90 percent horse manure and 10 percent luck."

It was the tightly bunkered, heavily contoured greens that incited most of the uproar. But Beman and Dye listened, and over the next decade they softened their course. Today it is one of golf's greatest comeback stories—both the pros and amateurs praise it as one of the finest in the world.

THE TV HOLES

Expect birdies:
11, 12, 16

Expect bogeys:
14, 18

Above: 11th hole
Right: 17th hole

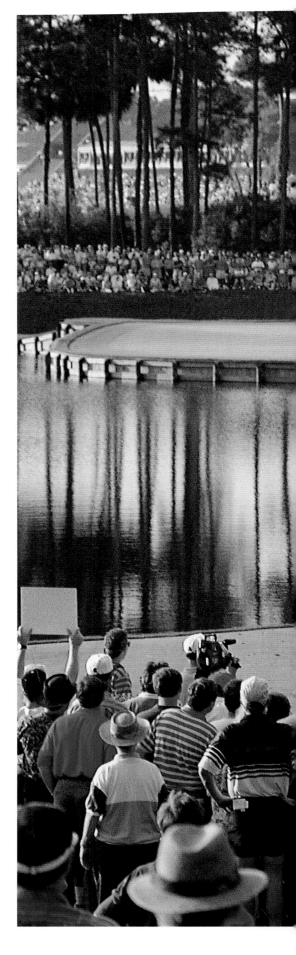

What to Watch For . . .

GREENSTANDS
This Stadium Course actually has stadium seating. Spectators at the first tee and 18th green watch the action from the comfort of enormous mounds that have been sculpted and terraced like wedding cakes, the rows of seats bulkheaded with wooden stakes and planking. Occasionally at 18, when a player pushes his approach shot, the fans have to clear out so the hapless pro can wedge his third shot from Section 13/Row 4/Seat J.

SKYBOXES
Commercialized professional golf finds its tacky epitome in the string of corporate hospitality cabins that loom above the left side of the island 17th hole. Each is equipped with comfortable chairs and a full-service bar.

THE NAME GAME
Symbolic of the struggle to raise the prestige of this event is the PGA Tour's manipulation of the tournament name. Originally, it was known as the Tournament Players Championship, a less-than-riveting mouthful whose abbreviation (TPC) quickly became confused with the network of Tournament Players Club courses. The Tour then shortened the name to THE PLAYERS Championship, hoping press and fans would compress it still further to THE PLAYERS (as in The Masters). In an attempt to hasten history with typography, they refer to their event everywhere in print as THE PLAYERS Championship.

EVERYONE WHO'S ANYONE
This is traditionally the strongest field of the year. All eligible U.S. PGA Tour players are invited—indeed, semi-required—to attend, and since the purse is the largest of any regular Tour event, few decline. The leading internationals are invited too, and many of them show up, using this as a final tuneup for The Masters, two weeks later.

A Watery Grave
In the blustery opening round of the 1984 Players Championship, 64 balls plunked into the water surrounding the 17th green. The scoring average for the day was 3.79, the highest ever recorded for a hole on the PGA Tour.

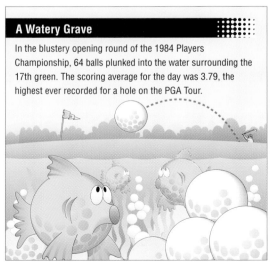

TPC at Sawgrass

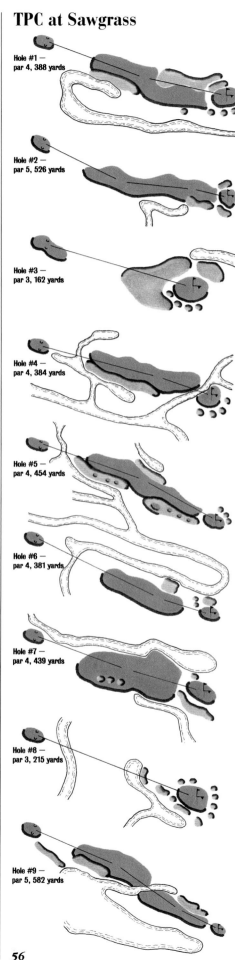

Hole #1 —
par 4, 388 yards

Hole #2 —
par 5, 526 yards

Hole #3 —
par 3, 162 yards

Hole #4 —
par 4, 384 yards

Hole #5 —
par 4, 454 yards

Hole #6 —
par 4, 381 yards

Hole #7 —
par 4, 439 yards

Hole #8 —
par 3, 215 yards

Hole #9 —
par 5, 582 yards

TOURNAMENT RATINGS

COURSE DIFFICULTY

Avg. winning score: 14.4 under par	26th on Tour
USGA course rating: 74.0 (2.0 over par)	28th on Tour
Overall rating: Moderate	30th on Tour

PRESTIGE

Field strength (18.8/25.0*)	5th on Tour*
Winner quality (1.050)	5th on Tour
Course difficulty (above)	30th on Tour
Plus factors: Course rated 46th in U.S., large purse, near-major status, 10-year exemption to winner, international field	
Overall rating	5th on Tour

*Based on Sony Ranking comparison with major championships

This is not a long course—less than 7000 yards—but accuracy is paramount, both from the tee and into the green.

And Beman saved most of the excitement for the finale. On no finishing stretch is a lead less secure than over the last three holes—a par five, par three, and par four, all guarded by water.

Sixteen is reachable in two, but even more reachable is the lake that runs down its right side. No short

___

18th hole

Practical Matters

FOR TICKET INFORMATION
The Players Championship
103 TPC Blvd.
Ponte Vedra, FL 32082

COURSE
TPC at Sawgrass—Stadium Course

ACCESS
Resort course with members, open to the public

COURSE RATING

Tees	Pro	Member
Yardage	6857	6394
Rating	74.0	71.9
Slope	135	130

GREEN FEES
$106 for guests of members;
$145 for resort guests
(rates include cart)
For more information:
(904) 273-3235

PRO-AM
None
For more information:
(904) 285-3700

hole is more intimidating than the famed island 17th. Number 18 is the toughest hole on the course, arcing 440 yards along the edge of a lake. Going into these holes, a player can be three strokes ahead of the field and lose—easily—and, just as easily, a player can be three behind and steal it away.

Local Knowledge

BEATING BIG BUNKERS

Until 1994, one of the salient features of the TPC at Sawgrass was the waste bunker—in fact dozens of them—vast tracts of unraked sand where players were allowed to ground the club before playing their shots.

These days, those waste bunkers are simply bunkers—the sand is neatly raked, but you may not ground your club. But they remain a daunting aspect of the challenge at this course.

However, the fact is, they're more intimidating than intrinsically difficult. Since the base of the bunker is shallow, you rarely get a bad lie—the ball sits up just as it does in the fairway, allowing you to make clean contact. Nonetheless, you should take care: Use one club more than you would from a fairway lie, and keep your swing compact, with a bit less lower body movement than normal. A slightly wider-than-usual stance will help keep the legs quiet.

If you often hit fat or topped shots from these lies, try setting up in a slightly open stance, with your feet and body aligned left of the target. This "slice stance" facilitates a more downward impact, so you'll be less likely to hit behind the ball (for a fat shot) or up and over it (for a top).The open stance will also encourage a slightly higher trajectory, which will help you fly the ball over the bunker's lip. Just expect a bit less yardage, along with some left-to-rightward drift.

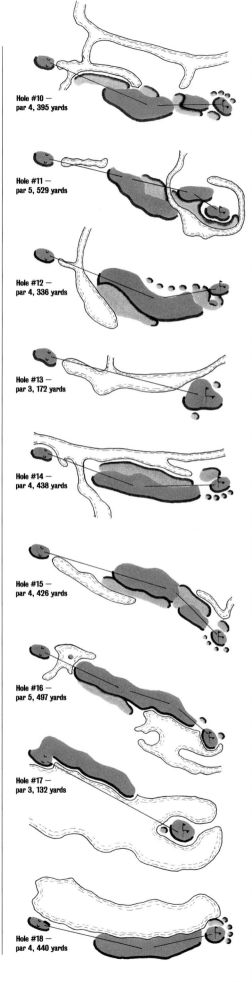

Hole #10 —
par 4, 395 yards

Hole #11 —
par 5, 529 yards

Hole #12 —
par 4, 336 yards

Hole #13 —
par 3, 172 yards

Hole #14 —
par 4, 438 yards

Hole #15 —
par 4, 426 yards

Hole #16 —
par 5, 497 yards

Hole #17 —
par 3, 132 yards

Hole #18 —
par 4, 440 yards

Freeport-McMoRan Classic

ENGLISH TURN GOLF AND COUNTRY CLUB

B.L.O.B. That's the advice for those taking on English Turn Golf & Country Club: Bring Lots of Balls. This is a golf course with more water hazards (21) than holes.

Those hazards weren't there in 1988—but Jack Nicklaus was. His golf course design company came to this flat area on the Mississippi delta, excavated a moat, funneled water throughout the property, and molded over a million cubic yards of dirt into one of the most distinctive layouts on the Tour.

Throughout his architectural career, Nicklaus has been accused of designing courses with his own game in mind. In most cases the criticism has been unjust, but with English Turn a strong case can be made. It is long, its 10 par fours averaging more than 415 yards in length, the way Jack likes them. With many greens guarded by lakes, it calls for high-flying approach shots that land softly—the way Jack plays them. And its speedy greens are full of severe contours, calling for nerves of steel—just like Jack's.

Still, most critics who have played English Turn agree that this is one of Jack's best designs. Nicklaus claims it was the most challenging piece of property he's had to work with and is proud of the "pace" of his routing, in which the tough holes alternate with less tough ones.

The most dramatic hole on the course is 15, a par five that plays 542 water-flanked yards to an island green. Under normal conditions, it's reachable in two, but even the strongest hitters will have to go at it with long irons. Speaking of the strongest players, the mighty John Daly has a record here, but one he'd rather not own. In the second round of the 1994 tournament, Daly hit

THE TV HOLES

Expect birdies:
11

Expect bogeys:
18

18th hole

What to Watch For . . .

GOURMET CUISINE
New Orleans's famed restaurants offer their specialties at a "fan enhancement area" amid the corporate hospitality tents.

REPTILES
In the first year the tournament was held here, play at the 11th hole was suspended so officials could coax a water moccasin off the green, and in 1992 a marshal at the 14th hole had to call for help to corral an alligator that had taken up residence in the rough at number 14.

A NORMAN CONQUEST
In the first four years the tournament was held at English Turn, Greg Norman failed to win but finished second three times, most agonizingly in 1991, when David Frost blasted from a greenside bunker and into the hole for a birdie that gave him a one-stroke victory. A win by the Great White Shark would seem inevitable.

COMPLAINING PROS
A *GOLF Magazine* survey of 70 PGA Tour players found that this was the least popular tournament on the U.S. Tour, and that New Orleans was the city the pros liked second least. Only Los Angeles was less popular.

Tough Assignments			
Hardest Holes on the PGA Tour:			
Course	**Hole**	**Par**	**Avg. Score**
English Turn G & CC	**18**	**4**	**4.493**
Spyglass Hill GC	8	4	4.419
Spyglass Hill GC	16	4	4.415
Westchester CC	12	4	4.411
Bay Hill Club	18	4	4.409

English Turn Golf and Country Club

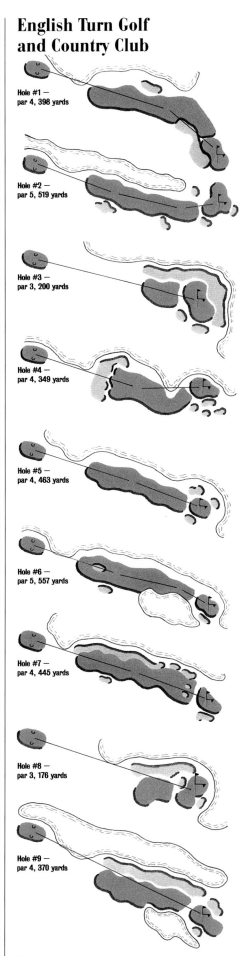

Hole #1 —
par 4, 398 yards

Hole #2 —
par 5, 519 yards

Hole #3 —
par 3, 200 yards

Hole #4 —
par 4, 349 yards

Hole #5 —
par 4, 463 yards

Hole #6 —
par 5, 557 yards

Hole #7 —
par 4, 445 yards

Hole #8 —
par 3, 176 yards

Hole #9 —
par 4, 370 yards

15th hole

four tee shots into the water, finally reached the back greenside bunker in 10, and got up and down for a 12. Daly posted an 84 for the day and got the weekend off.

Any birdies earned at 15 will be needed, because the final hole at English Turn is not only the hardest on the course, it is one of the hardest on the entire PGA Tour. It stretches 471 yards, and the tee shot must be threaded between water and a huge waste bunker on the left and a swarm of pot bunkers on the right. After that it's an approach of over 200 yards to a firm, shallow green cinched by sand. This is a hole where even the pros make bogey as often as par. In the 1992 tournament, only a handful of 3's were made here, but

one of them came at the moment of truth. After hitting his second shot into the left-hand bunker, South African David Frost splashed the ball out of the sand and into the hole for a birdie that edged luckless Greg Norman by a single stroke.

TOURNAMENT RATINGS

COURSE DIFFICULTY

Avg. winning score: 12.2 under par	15th on Tour
USGA course rating: 74.2 (2.2 over par)	25th on Tour
Overall rating: Moderate	23rd on Tour

PRESTIGE

Field strength (7.2)	36th on Tour
Winner quality (.780)	16th on Tour
Course difficulty (above)	23rd on Tour
Plus factors: None	
Overall rating	29th on Tour

Practical Matters

FOR TICKET INFORMATION
Freeport McMoRan Classic
110 Veterans Blvd.
Suite 170
Metairie, LA 70005

COURSE
English Turn Golf and
Country Club

ACCESS
Private course: In-town guests must play with a member; out-of-town guests must be introduced by a member. Occasionally, visitors can secure tee times by having their hotel call the pro shop.

COURSE RATING

Tees	Pro	Member
Yardage	7078	6449
Rating	74.2	71.0
Slope	141	131

GREEN FEES
$65 weekdays, $95 weekands

PRO-AM
Spots open to the public? Yes
Handicap: Maximum of 21
Format: Best ball of team
Entry fee: $2500
For more information:
(504) 391-8018

Local Knowledge

ESCAPING THE POTS

Haunting the right side of the drive zone at number 18 is a nest of pot bunkers. When a drive lands in them, reaching the green becomes little more than a dream. Pot bunkers abound on the links courses of Great Britain and Ireland, but in the U.S. they are relatively uncommon. When you find one, the best idea is to take your medicine. Don't try for a heroic shot of any appreciable distance—just be sure to get the ball back into play.

In the most severe cases, when you have a high lip in front of you, the right move may be to play out to the side, or even back toward the tee, rather than risking failure to clear the lip.

Assuming you have a reasonable lie—play the ball from a wide-open stance, and build some extra trajectory into your sand wedge (or third wedge) by opening the blade and laying it back so that the clubface at address is parallel to the surface of the bunker. The swing should be an up-and-down chopping motion, beginning with an early cocking of the wrists. Hit down sharply about an inch behind the ball—give it plenty of force— and be sure to finish the swing. If you "quit" on this shot, your ball won't get out of the pot.

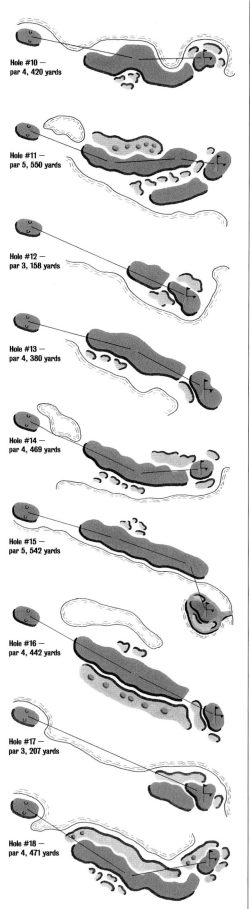

Hole #10 — par 4, 420 yards

Hole #11 — par 5, 550 yards

Hole #12 — par 3, 158 yards

Hole #13 — par 4, 380 yards

Hole #14 — par 4, 469 yards

Hole #15 — par 5, 542 yards

Hole #16 — par 4, 442 yards

Hole #17 — par 3, 207 yards

Hole #18 — par 4, 471 yards

MCI Heritage Classic

HARBOUR TOWN GOLF LINKS

You'd think the tournament that runs one week after The Masters would be a crashing, inevitable letdown. Not so the Heritage Classic.

Just a three–hour drive from Augusta, Georgia, is Hilton Head Island, South Carolina. Each April, one day after the season's first major championship, an international field of players begins to assemble here —a field greater in number and of no lesser quality than the one that convened at Augusta. From Thursday through Sunday they put on a show of shotmaking that, in most years, boils down to a final–nine battle rivaling the stretch run at The Masters. And when the smoke clears, the man on top is invariably a player of the very highest caliber.

They come here each year for one surpassing reason: the golf course. At the eastern tip of this island is the Harbour Town Golf Links, a layout that may be the best-loved playing field on the PGA Tour. Designed in 1969 by Pete Dye, with consultation from then-budding architect Jack Nicklaus, Harbour Town has been called the first modern American golf course. Dye resisted the

THE
TV
HOLES

Expect birdies:

Nowhere

Expect bogeys:

11

18th hole

What to Watch For . . .

WEDGE WIZARDRY
The greens here are about 20 percent smaller than at most Tour stops. As a result, even the pros miss their targets a good part of the time. This gives us a chance to appreciate their greenside artistry.

NOT JUST WINNERS—CHAMPIONS
Arnold Palmer won the first Heritage Classic in 1969, and that set a pattern. In 19 of this event's first 25 years, the victor was a player with at least one major championship on his résumé, and in three of the six other years (1987, 1991, and 1992) the winner has been Davis Love III, a player widely agreed to have at least one major title in his future.

ERSATZ SCOTLAND
The folks in South Carolina's Low Country claim that golf had its American origins here with a settlement of Scottish merchants in the late 18th century— hence the name "Heritage." The Harbour Town club- house is the rechartered home of the South Carolina Golf Club and it houses a valuable collection of antique clubs imported from Scotland. A parade of bagpipers begins the tournament, and each champion receives a tartan blazer.

A START WITH A BANG
Another aspect of the tradition is the "playing-in" of the defending champion, a ceremony that mimics the annual rite at the Royal & Ancient Golf Club of St. Andrews, Scotland, where each new captain (equiva- lent of a club president) plays himself into office by hitting a ceremonial tee shot from the first tee of the Old Course. At Harbour Town, as at St. Andrews, a cannon blast is fired at the moment of impact.

"Caddie, Dust Off My Putter!"

Fewest Putts for 72 Holes on the PGA Tour:

Putts	Player	Tournament
93	Kenny Knox	1989 MCI Heritage Classic
94	George Archer	1980 Sea Pines Heritage Classic
99	Bob Menne	1977 Tournament Players Championship
	Steve Melnyk	1980 Sea Pines Heritage Classic
	Greg Norman	1990 USF&G Classic

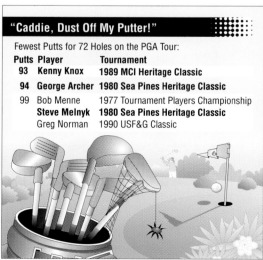

Harbour Town Golf Links

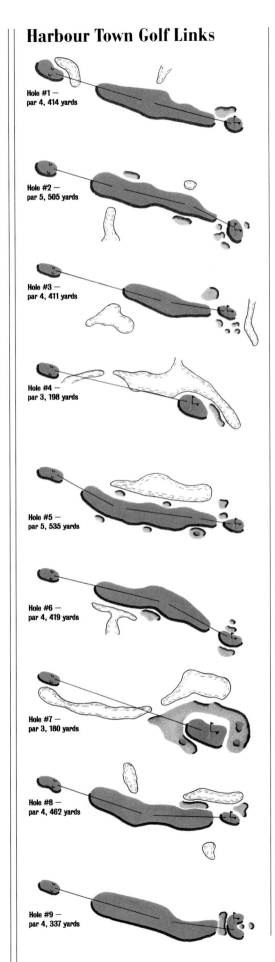

Hole #1 —
par 4, 414 yards

Hole #2 —
par 5, 505 yards

Hole #3 —
par 4, 411 yards

Hole #4 —
par 3, 198 yards

Hole #5 —
par 5, 535 yards

Hole #6 —
par 4, 419 yards

Hole #7 —
par 3, 180 yards

Hole #8 —
par 4, 462 yards

Hole #9 —
par 4, 337 yards

American penchant for long, expansive courses and instead crafted a tight, cozy journey through the low-lying marshland, threading his narrow fairways through stands of oak, pine, and Spanish moss, and placing his greens in menacing proximity to a dozen ponds and lagoons.

Minimalism is the keynote here. Only 6912 yards, this par 71 sets no records on the odometer but is plenty long on challenge. The fairways are slender, the greens are small, and when the wind blows off nearby Calibogue Sound, every target shrinks still further. Only 45 bunkers mark Harbour Town, but every one is cunningly placed. They come in all shapes and sizes—from the tiny pots guarding the ninth and 14th greens to the white moat encircling the dance floor at number seven.

This may be the ultimate shot-maker's course. It can't be pummeled into submission with booming drives and towering irons, but must be caressed with soft fades, controlled draws, and deft pitches. Says co-designer Nicklaus, "I get angrier here than anywhere else.... This place is designed for some shots I'm not supposed to be able to hit, and that's a challenge. Then, when I can't hit them, it just burns my rear end."

No course has a more beguiling quartet of par threes, and the last of them, number 17, is always pivotal. It plays 192 yards over water and then

an immense bunker that is bulkheaded with architect Dye's signature railroad ties. Late on Sunday, the tee shot plays dead into the setting sun, making club selection a particular challenge.

More often than not, the tournament hinges on Harbour Town's final hole, a 478–yard par four that winds along the marshy edge of the Sound, its tee on one promontory, the drive zone on a spit of land, and the bulkheaded green rising from the bog. Into a strong wind, it is unreachable even to the pros, and even under perfect conditions it is a tough place to have to make a par.

Practical Matters

FOR TICKET INFORMATION
MCI Heritage Classic
79 Lighthouse Road
Suite 414
Hilton Head, SC 29928

COURSE
Harbour Town Golf Links

ACCESS
Resort course, open to the public

COURSE RATING

Tees	Pro	Member
Yardage	6912	6119
Rating	74.0	70.0
Slope	136	126

GREEN FEES
$165.90; after 1:00 pm $105;
after 4 pm $95.55
For more information:
(803) 842-8484

PRO–AM
Spots open to the public? Yes
Handicap: Maximum of 21
Format: Best ball of team
Entry fee: $2950
For more information:
(803) 671-2448

Local Knowledge

BATTLING BAHIAGRASS

The rough doesn't get much rougher than at Harbour Town. Whereas the tees, fairways, and greens here are sown with strains of the bermudagrass that is common to this part of the country, the areas beyond the straight and narrow are thick with bahiagrass, a rare breed of weed that drives golfers crazy.

You can't get cute with this stuff. Don't even think about finessing the ball out with a soft swing. Instead, your object should be to insure clean and solid contact. You can minimize the effect of the grass by positioning the ball a couple of inches to the rear of its usual point in your stance. This will set up a steep up-and-down swing, with the club coming down on the back of the ball instead of sweeping through the grass. Stand a bit closer to the ball as well—this will have the same effect.

In extremely deep lies, calling for you to gouge out with a short iron or wedge, close the clubface of your club a few degrees—as you would for a buried lie in sand. And to insure firm impact with any lie, increase your left-hand grip pressure. This will help you hold the club square and resist the grasp of the bahia.

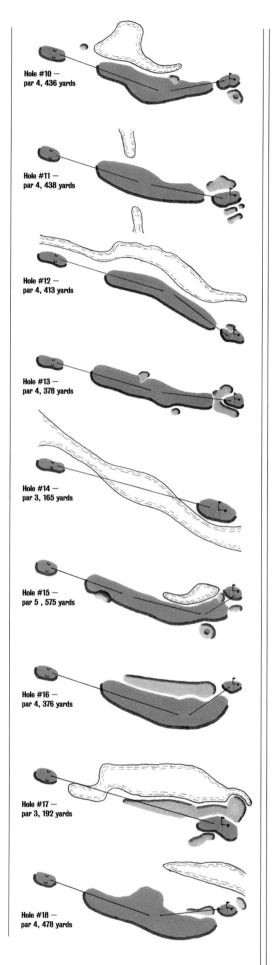

Hole #10 —
par 4, 436 yards

Hole #11 —
par 4, 438 yards

Hole #12 —
par 4, 413 yards

Hole #13 —
par 4, 378 yards

Hole #14 —
par 3, 165 yards

Hole #15 —
par 5 , 575 yards

Hole #16 —
par 4, 376 yards

Hole #17 —
par 3, 192 yards

Hole #18 —
par 4, 478 yards

Shell Houston Open

TPC AT THE WOODLANDS

I f you're expecting classic Texas—a lonely windswept prairie or a range of rugged hills—forget it. And if you're expecting classic Houston—the steel-and-concrete boom town —you can forget that too. Despite its address, this event isn't played in Houston, Texas, it's played at The Woodlands.

About a half hour from the city center, The Woodlands is a huge residential development created in the late 1970s. A network of quiet, tree-lined streets dotted with spacious homes, it could as easily be a suburb of Chicago or San Francisco or Jacksonville. In the center of this calculated community is a prime component of former Commissioner Deane Beman's infrastructure, the TPC at The Woodlands. In 1984 the Tour took over this Devlin/Von Hagge course, toughened it up a bit, made it spectator-friendly, and put it back in service for the 1985 Houston Open. Ray Floyd won that year, Curtis Strange the next, and this has been a mainstay on the Tour schedule ever since.

The pros like this course, partly because they make more birdies here than almost anywhere on the Tour. There are no killer holes, the statistically toughest test being the par-three 14th, which plays just a tenth of a stroke over par for the pros.

THE TV HOLES

Expect birdies:
13, 15

Expect bogeys:
Nowhere

14th hole

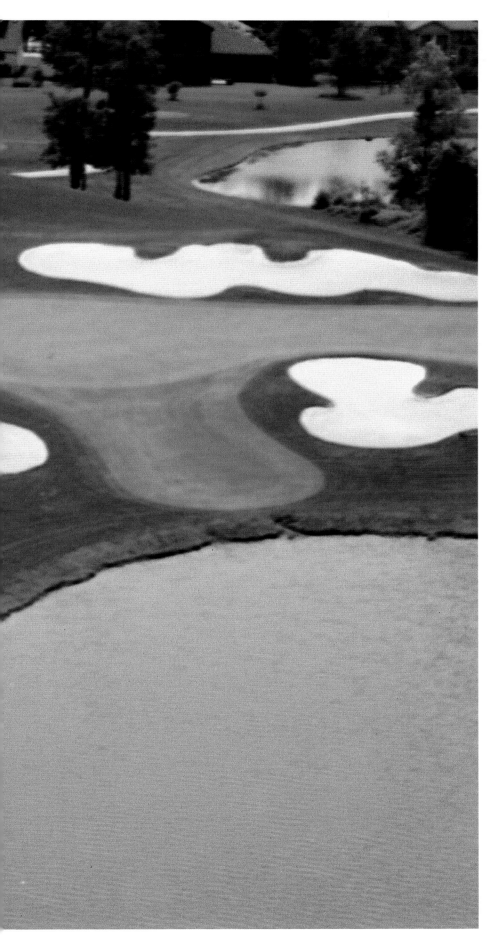

What to Watch For . . .

BREAKTHROUGHS

From 1990 to 1994, five straight Houston champions were first-time winners.

LOUSY WEATHER

In recent years, rainy days have been the rule here. Twice since 1990 the tournament has been shortened to 54 holes, and a third time (1991) the rain was so heavy that the entire tournament was rained out (the first time that had happened on Tour since 1966—at the Houston Open). But the Tour granted a mulligan and everyone returned to The Woodlands in November, when Fulton Allem won after a full 72 holes—despite a first round delayed by fog.

MOVES ON THE FIVES

Those who lose this tournament usually will collapse at the water-guarded 17th and 18th, but the winners tend to make their moves earlier, on the pair of back-nine par fives. Holes 13 and 15 are pushovers for the pros, yielding hundreds of birdies and more than a few eagles every year.

VITTLES

In case you forget this is South Texas, check out the practice tee, where the players are invited to fuel themselves for the day with a heapin' helpin' of barbecue.

PRO–AM–AM–AM–AM–AM

This tournament has not one pro-am, but five of them, two on Monday and three on Wednesday. For the pros, Tuesday is a day of rest.

Like Déjà Vû All Over Again

Gary Player won the Houston Open in 1978 for his third victory in a row. It's the last time a player has won in three consecutive weeks on the PGA Tour.

TPC at The Woodlands

Hole #1 —
par 5, 515 yards

Hole #2 —
par 4, 365 yards

Hole #3 —
par 3, 165 yards

Hole #4 —
par 4, 413 yards

Hole #5 —
par 4, 457 yards

Hole #6 —
par 5, 577 yards

Hole #7 —
par 4, 413 yards

Hole #8 —
par 3, 218 yards

Hole #9 —
par 4, 427 yards

17th hole

However, the last two holes constitute a worthy closing gauntlet. At 383 yards, 17 is one of the finer short par fours on the Tour. The pros tee off with long irons to position themselves at the knee of this leftward dogleg. This leaves a slightly downhill lie for the short-iron shot to a wide but extremely shallow green with water in front, a bunker to the rear.

Eighteen is another example of what has become the classic PGA Tour finishing hole, a lengthy par four that winds along water to a complex putting green. The golf courses at Doral, Sawgrass, Harbour Town, Scottsdale, Bay Hill, Colonial, and Southwind end in much the same way, but each of those holes is an excellent place to finish a tournament, and so, emphatically, is this one.

TOURNAMENT RATINGS

COURSE DIFFICULTY

Avg. winning score:	
13.9 under par	25th on Tour
USGA course rating:	
73.6 (1.6 over par)	34th on Tour
Overall rating:	
Moderate	31st on Tour

PRESTIGE

Field strength (8.2)	32nd on Tour
Winner quality (.500)	33rd on Tour
Course difficulty (above)	31st on Tour
Plus factors: None	
Overall rating	35th on Tour

Practical Matters

FOR TICKET INFORMATION
Houston Golf Association
1830 South Millbend Drive
The Woodlands, TX 77380

COURSE
TPC at The Woodlands

ACCESS
Open to the public

COURSE RATING

Tees	Pro	Member
Yardage	7045	6387
Rating	73.6	70.5
Slope	135	127

GREEN FEES
$70 weekdays, $85 weekends, including cart
For more information:
(713) 367-7285

PRO-AM
Spots open to the public? Yes
Handicap: Maximum of 21
Format: Best ball of team
Entry fee: $3000
For more information:
(713) 367-7999

Local Knowledge

HOW TO LAY UP

Par fives such as The Woodlands's first and 13th—with greens surrounded by sand and water—discourage the average golfer from trying to get home in two. But in executing this sound strategy, many players make a tactical mistake—they try to advance the ball as far as possible, leaving it at the edge of the fronting hazard, so their third shot is a relatively short one.

There's usually little point in such a shot. For one thing, you might hit your layup too long and reach the trouble. For another, even if you place the shot where you want, the ensuing partial-wedge shot is, for most players, more difficult than a full wedge, especially when it must be lofted over an intervening hazard.

There's an old saying, "If you're going to lay up, then lay up." Leave the ball well short of the trouble, and leave it in a place that will allow you to make a full and aggressive third shot. In this sense, golf is similar to pocket billiards. You plan and play each shot in such a way that it makes your next shot easier.

If you know that you hit a full pitching wedge, say 100 yards, then on your second shot choose a club that will leave you about 100 yards to the pin. Planning like this is the essence of smart course management.

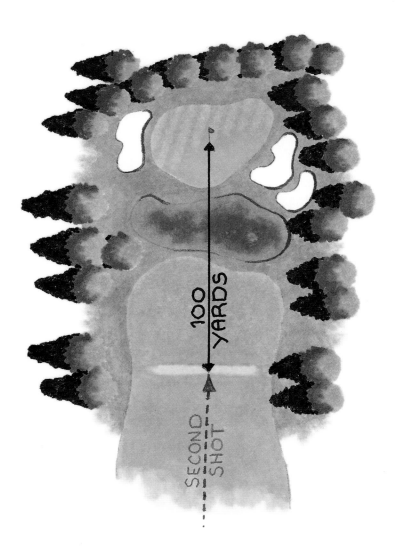

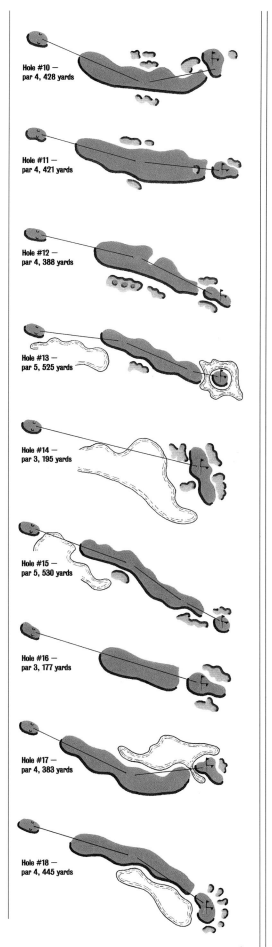

Hole #10 —
par 4, 428 yards

Hole #11 —
par 4, 421 yards

Hole #12 —
par 4, 388 yards

Hole #13 —
par 5, 525 yards

Hole #14 —
par 3, 195 yards

Hole #15 —
par 5, 530 yards

Hole #16 —
par 3, 177 yards

Hole #17 —
par 4, 383 yards

Hole #18 —
par 4, 445 yards

Kmart Greater Greensboro Open

FOREST OAKS COUNTRY CLUB

t's party time in tarheel territory.

The population of the greater Greensboro area is barely a million, but each spring more than 250,000 of those good folks show up at the Forest Oaks Country Club for the biggest bash of the year.

Civic pride, spring fever, and plenty of cold beer combine to make this a very festive, occasionally rowdy, place to watch golf. Party central is the 17th hole, a 188-yard par three backed by a bleacherful of exuberant fans, many of whom camp there the whole day, enjoying their beverage of choice and

amusing themselves with a little game of chance: As each group of players approaches the tee, the fans bet which pro will hit the ball closest to the hole. The balls that descend toward this green are therefore met with a bibulous roar that is unique in the world of golf.

Meanwhile, plenty of serious golf is played up and down the hills of this Ellis Maples design. A par 72 that greets the pros with less than 7000 yards on the card, it usually plays longer thanks to rolling terrain and spring winds. But the key to this course is its greens, which undulate severely and measure

T H E
TV
H O L E S

Expect birdies:

13

Expect bogeys:

14

What to Watch For . . .

COMEBACKS
This is a course where par is good, where the field tends to bunch up, and where a hot round on Sunday can go a long way. In 1990, Steve Elkington came from six strokes back to win. A year later, Mark Brooks came from seven behind to force a playoff, which he won. In 1992, Davis Love's course-record 62 catapulted him from three behind to a six-stroke victory, and in 1993, Rocco Mediate came from four behind for victory.

OUTDOOR LIFE
In keeping with the good-old-boy atmosphere, two special attractions are arranged for the Tour players: a fishing tournament and a skeet-shooting competition.

THE CLUB BUS
Check out the parking lot near the entrance to Rte. I-40 and you'll see a big yellow school bus. Inside it you'll find no children, but you will see hundreds of golf clubs, new and used. The mobile pro shop of Tony Winstead is an institution at the GGO. Among his best customers: Lee Trevino, Lanny Wadkins, and Mark Calcavecchia.

GOOD OLE BOY #1
The man whose legend dominates this tournament is Sam Snead, the natural athlete who came out of the West Virginia hills to win a record 81 events on the U.S. Tour. An incredible eight of Snead's victories came at Greensboro, the first in 1938 and the last in 1965.

3rd hole

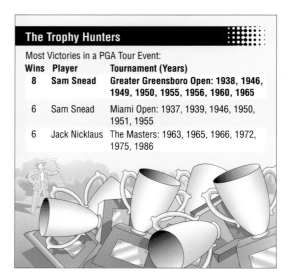

The Trophy Hunters		
Most Victories in a PGA Tour Event:		
Wins	**Player**	**Tournament (Years)**
8	Sam Snead	Greater Greensboro Open: 1938, 1946, 1949, 1950, 1955, 1956, 1960, 1965
6	Sam Snead	Miami Open: 1937, 1939, 1946, 1950, 1951, 1955
6	Jack Nicklaus	The Masters: 1963, 1965, 1966, 1972, 1975, 1986

Forest Oaks Country Club

Hole #1 —
par 4, 407 yards

Hole #2 —
par 5, 511 yards

Hole #3 —
par 4, 409 yards

Hole #4 —
par 3, 190 yards

Hole #5 —
par 4, 415 yards

Hole #6 —
par 4, 386 yards

Hole #7 —
par 4, 372 yards

Hole #8 —
par 3, 215 yards

Hole #9 —
par 5, 574 yards

about 25 percent larger than at most PGA Tour courses. Club selection on approach shots is a constant challenge, and in every round every player has to stand over a few snakes. Imagine putting on a surface the size of a baseball diamond, with your ball at second base, the cup at home plate, and the pitcher's mound in between—that's the kind of assignment the pros get at Forest Oaks.

For its first 50 years, the GGO resisted the temptation of corporate sponsorship, but in the late 1980s, as the Tour pressed them to keep pace with the escalating purses of other events, the Greensboro Jaycees entertained several suitors. The result was a marriage made in heaven—Kmart, the mass marketer to middle America—became the title sponsor. After all, Kmart shoppers have been coming to this tournament for five decades. The only better choice would have been Jack Daniels.

TOURNAMENT RATINGS

COURSE DIFFICULTY

Avg. winning score:	
10.5 under par	9th on Tour
USGA course rating:	
73.9 (1.9 over par)	31st on Tour
Overall rating:	
Moderate	19th on Tour

PRESTIGE

Field strength (9.1)	27th on Tour
Winner quality (.720)	20th on Tour
Course difficulty (above)	19th on Tour
Plus factors: None	
Overall rating	24th on Tour

13th hole

72

Local Knowledge

PUTTS THAT AREN'T PUTTS

Any time you play a course with greens the size of those at Forest Oaks, you're bound to encounter one of golf's weirdest beasts: the mammoth putt. When you're crouched over a ball that's 50 feet or more from the hole, you're facing an unnatural assignment, a shot that's too long to be stroked, too short to be hit.

The first rule, especially if you have a pro-type arm-and-shoulder stroke, is to allow some wrist action. This is one time to loosen it up a bit—allow a little natural hinging and unhinging of the wrists at the end of your back-swing.

Rule number two: Concentrate on distance rather than direction. Most three-putts begin when the approach putt is left several feet too long or short of the hole. If you can get your distance right, you'll rarely have more than a couple of feet for your second putt.

Finally, to simplify things, divide the putt in half. If you have a 60-footer, walk to a point about 30 feet from the hole and read the putt from there. Since the ball rolls more slowly as it nears the hole, it will be most susceptible to the slope and grain of the green during the second half of its journey. Once you have a feel for those last 30 feet, go back to the ball and focus your mind and muscles on striking a 60-foot putt that rolls over that halfway point.

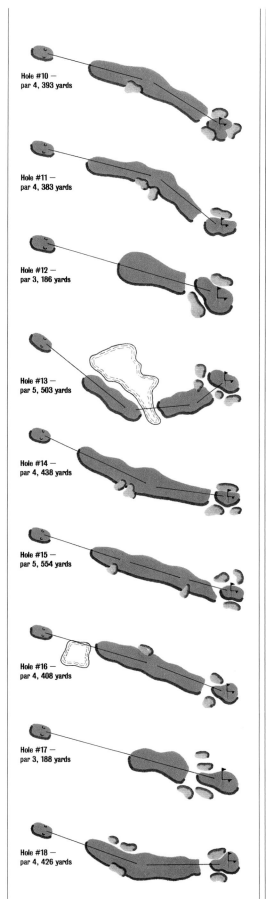

Hole #10 — par 4, 393 yards

Hole #11 — par 4, 383 yards

Hole #12 — par 3, 186 yards

Hole #13 — par 5, 503 yards

Hole #14 — par 4, 438 yards

Hole #15 — par 5, 554 yards

Hole #16 — par 4, 408 yards

Hole #17 — par 3, 188 yards

Hole #18 — par 4, 426 yards

Practical Matters

FOR TICKET INFORMATION

Kmart Greater Greensboro Open
P.O. Box 908
Greensboro, NC 27402

COURSE

Forest Oaks Country Club

ACCESS

Private course, but guests with club affiliations are welcome

COURSE RATING

Tees	Pro	Member
Yardage	6958	6326
Rating	73.9	70.9
Slope	129	123

GREEN FEES

$25 weekday, $50 weekend if playing with member; $50 any day if introduced by member; $100 to members of other clubs, with no introduction
For more information:
(910) 674-2241

PRO-AM

Spots open to the public?
Yes, for both Monday and Wednesday
Handicap: Maximum of 21
Format: Monday: Scramble;
Wednesday: Best ball of team
Entry fee: $5000
For more information:
(910) 379-1570

BellSouth Classic

ATLANTA COUNTRY CLUB

You can judge this book by its cover. Step onto the first tee of the Atlanta Country Club, and you'll discover immediately the quintessence of the course. A pair of bunkers and a thick stand of trees loom on the right side of the narrow fairway. To the left are more trees, another bunker, and a lake. Four words summarize your mission: Drive the ball straight.

In the 1980s, this event was sponsored by Georgia Pacific, and the paper conglomerate might easily have used the course to stoke its mills. Thousands

of pines and oaks line the fairways of this rolling layout that architect Willard Byrd carved from a forest in 1965. The ubiquitous trees, together with 63 bunkers and a dozen water hazards, make this one of the most claustrophobically daunting assignments in golf.

Water lurks at the edge of nine greens, most scenically at the 13th, a 156-yard par three where a tee shot that misses left will find a sheer rock face that drops off 15 feet to a patch of grass that drops again to a striking waterfall. To the right of the green is the remains of a Confederate mint which

THE
TV
HOLES

Expect birdies:
11
Expect bogeys:
15

What to Watch For . . .

PARASOLS AND JULEPS

For Atlantans, this isn't a golf tournament, it's the city's biggest lawn party, and when it comes to girl-watching the Tour pros claim it's hard to beat the BellSouth southern belles.

FATALITIES AT 15

The killer in the stretch run is a 452-yard dogleg right with a creed that menaces both the tee shot and approach. In 1982, the top four finishers played this hole on Sunday with a 5, a 6, a 7, and an 8.

THE ANTI-STADIUM

Since the Atlanta Country Club was carved from a forest, each hole is self-contained in a sheath of pines and oaks. The best options for spectating: Follow your favorite player from start to finish; walk the course backwards and catch several groups as they play toward you; or arrive early and stake out a good spot at the dramatic 18th hole.

THE NELSONS

Not Ozzie & Harriett—Larry and Gayle. The U.S. Open and PGA Champion is a longtime member of the ACC, and he and his family live alongside the 18th fairway. The proximity has paid off for Nelson— he has won this event twice.

18th hole

He Burned Up Atlanta

Nobody has ever won the BellSouth Classic in consecutive years. Jack Nicklaus, however, won the 1973 Atlanta Classic and the 1974 Tournament Players Championship at the same course, the Atlanta CC

Atlanta Country Club

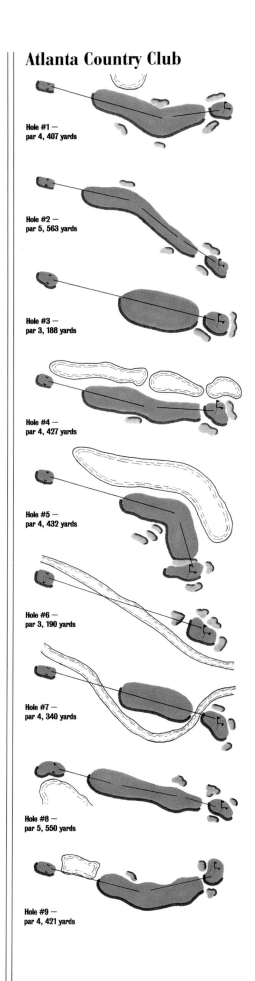

Hole #1 —
par 4, 407 yards

Hole #2 —
par 5, 563 yards

Hole #3 —
par 3, 188 yards

Hole #4 —
par 4, 427 yards

Hole #5 —
par 4, 432 yards

Hole #6 —
par 3, 190 yards

Hole #7 —
par 4, 340 yards

Hole #8 —
par 5, 550 yards

Hole #9 —
par 4, 421 yards

was torched by Union armies during a Civil War skirmish on this property in 1865.

Today's battles climax at the 18th, a hole that may have more potential for drama than any finisher on the Tour. A short (499-yard) par five, it runs along the right bank of a lake that pokes its nose in front of a shallow green surrounded by bunkers. Since this hole is very reachable, eagles are common; but since it's fraught with peril, 6s and 7s are not uncommon. Anything can happen here—as John Daly proved in 1994 when he birdied the hole for victory after a 300-yard drive and a second shot hit with an 8-iron.

Practical Matters

FOR TICKET INFORMATION
The BellSouth Classic
380 Interstate North Parkway
Suite 160
Atlanta, GA 30339

COURSE
Atlanta Country Club

ACCESS
Private course—you must play with a member

COURSE RATING

Tees	Pro	Member
Yardage	7018	6452
Rating	74.3	71.6
Slope	142	134

GREEN FEES
$75, including cart
For more information:
(404) 953-2100

PRO-AM
Spots open to the public? Yes
Handicap: Maximum of 21
Format: Best ball of team
Entry fee: $3250
For more information:
(404) 951-8777

13th hole

Local Knowledge

GET YOUR THINKING STRAIGHT

Few golf courses present as tight a driving challenge as the Atlanta Country Club, but on virtually every course there is at least one hole where accuracy off the tee is vital.

The average player lives in fear of such situations, and that's bad, because fearing leads to steering and steering leads to veering. This is one place where you need to make a calm and confident swing.

Assuming you have reasonably sound fundamentals, the best way to encourage such a swing is with a bit of mental preparation. Fundamentally, you should get your mind off the negative consequences of a poor shot and focus on a positive result. Pick out a specific point in the fairway where you'd like your ball to finish, and then visualize your ideal drive, flying and rolling to that spot. Keep your mind focused on this and there will be no room for negative thinking or fearful swings.

Another mental trick is to pretend you're standing on the tee of a very easy driving hole, a hole where you always hit a good shot. The best time to do this is in the last few seconds before you take the club back. After all, your ball on the tee looks the same as it does on that easy hole—so tell yourself that's where you are. This positive focus should produce a confident swing and a straight drive.

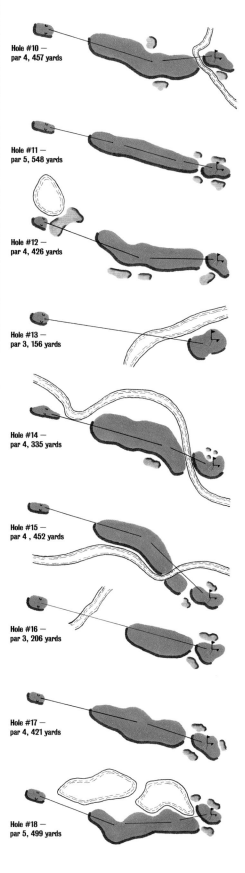

Hole #10 —
par 4, 457 yards

Hole #11 —
par 5, 548 yards

Hole #12 —
par 4, 426 yards

Hole #13 —
par 3, 156 yards

Hole #14 —
par 4, 335 yards

Hole #15 —
par 4 , 452 yards

Hole #16 —
par 3, 206 yards

Hole #17 —
par 4, 421 yards

Hole #18 —
par 5, 499 yards

GTE Byron Nelson Classic

TPC AT LAS COLINAS

A mong golf's living Hall of Famers, the most approachable is the gentleman rancher from Ft. Worth, Byron Nelson. Throughout his career, and afterward, the softspoken Nelson lived in the shadow of his charismatic contemporaries Ben Hogan and Sam Snead, the third leg of that great triumvirate. But Nelson's playing record speaks for itself, most emphatically his 1945 season—that year he won 18 tournaments, an astonishing 11 of them in succession.

In 1968, Nelson got a measure of the recognition he deserves when the Dallas Open changed its name to the Byron Nelson Golf Classic, making Lord Byron the first player to have a Tour event named in his honor.

Today the course on which this event is played—the TPC at Las Colinas—is a monument to the character of Byron Nelson. Las Colinas is a resort course, open to all with bias toward none. Its fairways are generous, its greens are accessible, and from the first tee to the 18th green there is not a hint of flamboyance or severity. Upon closer inspection, however, there is much to appreciate. With Las Colinas as with Byron Nelson, familiarity breeds respect.

The course was designed by Jay Morrish with consultation from Ben Crenshaw and Nelson himself, and the two Texans made sure that the routing paid homage to the winds of the Lone Star State. Most of the long holes play with the prevailing southerly breeze, most of the short

THE TV HOLES

Expect birdies:
16

Expect bogeys:
14

18th hole

What to Watch For . . .

A MEAN MOTHER

Since 1967, the Nelson has experienced 25 different suspensions of play due to rain, lightning, and, in 1974, fog. It has had nine rounds canceled entirely and twice has been forced to play 36 holes in one day. Two tournaments finished on Monday and one on Tuesday. Only six times in 28 years has the tournament managed four straight days without disruption by Mother Nature.

LORD BYRON

Not only is the tournament's namesake present in person all week, but a nine-foot-high statue of Nelson lords it over the entrance to the club. There's also a tree named after him—in 1993, the 30-foot-high Nelson Oak was planted on the left side of the drive zone at 18. Players must give it a wide berth, or their approach to the green will be blocked.

HOT SELLERS

The tournament is co-sponsored by the Salesmanship Club of Dallas, a group of 500 civic-minded business-men whose official uniform includes fire-engine-red slacks. But they do their job—this is the Tour's top fund-raiser for charity.

TAPE-MEASURE BLOWS

When the wind kicks up *here*, the ball can really travel, especially when the fairways are a bit hard. In 1984, Dave Eichelberger cranked one down-gale drive that measured 397 yards, an all-time PGA Tour record.

INTRAMURAL ATHLETICS

About a third of the tournament field stays at the luxurious Four Seasons Resort Hotel, which over-looks the 18th hole, and the pros aren't shy about using the hotel's sports facilities. On most afternoons, you can find a tennis match or a 3-on-3 basketball gameful of PGA Tour players.

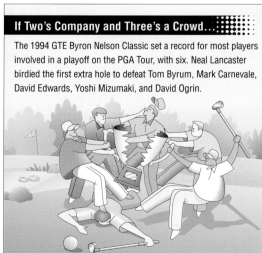

If Two's Company and Three's a Crowd...

The 1994 GTE Byron Nelson Classic set a record for most players involved in a playoff on the PGA Tour, with six. Neal Lancaster birdied the first extra hole to defeat Tom Byrum, Mark Carnevale, David Edwards, Yoshi Mizumaki, and David Ogrin.

TPC at Las Colinas

Hole #1 —
par 4, 352 yards

Hole #2 —
par 3, 176 yards

Hole #3 —
par 4, 460 yards

Hole #4 —
par 4, 428 yards

Hole #5 —
par 3, 176 yards

Hole #6 —
par 4, 396 yards

Hole #7 —
par 5, 533 yards

Hole #8 —
par 4, 451 yards

Hole #9 —
par 4, 406 yards

holes play against it, and very few play across it. Despite a helping wind at the third hole, this 460-yard par four is the hardest hole on the course, playing alongside a creek. On the inward nine, the wind and wet combine to menace the approach to the 14th hole, where the approach is played over the drink to a perched green.

This is also one of the Tour's best tests of short-game prowess. Since wind is such a factor, all but two of the greens (5 and 14) allow for bounce-on approaches. And since this is a Stadium Course, many of the greens are surrounded by mounds and grass bunkers. To complicate matters further, the greenkeepers vary the greenside mowing patterns to keep players off guard. You might pitch to one green, then, from a similar distance and lie, chip to the next, putt to a third, and hit a flop shot to a fourth. All of which makes this sneaky-tough in the tradition of Pinehurst #2. According to Las Colinas's Director of Golf, Mike Abbott, "A pro can shoot 80 here and wonder why it wasn't 70."

15th hole

TOURNAMENT RATINGS

COURSE DIFFICULTY

Avg. winning score: 10.7 under par	11th on Tour
USGA course rating: 73.5 (3.5 over par)	8th on Tour
Overall rating: Severe	9th on Tour

PRESTIGE

Field strength (10.5)	20th on Tour
Winner quality (.900)	10th on Tour
Course difficulty (above)	9th on Tour
Plus factor: Hosted by Byron Nelson	
Overall rating	14th on Tour

Local Knowledge

ON KNOWING THE MOWING

Maintenance procedures can have an effect on the way your ball reacts at impact, and you should be particularly aware of this around the green, especially on courses such as Las Colinas, where part of the challenge is in dealing with the mowing patterns that vary from hole to hole.

If mowers have cut the grass in such a way that it pushes against the front of your ball, you can expect some resistance if you try to putt the ball or hit a low chip or pitch. The blades of grass will tend to impede impact a bit, imparting extra backspin that can make the ball skip or veer off line. In such a situation, you might want to opt for a more lofted shot that slips the ball quickly upward and over the grass.

If, on the other hand, the grass has been mown so that the blades point in the same direction as your shot—in effect, the mower has created a "grain" in your favor—you'll have little or no resistance from the grass and you'll therefore have more options. The smartest shot might be a running chip or even a putt, to get the ball rolling smoothly toward the hole.

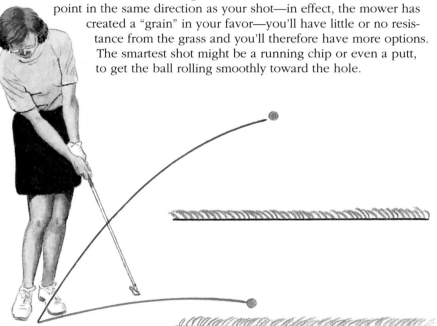

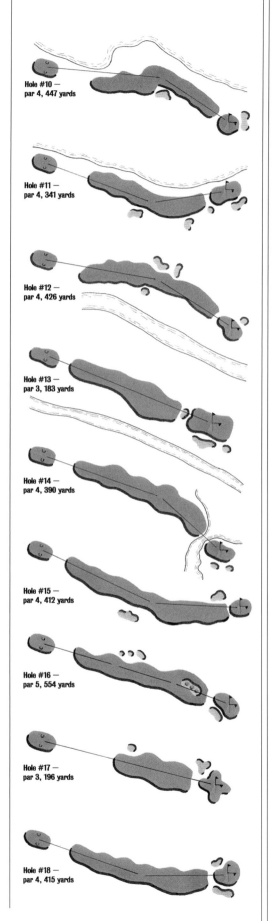

Hole #10 —
par 4, 447 yards

Hole #11 —
par 4, 341 yards

Hole #12 —
par 4, 426 yards

Hole #13 —
par 3, 183 yards

Hole #14 —
par 4, 390 yards

Hole #15 —
par 4, 412 yards

Hole #16 —
par 5, 554 yards

Hole #17 —
par 3, 196 yards

Hole #18 —
par 4, 415 yards

Practical Matters

FOR TICKET INFORMATION
Salesmanship Club of Dallas
400 S. Houston St.
350 Union Station
Dallas, TX 75202

COURSE
TPC at Las Colinas

ACCESS
Resort course, open to guests of the Four Seasons Hotel

COURSE RATING

Tees	Pro	Member
Yardage	6899	6500
Rating	73.5	71.4
Slope	135	129

GREEN FEES
$85
For more information:
(214) 717-0700

PRO-AM
Spots open to the public? Yes, but you must play in a qualifying tournament
Handicap: Maximum of 21
Format: Best ball of team
Entry fee: Several tiers (Sunday, Monday, and Wednesday): $2000–$4250
For more information:
(214) 742-3896

Buick Classic

WESTCHESTER COUNTRY CLUB
[WEST COURSE]

Welcome to New York. As the lyric says, "If you can make it there, you'll make it anywhere."

"There" is the West Course of the Westchester Country Club, a compact layout that may be—yard for yard—the hardest course on the PGA Tour. At just 6779 yards, and with water only faintly in play, it doesn't look tough on paper. But consider this: Whereas 21 acres of this course are fairway, 80 acres are rough, and at tournament time in early June that rough is in midseason form—healthy and thick. Combine that with a series of long, tightly treelined par fours culminating in small greens, and the result can be a struggle.

As such, the Buick Classic has come to be regarded as ideal preparation for the U.S. Open, which directly follows it on the schedule. Expect to see irons hit from some of these tees, and expect to see some serious scrambling when the approach shots miss the greens. Westchester was designed three-quarters of a century ago by three-time U.S. Amateur Champion Walter Travis, and he routed his holes up and down rugged rocky hills and through thick stands of pines, oaks, and maples.

THE TV HOLES

Expect birdies:
18
Expect bogeys:
11, 12, 15, 16

Right: 1st hole

What to Watch For . . .

FOREIGN INVASION
Since this tournament is often played one week before the U.S. Open—and course conditions usually resemble the USGA's setup—several international players come here for a last-minute tune-up.

BOGEYS
No other PGA Tour course has as many difficult holes on its incoming stretch. In most years, at least four holes rank among the Tour's top two dozen or so in difficulty.

THE COURSE WITHIN A COURSE
Spectators who wander away from the back-nine action risk tumbling into a minibunker. In an area between the 11th and 18th holes is a pitch-and-putt course. Westchester also has another regulation 18-hole layout—the South Course —which is used for the overflow of the pro-am.

A 300-ROOM CLUBHOUSE
Perhaps the most imposing 19th hole in golf, it was originally the Westchester Biltmore Hotel. Today, most of its rooms house permanent residents along with a handful of local businesses.

GILDER'S PLAQUE
Embedded in the center of the 18th fairway is a plaque that commemorates the shot played by Bob Gilder in the third round of the 1982 Classic. Leading the tournament at the time, Gilder slugged a 3-wood second shot 251 yards into the hole for a double eagle. It gave him a record 54-hole total of 192 and spurred him to a record victory total of 261. No other player has come within four shots of that mark.

One Nasty Course
Westchester CC has five of the 19 hardest holes on the PGA Tour. No other course has more than two.

Hole	Par	Avg. Score	PGA Tour Rank
12	4	4.411	4
11	4	4.382	7
15	4	4.343	12
8	4	4.319	17
4	4	4.316	19

Westchester Country Club

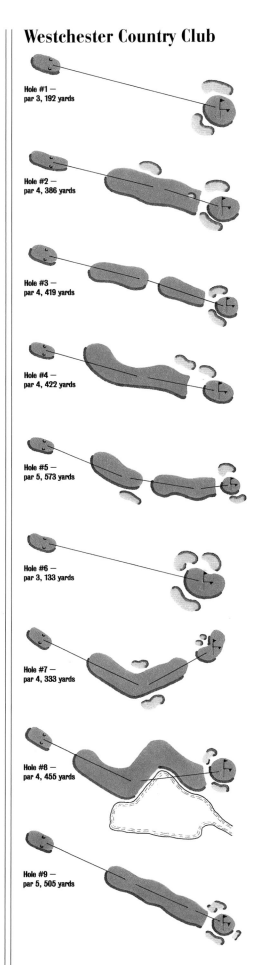

Hole #1 —
par 3, 192 yards

Hole #2 —
par 4, 386 yards

Hole #3 —
par 4, 419 yards

Hole #4 —
par 4, 422 yards

Hole #5 —
par 5, 573 yards

Hole #6 —
par 3, 133 yards

Hole #7 —
par 4, 333 yards

Hole #8 —
par 4, 455 yards

Hole #9 —
par 5, 505 yards

The Westchester clubhouse

Practical Matters

FOR TICKET INFORMATION
The Buick Classic
P.O. Box 200
Rye, NY 10580

COURSE
Westchester Country Club
(West Course)

ACCESS
Private club—you must play
with a member

COURSE RATING

Tees	Pro	Member
Yardage	6779	6335
Rating	73.4	71.8
Slope	139	135

GREEN FEES
$75
For more information:
(914) 967-6000

PRO–AM
Spots open to the public? Yes
Handicap: Maximum of 21
Format: Best ball of team
Entry fee: Three-tiers:
$3500, $2000, $1500
For more information:
(800) 765-4742

For the tournament, the front and back nines of the course are reversed, with some interesting results. First, the course begins with a par three. Second, the back nine starts with a drivable par four (though few try, except when the hole becomes the site of a sudden-death playoff). But if low scores are to be made, they must be made on the front nine, because the home stretch is a gauntlet of brutes, with no real respite until the home hole, a reachable par five where every pro has a reasonable chance of making a 3 . . . or a 6.

TOURNAMENT RATINGS

COURSE DIFFICULTY

Avg. winning score:
10.6 under par   10th on Tour

USGA course rating:
73.4 (2.4 over par)   22nd on Tour

Overall rating:
Moderate   14th on Tour

PRESTIGE

Field strength (10.1)	21st on Tour
Winner quality (.860)	11th on Tour
Course difficulty (above)	14th on Tour
Plus factors: None	
Overall rating	16th on Tour

Local Knowledge

THE LOB SHOT

When the rough is thick and the greens are small, fast, and crowned, as most of them are at Westchester, you often find yourself facing a short recovery shot that must be hit from a fluffy lie and stop soon after it lands on the putting surface. That's a tough assignment unless your shotmaking arsenal includes the lob.

The lob in golf is the same as in tennis, a high, soft, floating ball that thuds to earth with relatively little spin. It is played most easily from light rough, where you can slip the face of your sand wedge or lofted wedge under the ball without fear of hitting the shot thin.

The proper technique is very similar to the explosion shot from sand. You set up in an open stance—your feet, knees, hips, and shoulders pointing well left of the target—and the ball positioned about midway between your feet. When you're very close to the green and need extra loft, turn the face of your club open a few degrees. As for the swing, you can play a wristy shot or hit it with "quiet," almost stiff wrists, according to your personal comfort and preference. The important thing is tempo—make the slowest, laziest up-and-down move you possibly can. It is this languid tempo that creates the soft, high flight.

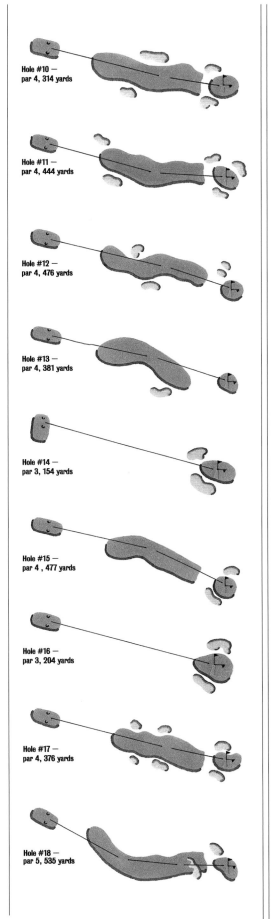

Hole #10 —
par 4, 314 yards

Hole #11 —
par 4, 444 yards

Hole #12 —
par 4, 476 yards

Hole #13 —
par 4, 381 yards

Hole #14 —
par 3, 154 yards

Hole #15 —
par 4 , 477 yards

Hole #16 —
par 3, 204 yards

Hole #17 —
par 4, 376 yards

Hole #18 —
par 5, 535 yards

Colonial National Invitation

COLONIAL COUNTRY CLUB

A half century ago, Cary Middlecoff declared Colonial Country Club "the hardest par 70 in the world." That is no longer the case, but this course on Ft. Worth's Trinity River remains one of the game's superb tests, and a victory here is high on every player's wish list.

A big reason is tradition. The Colonial began in 1946, when Ben Hogan fired a 65 in the final round to come from six strokes behind for a one-stroke victory. Snead, Palmer, Nicklaus, and Trevino all have won here—and it

is here and only here—at Colonial—that this event has been played. No course on the Tour has a longer-running tenure as a tournament site.

One of only a handful of par-70s on the Tour, Colonial was designed by John Bredemus in 1935 and over the decades has been reworked by Perry Maxwell, Dick Wilson, Robert Trent Jones, Bob Cupp, and Jay Morrish. But the essential challenge remains—7100 yards of shotmaking, built around a collection of long, taut par fours that culminate at smallish, well-bunkered greens. It's a course for shotmakers, particularly

THE
TV
HOLES

Expect birdies:
11

Expect bogeys:
Nowhere

What to Watch For . . .

BIG BEN

Hogan won not only the inaugural Colonial, he won here a record six times, his last victory coming in 1959 at the age of 46. No other player has won it more than twice. On the main floor of the Colonial clubhouse is the Ben Hogan Trophy Room, containing many of his prizes and memorabilia.

THE WALL OF FAME

Near the first tee is a permanent tribute to the men who have won at Colonial. The Wall of Champions holds plaques for each of the victors, starting with Craig Wood in the 1941 U.S. Open and including every winner of the Tour event since Hogan in 1946.

ROUGH STARTS

The front nine of this course is harder than the back, and the three most difficult tests on the course occur at holes three to five, known as the Horrible Horseshoe.

YOUTH MOVEMENT

This is one of the few remaining invitationals on the PGA Tour. As such, the field usually includes a few surprises. Each year invitations are extended to two amateurs. In addition, the former Colonial champions choose two promising newcomers who have never been invited. In 1967, one of the Champions' Choices was Dave Stockton, who opened with a 65 and went on to win the tournament.

FREEBIES

There is no charge for tickets on Monday and Tuesday, nor is there a charge for the pro-am, per se. You simply must buy (or sell) $4500 worth of tournament tickets.

18th hole

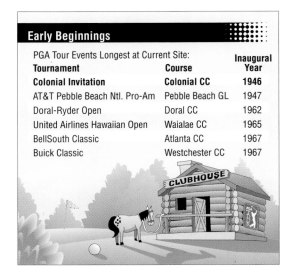

Early Beginnings

PGA Tour Events Longest at Current Site:

Tournament	Course	Inaugural Year
Colonial Invitation	Colonial CC	1946
AT&T Pebble Beach Ntl. Pro-Am	Pebble Beach GL	1947
Doral-Ryder Open	Doral CC	1962
United Airlines Hawaiian Open	Waialae CC	1965
BellSouth Classic	Atlanta CC	1967
Buick Classic	Westchester CC	1967

Colonial Country Club

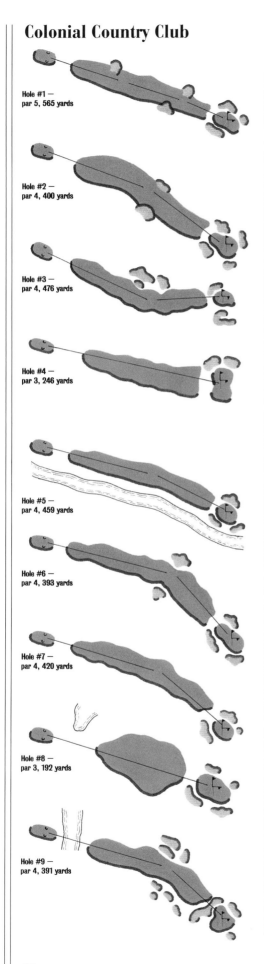

Hole #1 —
par 5, 565 yards

Hole #2 —
par 4, 400 yards

Hole #3 —
par 4, 476 yards

Hole #4 —
par 3, 246 yards

Hole #5 —
par 4, 459 yards

Hole #6 —
par 4, 393 yards

Hole #7 —
par 4, 420 yards

Hole #8 —
par 3, 192 yards

Hole #9 —
par 4, 391 yards

16th hole

those who can move the ball from left to right. Ten of the 14 par fours and fives favor a fade from the tee, so it's little surprise that this event was dominated by the ultimate fader, Hogan, and has been won twice by Bruce Lietzke and Lee Trevino.

Hogan's 65 held up for 25 years as the lowest score ever shot at Colonial, but in recent years the pros have tamed the course regularly. The record is now 62, shot by more than one player, and in 1987 Keith Clearwater won the tournament by shooting back-to-back 64s on Sunday. But as the scores go down, the prestige of the prize at Colonial remains high.

Practical Matters

FOR TICKET INFORMATION
Colonial Country Club
3735 Country Club Circle
Ft. Worth, TX 76109

COURSE
Colonial Country Club

ACCESS
Private club—you must play
with a member

COURSE RATING

Tees	Pro	Member
Yardage	7010	6486
Rating	73.7	70.9
Slope	132	126

GREEN FEES
$75 weekdays, $100 weekends
For more information:
(817) 927-4221

PRO-AM
Spots open to the public? Yes
Handicap: Maximum of 21
Format: Best ball of team
Entry fee: Free to anyone who buys
or sells $4500 worth of tickets
For more information:
(817) 927-4280

TOURNAMENT RATINGS

COURSE DIFFICULTY

Avg. winning score: 11.7 under par	13th on Tour
USGA course rating: 73.7 (3.7 over par)	6th on Tour
Overall rating: Severe	12th on Tour

PRESTIGE

Field strength (15.5)	8th on Tour
Winner quality (.620)	26th on Tour
Course difficulty (above)	12th on Tour
Plus factors: Invitational, course rated 30th in U.S., same site since 1946	
Overall rating	11th on Tour

Local Knowledge

CONTROLLING A FADE

It's not surprising that Ben Hogan mastered this course. No course favors a controlled fade more than Colonial, and no player controlled a fade better than Hogan.

Assuming you don't already have a fade—or its unattractive cousin, the slice—it is not a difficult shot to learn. The idea is to impart clockwise spin to the ball. To do that, it's simplest to address the ball in an open stance, with your feet, knees, hips, and shoulders aligned to the left of your target while keeping your clubface aligned directly at the target. This setup position will encourage you to take the club away from the ball on an outside path instead of straight back, and will result in a downswing that cuts across the ball from out to in, imparting the clockwise spin which makes the ball drift from left to right.

The more fade—or slice—you want, the more you should open your stance.

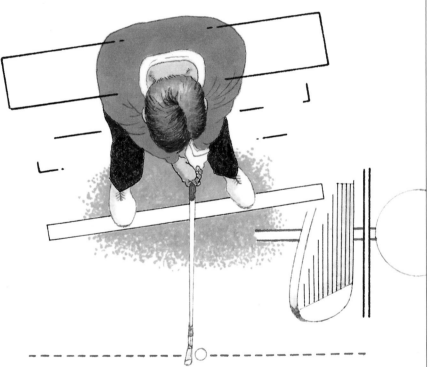

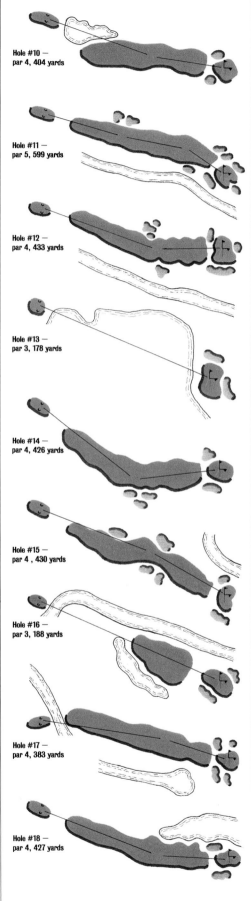

Hole #10 —
par 4, 404 yards

Hole #11 —
par 5, 599 yards

Hole #12 —
par 4, 433 yards

Hole #13 —
par 3, 178 yards

Hole #14 —
par 4, 426 yards

Hole #15 —
par 4 , 430 yards

Hole #16 —
par 3, 188 yards

Hole #17 —
par 4, 383 yards

Hole #18 —
par 4, 427 yards

The Memorial Tournament

MUIRFIELD VILLAGE GOLF CLUB

Not long ago, Jack Nicklaus was asked a question he had never pondered: "Where do you want your ashes spread?" He hesitated only a second or two, then said "Muirfield Village." The answer was no surprise. This is his hometown, his course, the site of two of his most cherished victories, and ultimately, his monument to himself.

When in 1966 Nicklaus first walked across this 170-acre tract of rolling farmland near Columbus, Ohio, he had one goal in mind: a golf course that would challenge the best players in the world. He designed it himself, in collaboration with architect Desmond Muirhead, and when the course opened in 1974, it was both the toughest and most perfectly conditioned test the Tour had seen in many years. A decade passed before any player posted a four-round total of less than 280. Today, after a number of changes by Nicklaus, the Muirfield Village Golf Club has eased a bit—it now ranks about midway on the Tour's list of most difficult tracks—but the lower scores are due in part to the consistently superb condition of this course.

Nicklaus named his course after the site of his first British Open victory, but he modeled his tournament after another major championship. From the tough ticket policy to the invitational format, to the very name of the event, The Memorial mimics The Masters.

In the same way, the holes of Muirfield Village evoke the holes of Augusta National Golf Club. The feeling from the tee is expansive—broad, meticulously manicured fairways that roll and tumble. As at Augusta, the hard work begins on the approach shots, which must flirt with water or sand and find the right sectors of the fiendishly fast greens. Indeed, the combined challenge of bunkers and greens is even more daunting than at The Masters. The best example of this challenge is number 14, a short par four where the slender green is pinched by a stream at the front and a bunker to the rear. The approach is a short

THE TV HOLES

Expect birdies:

15

Expect bogeys:

18

12th hole

What to Watch For . . .

A GARDEN SPOT
When writer Dan Jenkins attended the first Memorial, he said Muirfield Village was "in such immaculate condition that people would sooner have dropped cigarette butts on their babies' tummies."

MEMORIALIZING
Each year, the tournament selects a person who has played golf "with conspicuous honor" and adds him or her to the list of Memorial honorees via a special induction ceremony on Wednesday afternoon.

A LIMITED MENU
Don't expect to find any hot dogs or hamburgers at the concession stand. The host—a diligent dieter since his early Tour days—doesn't like the smell of food cooking when he's playing golf.

PRACTICE MADE PERFECT
The driving range at Muirfield Village is recognized as the finest on the PGA Tour—25 acres with the teeing ground encircling the landing area to allow a player to practice into the wind, downwind, or crosswind.

NOT-SO-SUDDEN DEATH
The Memorial is the only tournament on the Tour to settle its ties with a four-hole playoff where the low total for the four holes wins. If a tie persists, sudden-death takes effect. This method is also used at the British Open.

NICKLAUSIANA
Ultimately, this Memorial is to Jack. The clubhouse is crammed with memorabilia from his career, and near the first tee is a life-size Nicklaus statue (awarded to him by *GOLF Magazine* as the Player of the Century). Soon, it will all go into a Nicklaus Museum on the grounds.

Home Field Disadvantage

Muirfield VIlage was the site of the only U.S. Ryder Cup loss on American soil (1987).

Muirfield Village Golf Club

Hole #1 —
par 4, 446 yards

Hole #2 —
par 4, 452 yards

Hole #3 —
par 4, 392 yards

Hole #4 —
par 3, 204 yards

Hole #5 —
par 5, 531 yards

Hole #6 —
par 4, 430 yards

Hole #7 —
par 5, 549 yards

Hole #8 —
par 3, 189 yards

Hole #9 —
par 4, 410 yards

12th hole

one, but it calls for the player to choose the right club, then hit the right club right.

Each of the par-five holes is reachable in two shots by the Tour's longest hitters, and the last of them—number 15—is the easiest hole on the course (as is the 15th at Augusta), yielding a few eagles each year. But Jack gets his revenge at the home hole, an uphill dogleg of 437 yards. On Sunday, the pin is usually positioned at the left-front of the green, just behind a six-foot-deep bunker. Few players who find that are able to salvage par. In 1993, however, Paul Azinger worked a miracle, blasting softly and deftly over the bunker's lip so that his ball trickled down the slope of the green and into the hole. The sensational birdie was just enough to give Azinger a one-stroke victory.

TOURNAMENT RATINGS

COURSE DIFFICULTY

Avg. winning score:	
12.9 under par	19th on Tour
USGA course rating:	
75.5 (3.5 over par)	8th on Tour
Overall rating:	
Moderate	15th on Tour

PRESTIGE

Field strength (15.6)	7th on Tour
Winner quality (1.026)	7th on Tour
Course difficulty (above)	15th on Tour
Plus factors: Invitational, hosted by Jack Nicklaus, course rated 15th in U.S.	
Overall rating	6th on Tour

Practical Matters

FOR TICKET INFORMATION
Memorial Tournament
P.O. Box 396
Dublin, Ohio 43017

COURSE
Muirfield Village Golf Club

ACCESS
Private course—you must play with a member

COURSE RATING

Tees	Pro	Member
Yardage	7104	6468
Rating	75.5	73.3
Slope	145	139

GREEN FEES
$100
For more information:
(614) 889-6700

PRO-AM
None

Local Knowledge

TWO SEAM SHOTS

The fast surfaces of Muirfield Village require a soft touch around the green, but when your ball comes to rest on the seam between the fringe and rough, a soft touch becomes difficult. Normally, this situation calls for a downward pop with the putter or a crisp chip, and those shots can launch the ball with too much pace.

However, two other shots have been developed by the Tour players in recent years, and they're worth a try. First, the bellied wedge: Using your putting stance and stroke, strike the ball at its equator with the leading edge of your sand wedge. The heavy clubhead of the wedge will glide through the rough grass smoothly and unimpeded, and will enable you to strike the ball solidly. This takes some practice, but it's a shot that's worth practicing.

If you can't master the bellied wedge, you might have another option, depending on the design of your putter. If you have a putter that's squared off at the toe, turn the clubface 90 degrees and stroke the ball with the toe of the club. The putter, when held this way, is a fraction of its normal width and thus it penetrates the heavy grass rather than being twisted by it. Fred Couples uses this shot very effectively, but you don't need his innate talent to make it work for you—just a flat-toed putter and a bit of practice.

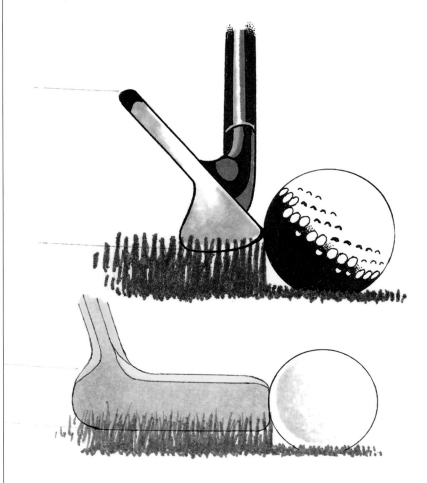

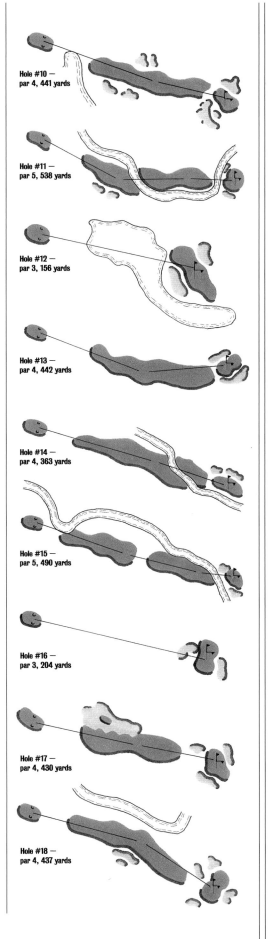

Hole #10 — par 4, 441 yards

Hole #11 — par 5, 538 yards

Hole #12 — par 3, 156 yards

Hole #13 — par 4, 442 yards

Hole #14 — par 4, 363 yards

Hole #15 — par 5, 490 yards

Hole #16 — par 3, 204 yards

Hole #17 — par 4, 430 yards

Hole #18 — par 4, 437 yards

Kemper Open

TPC AT AVENEL

This course had a tough act to follow. In 1987, the Kemper Open ended a seven-year run at famed Congressional Country Club and moved a few miles down the road to the brand-new Tournament Players Club at Avenel. In exchange for a course that had hosted both the U.S. Open and the PGA Championship came a course that had not hosted as much as a member-guest.

On a rolling tree-clad tract of land, architect Ed Ault routed his layout in the manner of classics such as Royal Birkdale, Seminole, and Winged Foot, its two discrete nine-hole loops emanating in different directions from the clubhouse. The early rumor was that this would be the finest Stadium Course to date.

The pros didn't see it that way. At the inaugural Kemper Open at Avenel, Greg Norman issued a barrage of complaints about the design and condition of the course, and several of his Tour colleagues stood with him. The Tour listened, and over the next few years wholesale changes were made. Entire fairways were moved, rebunkered, and reshaped, and nearly 150 yards were added to the course. Today, the decade-old

THE TV HOLES

Expect birdies:
13, 14

Expect bogeys:
12

9th hole

What to Watch For . . .

KNIGHT MUSIC

Anyone who has forgotten that this is Washington D.C.'s neighborhood tournament will get a reminder at the end of the tournament when a military band marches over the rise at 18 and caps the closing ceremonies with a brief concert.

ARNIE'S PLAQUE

Arnold Palmer won the inaugural Kemper Open in 1968, but that was at Pleasant Valley in Massachusetts. At Avenel he is immortalized for the two days in 1983 when, during practice rounds for the Chrysler Cup matches, he scored back-to-back holes in one at the third hole. Arnie used a 5-iron both days (the hole was then 187 yards—now it's 239). The odds on anyone—even Arnold Palmer—making two aces consecutively on the same hole are roughly 9 million to one.

WET SHOTS

Since the creek that snakes through this property is relatively shallow, it's not uncommon to see the pros play water blasts out of it rather than accepting a penalty stroke. The Tour players know that this shot is not much harder than an explosion from a buried lie in sand, as long as at least some part of the ball protrudes above the water's surface. A few aggressive players will even try this shot when the ball is completely submerged.

HOSPITALITY HILL

High above the 18th green, a ring of state-of-the-art corporate tents insures that the politicians, bureaucrats, and other denizens of our nation's capital are lobbied in style.

Portable Champions		
PGA Tour Players Winning the Same Tournament on Two Different Courses, Since 1980:		
Chip Beck	USF&G Classic/Freeport-McMoRan Classic: Lakewood CC (1988) English Turn G&CC (1992)	
Bill Glasson	**Kemper Open: Congressional CC (1985) TPC at Avenel (1992)**	
Curtis Strange	Houston Open: Woodlands CC (1980), TPC at The Woodlands (1988)	

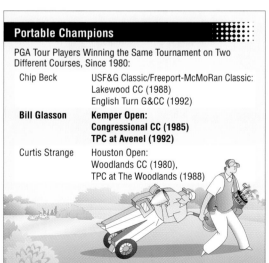

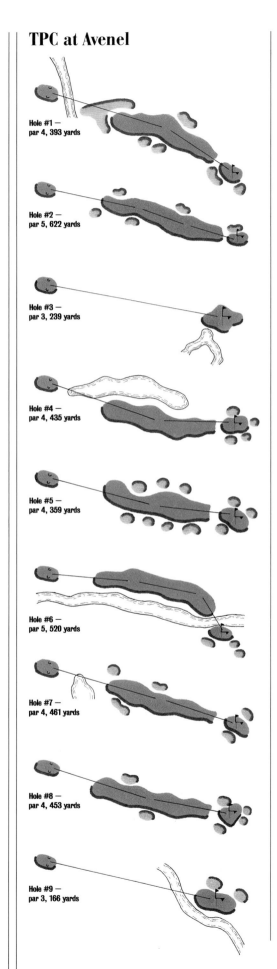

Hole #1 —
par 4, 393 yards

Hole #2 —
par 5, 622 yards

Hole #3 —
par 3, 239 yards

Hole #4 —
par 4, 435 yards

Hole #5 —
par 4, 359 yards

Hole #6 —
par 5, 520 yards

Hole #7 —
par 4, 461 yards

Hole #8 —
par 4, 453 yards

Hole #9 —
par 3, 166 yards

7th hole

course has matured, its bentgrass greens and zoysia fairways reach peak condition at tournament time, and its lush rough gives the pros a full but fair challenge.

One key to the course is variety.

TOURNAMENT RATINGS

COURSE DIFFICULTY

Avg. winning score: 12.6 under par	16th on Tour
USGA course rating: 74.0 (3.0 over par)	16th on Tour
Overall rating: Moderate	17th on Tour

PRESTIGE

Field strength (6.7)	38th on Tour
Winner quality (.560)	28th on Tour
Course difficulty (above)	17th on Tour
Plus factors: None	
Overall rating	34th on Tour

The par threes range in length from 165 to 239 yards, the fours go from 301 to 472, and one par five weighs in at 622. A stream lurks through the early holes of the back nine, where the toughest and easiest holes on the course occur back to back, and it is this area of the course that produces the most excitement in the stadium. Number 12 stretches 472 treelined yards, with the stream lurking along the left side and then crossing in front of the fiercely sloped green. Bogeys and worse are not uncommon, but those who slip here have a chance to grab back a stroke or two at 13, a reachable (but water-guarded) par five and at 14, a reachable (but again, water-guarded) par four of just 301 yards. The remainder of the course—a trio of par fours and a 195-yard par three—winds through broad, open fairways shouldered by towering spectator mounds. The gallery at Avenel is afforded plenty of good viewing, even if they'll never see an Open or a PGA.

Local Knowledge

STADIUM CHIPPING

When you miss a green on a TPC course such as Avenel, your ball is likely to come to rest on the downslope of a spectator mound, a lie that adds complexity to your chip shot.

Downhill chips are shooters—they fly lower and hotter than chips from flat lies. Therefore, you should choose a more lofted club than you normally would. You should also play the ball about an inch farther back in your stance than you would from a level lie, since on a downhill lie your club will tend to "meet the ground" earlier in its swing. For most situations, these are the only changes you need make. However, from a severely downhill lie, add a bit of extra wrist action to your chipping motion to guard against a topped or skulled shot and to insure that you get your clubface squarely down to the back of the ball.

Practical Matters

FOR TICKET INFORMATION

Kemper Open
10000 Oaklyn Dr.
Potomac, MD 20854

COURSE

TPC at Avenel

ACCESS

Private course—you must be introduced by a member

COURSE RATING

Tees	Pro	Member
Yardage	7005	6462
Rating	74.0	72.0
Slope	133	129

GREEN FEES

$99, including cart
For more information:
(301) 469-3737

PRO-AM

Spots open to the public? Yes
Handicap: Maximum of 21
Format: Best ball of team
Entry fee: $3000
For more information:
(301) 469-3737

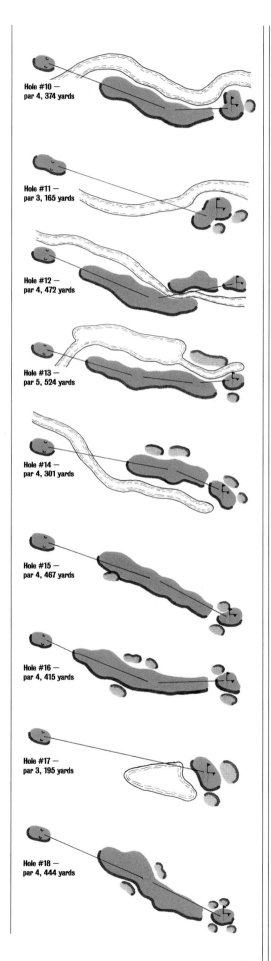

Hole #10 —
par 4, 374 yards

Hole #11 —
par 3, 165 yards

Hole #12 —
par 4, 472 yards

Hole #13 —
par 5, 524 yards

Hole #14 —
par 4, 301 yards

Hole #15 —
par 4, 467 yards

Hole #16 —
par 4, 415 yards

Hole #17 —
par 3, 195 yards

Hole #18 —
par 4, 444 yards

Canon Greater Hartford Open

TPC AT RIVER HIGHLANDS

For the past decade or so, this event has been a tale of three sites, all on the same land. In the beginning there was Edgewood, a flat, relatively featureless course designed in 1928 by a cousin of famed architect Donald Ross. Then came the TPC of Connecticut, a modified revamp of the original layout at the hands of Pete Dye. Hired to build a course that would test the Tour pros—but hampered by an insufficiency of space—Dye got his job about half right, fashioning a modern target-style back nine while making few major changes to the front. When it opened in 1984, critics called it Jekyll and Hyde Country Club.

So in 1990 the Tour stepped back in, ponied up $4 million, bought 52 more acres of property, and changed every hole on the course. Tour agronomist Bobby Weed did the job, fashioning seven new holes, adding two lakes and 80 bunkers, and lengthening the course slightly while at the same time reducing its par from 71 to 70. Even its name was changed—to the TPC at River Highlands—to reflect the dramatic tract of land on which the new holes are routed, a ridge that runs 70 feet

18th hole

THE TV HOLES

Expect birdies:
Nowhere

Expect bogeys:
10, 17, 18

What to Watch For . . .

MOST OF GREATER HARTFORD
This is, without question, the biggest sporting event in the state. It also attracts the largest galleries on the PGA Tour, about 250,000 a year.

PLAYOFFS
Since the first Insurance City Open in 1952, this tournament has gone into sudden death 15 times. That's better than once every three years and more often than any other event on the men's Tour. Arnold Palmer, a two-time winner, had to go extra innings for each of his victories.

THRILLS AND SPILLS
Each of the last four holes packs the potential for triumph or disaster, the 15th, 16th, and 17th encircling a lake and 18 playing a rambling 444 uphill yards. For the leader coming into these holes, even a cushion of four may not be enough.

PREVIEWING
Even the driving range is set up for easy spectating. It's a few steps from the clubhouse, smack between the first tee and the 18th green, with a broad, high spectator mound behind it. Several faux greens enable the pros to hone their accuracy with various clubs, and the entire landing area slopes severely downhill, so all the shots have majestic hang time. An enormous putting green sprawls alongside the range.

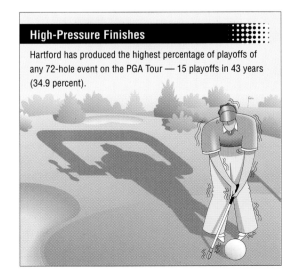

High-Pressure Finishes

Hartford has produced the highest percentage of playoffs of any 72-hole event on the PGA Tour — 15 playoffs in 43 years (34.9 percent).

TPC at River Highlands

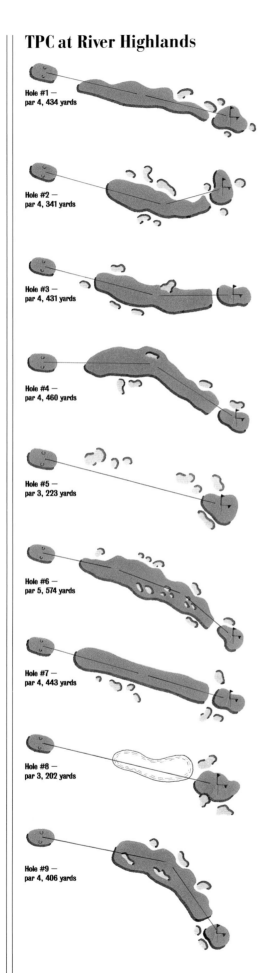

Hole #1 —
par 4, 434 yards

Hole #2 —
par 4, 341 yards

Hole #3 —
par 4, 431 yards

Hole #4 —
par 4, 460 yards

Hole #5 —
par 3, 223 yards

Hole #6 —
par 5, 574 yards

Hole #7 —
par 4, 443 yards

Hole #8 —
par 3, 202 yards

Hole #9 —
par 4, 406 yards

17th hole

above the beautiful Connecticut River.

Most of the new greens are small, and many are raised or crowned—those who miss them will need a well-oiled short game. Holes such as the downhill par-three 11th afford picturesque views of the river, but the pros will pause longest at 15, 16, and 17, where a lake stares them in the face. Then it's uphill into Connecticut's version of the Colosseum, a massive natural amphitheater that begins halfway up both sides of the fairway and curls around the back of the green. The hole can accommodate 50,000 spectators, and on Sunday afternoon it's full to capacity. Those who have won here say the roar that comes from that crowd is unlike any other sound in golf.

TOURNAMENT RATINGS

COURSE DIFFICULTY

Avg. winning score:	
9.0 under par*	6th on Tour
USGA course rating:	
73.4 (3.4 over par)	10th on Tour
Overall rating:	
Severe	7th on Tour

PRESTIGE

Field strength (8.2)	32nd on Tour
Winner quality (.580)	27th on Tour
Course difficulty (above)	7th on Tour
Plus factors: Huge crowds	
Overall rating	27th on Tour

*In four years since redesign

Practical Matters

FOR TICKET INFORMATION
TPC at River Highlands
Golf Club Road
Cromwell, CT 06416

COURSE
TPC at River Highlands

ACCESS
Private course—you must play with or be introduced by a member

COURSE RATING

Tees	Pro	Member
Yardage	6820	6518
Rating	73.4	72.0
Slope	135	131

GREEN FEES
$60–80
For more information:
(203) 635-2211

PRO-AM
Spots open to the public? Yes
Handicap: Maximum of 21
Format: Scramble
Entry fee: Two tiers: $2500 Wednesday; $1250 Monday
For more information:
(203) 246-4440

Local Knowledge

KNOW YOUR OWN STRENGTH

The TPC at River Highlands is a local knowledge course. Several greens call for uphill or downhill approaches, and on four holes if you leave your shot short, you'll be in water.

On such courses you need to make good club selections. That begins with an accurate knowledge of your distance capabilities with every club in your bag. Too many golfers have unrealistic notions about their own strength—they overestimate it for two reasons: 1) They assume that every shot will travel the distance of their best shot 2) They think of distance as the total of flight and roll. As a result, most amateurs miss greens by leaving the ball short.

To avoid this mistake and hit more greens, spend an hour or so taking some accurate readings on your distances. The best way to do this is by hitting several practice shots with each club. As you play the shots, estimate the distance that the ball rolls. Disregard the best and worst shots, and then pace off the distance to the area where the average of the others finished. (Note: The pace of the average male is a bit shorter than a yard, so take big steps.) This will give you your total distance, and when you subtract the roll of the shots, you will also know the carrying distance for each of your clubs. An accurate knowledge of your carrying distance is the key to smart club selection.

CLUB	DISTANCE*	CARRY
SW	85	80
PW	105	96
9	120	110
8	135	125
7	145	133
6	155	142
5	165	150

*in yards

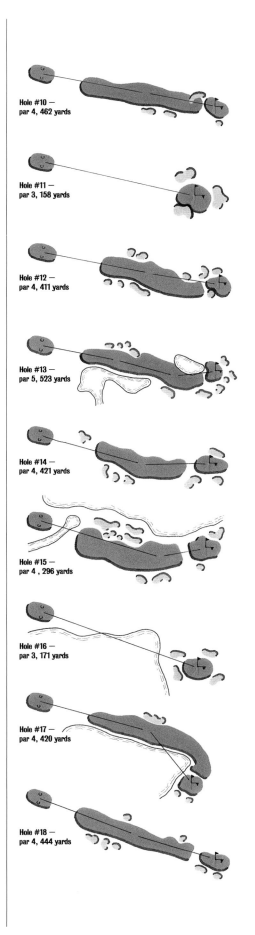

Hole #10 —
par 4, 462 yards

Hole #11 —
par 3, 158 yards

Hole #12 —
par 4, 411 yards

Hole #13 —
par 5, 523 yards

Hole #14 —
par 4, 421 yards

Hole #15 —
par 4 , 296 yards

Hole #16 —
par 3, 171 yards

Hole #17 —
par 4, 420 yards

Hole #18 —
par 4, 444 yards

Federal Express St. Jude Classic

TPC AT SOUTHWIND

The title sponsor may be Federal Express, but invariably it is the players who deliver at this tournament.

The steamy midsummer Memphis weather combines with a pliant golf course to produce some of the hottest scoring of each Tour season. Since the Tour arrived here in 1989, the average winning score has been 16 under par.

The TPC at Southwind was designed by Ron Prichard in 1988. He threaded his rolling zoysia fairways through 11 lakes and streams and among 87 bunkers of all shapes and sizes. Water comes into play on roughly half of the 35 tee-to-green swings, and sand is there on virtually all of them, especially around the smallish contoured greens. As such, this course of just over 7000 yards calls for accuracy more than might.

The core of this course is its collection of par fours, and four of the toughest lurk near the clubhouse. Holes one, nine, ten, and 18 are a quartet of water-menaced monsters that average 440 yards—stern places to start and finish. Much less demanding are the three "long" holes, numbers, 3, 5, and 16, which measure only 525, 527, and 528 yards, respectively, with water at only the fifth. Except for Waialae Country Club (site of the Hawaiian Open), which has four par fives, no tournament on the Tour yields more eagles than Southwind.

THE TV HOLES

Expect birdies:

16

Expect bogeys:

14

18th hole

What to Watch For . . .

LOW NUMBERS

Jay Delsing shot 61 here in 1993, and a half dozen players have posted 62s. But torrid scoring is a tradition in Memphis; back in 1977, it was in this event (although at a different course) that Al Geiberger posted the Tour's first score of 59.

REBEL QUELLS

At most PGA Tour events, gallery marshals control the crowds by raising paddles that read "QUIET PLEASE." Paddles are in use here, too, but they read "HUSH Y'ALL."

A TRIBUTE TO DANNY

The honorary chairman of this tournament, and for the two decades until his death its heart and soul, was entertainer and humanitarian Danny Thomas. Thomas founded the St. Jude Children's Research Hospital that is the event's sole beneficiary. On the grounds of the TPC at Southwind, a six-sided brick and granite memorial pays tribute to Danny.

Those Terrible Threes

Hardest Par-3s on the PGA Tour:

Course	Hole	Yards	Avg. Score
TPC at Southwind	14	231	3.365
Torrey Pines-North	6	160	3.318
Doral	13	246	3.314
Augusta National	12	155	3.298
Doral	4	237	3.262
TPC at Summerlin	8	239	3.253

TPC at Southwind

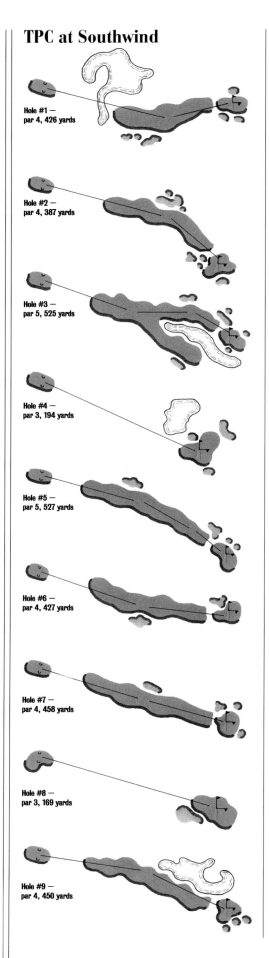

Hole #1 —
par 4, 426 yards

Hole #2 —
par 4, 387 yards

Hole #3 —
par 5, 525 yards

Hole #4 —
par 3, 194 yards

Hole #5 —
par 5, 527 yards

Hole #6 —
par 4, 427 yards

Hole #7 —
par 4, 458 yards

Hole #8 —
par 3, 169 yards

Hole #9 —
par 4, 450 yards

Remarkably, the hardest hole on the course is a par three. Number 14 plays 231 yards over a lake to a green with lots of slope. It is a hole in the tradition of the 12th at Augusta National, an all-or-nothing shot that looms in a player's mind from the moment he arrives at the course. In most years, this hole is statistically the toughest par three on the entire PGA Tour, playing to an average of roughly 3.5 strokes.

15th hole

TOURNAMENT RATINGS
COURSE DIFFICULTY

Avg. winning score:	
16.3 under par	32nd on Tour
USGA course rating:	
74.9 (3.9 over par)	3rd on Tour
Overall rating:	
Moderate	26th on Tour

PRESTIGE

Field strength (7.9)	35th on Tour
Winner quality (.860)	11th on Tour
Course difficulty (above)	26th on Tour
Plus factors: None	
Overall rating	26th on Tour

Local Knowledge

LOOK OUT FOR SUCKER PINS

On fully half of the approach shots at the TPC at Southwind, water comes into play—and into mind. And when the greenkeeping crew positions the pin in close proximity to that water, the assignment becomes doubly daunting.

In such situations, the biggest challenge is a mental one—restraint. Particularly when you have a short iron in your hand, there is a strong temptation to shoot aggressively at that pin. More often than not, that's a bad idea—you have more to lose than to gain.

The pros refer to these situations as "sucker pins," and if they rarely shoot at them, then certainly the average player should be equally prudent. When the flag is near water, a deep bunker, or other trouble, do yourself a favor and play safely for the fat part of the green. Accept the probability of two putts, and save your aggressive tactics for a more vulnerable target.

In only two cases should you consider shooting for a sucker pin: 1) when you have no choice—your back is to the wall in a match and you must deliver, and 2) when the situation strongly favors your shot pattern—in other words, when the pin is on the extreme right of the green and the controlled fade is your bread-and-butter shot, so you can let the ball drift across the width of the green and seek out the flag.

Practical Matters

FOR TICKET INFORMATION

Federal Express St. Jude Classic
TPC at Southwind
3325 Club at Southwind
Memphis, TN 38125

ACCESS

Private course—you must play with a member

COURSE

TPC at Southwind

COURSE RATING

Tees	Pro	Member
Yardage	7006	5867
Rating	74.9	68.9
Slope	135	118

GREEN FEES

$96
For more information:
(901) 748-0330

PRO-AM

Spots open to the public? Yes, but there is a waiting list
Handicap: Maximum of 21
Format: Best ball of team
Entry fee: $3500
For more information:
(901) 748-0534

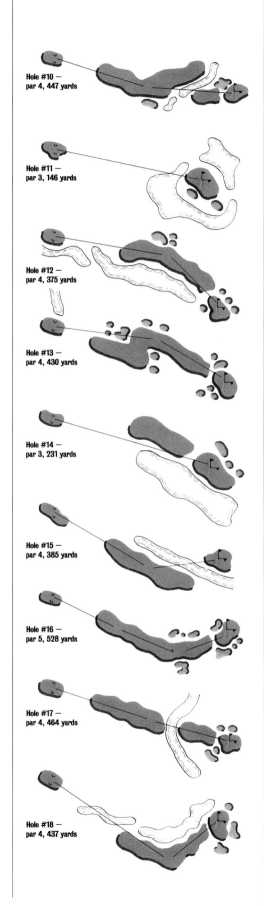

Hole #10 —
par 4, 447 yards

Hole #11 —
par 3, 146 yards

Hole #12 —
par 4, 375 yards

Hole #13 —
par 4, 430 yards

Hole #14 —
par 3, 231 yards

Hole #15 —
par 4, 385 yards

Hole #16 —
par 5, 528 yards

Hole #17 —
par 4, 464 yards

Hole #18 —
par 4, 437 yards

Motorola Western Open

COG HILL COUNTRY CLUB

The burning question is: Why do they call it the Western Open? This tournament hasn't been played west of Chicago for more than 30 years, and in its early days it wandered to Michigan, Texas, and all the way to New York.

And the answer is: This is the second-oldest event in American golf (only the U.S. Open predates it), and back when it started (1899), the American "West" referred to anything located to the left of the Alleghenies.

Back then, the Western Open was as important as today's major championships. Indeed, up until World War II it ranked just a notch below the U.S. Open in prestige. But times have changed. In the last half century, The Masters has overshadowed the Western, a corporate sponsor has been brought in to keep pace with the escalating purses, and the tournament has returned permanently to its Chicagoland home. Following a 16-year run at Butler National in Oak Brook, the Motorola Western Open has settled at a course in Lemont, Illinois.

Its name is Dubsdread—actually, that's the nickname for this course at the Cog

THE TV HOLES

Expect birdies:

11, 15

Expect bogeys:

13, 18

***

18th hole

What to Watch For . . .

KIDS
The pride of the Western Open—and the entire Western Golf Association—is the Evans Caddie Scholar Program. Begun by Chick Evans (the first player to win the U.S. Amateur and Open in the same year—1916) it is a fund that provides college tuition and board for Chicago-area caddies. Since 1930, over 6000 scholarships have been awarded; presently, nearly 1000 caddies are enrolled, thanks to contributions of $5 million a year. The Tour players are encouraged to use the caddie scholars this week, and many do. All proceeds of the tournament go to the fund.

HISTORY
Virtually every prominent American professional has won this tournament, and the very best have won it more than once: Hagen (5 times), Hogan (2), Nelson (2), Snead (2), Guldahl (3), Demaret (2), Casper (4), Palmer (2), Nicklaus (2), and Watson (3).

ALTERNATIVES
There are three other fine and challenging courses at Cog Hill, all of them open to the public.

DREAM TEAMS
Part of the pretournament festivities is a shootout among several pro-celebrity twosomes. Among the regulars: local boys Michael Jordan, Walter Payton, and Mike Ditka.

Tests of Time

Oldest Tournaments on the PGA Tour:

Tournament	Inaugural Year
U.S. Open	1895
Western Open	**1899**
Canadian Open	1904
PGA Championship	1916
Texas Open	1922
Los Angeles Open	1926
The Masters	1934
Phoenix Open	1935

Cog Hill Country Club – Dubsdread Course

Hole #1 —
par 4, 420 yards

Hole #2 —
par 3, 177 yards

Hole #3 —
par 4, 415 yards

Hole #4 —
par 4, 416 yards

Hole #5 —
par 5, 525 yards

Hole #6 —
par 3, 213 yards

Hole #7 —
par 4, 410 yards

Hole #8 —
par 4, 378 yards

Hole #9 —
par 5, 568 yards

Hill Country Club, and therein is another misnomer. For Cog Hill is not, strictly speaking, a private country club—it is open to the public, thanks to golf entrepreneur Joe Jemsek, whose life's work has been dedicated to improving the lot of Chicago's daily-fee players.

On rolling land clad with hundreds of sprawling oak trees, Jemsek and his chosen designers Dick Wilson and Joe Lee set out to design a course that would please the locals, yet—from its championship tees—test the best players in the world. The course they fashioned is not a long one for its par of 72—barely 7000 yards from the tips—but it calls constantly for accuracy, particularly into its small, sloping, and tightly bunkered greens.

Jemsek got the first half of his wish immediately—Dubsdread has delighted Chicago's golfers ever since it opened in 1964—but he had to wait until the Western arrived in 1991 to see just how it would test the big boys. The result was an unqualified success as the course won unanimous raves from the pros while the winning score—275—was exactly what it had been each of the two previous years at Butler.

The heart of the challenge is the trio of holes 12, 13, and 14, two lengthy par threes sandwiching a 446-yard par four that is corseted by

sand on the left, trees and out of bounds to the right. The three holes are known less than affectionately as Death Valley, and death is exactly what they dealt Greg Norman in that first Western Open here. Leading the tournament by four strokes as he came to the 12th tee, the Shark took three straight quick bogeys and eventually lost the tournament by one stroke to Russ Cochran.

But what is pain for the players is pleasure for the spectators. A large mound runs through these holes, affording galleryites a splendid view of the struggles.

TOURNAMENT RATINGS

COURSE DIFFICULTY

Avg. winning score: 13.8 under par		24th on Tour
USGA course rating: 75.4 (3.4 over par)		10th on Tour
Overall rating: Moderate		25th on Tour

PRESTIGE

Field strength (11.9)		19th on Tour
Winner quality (.840)		13th on Tour
Course difficulty (above)		25th on Tour
Plus factors: History (event began 1899)		
Overall rating		15th on Tour

Practical Matters

FOR TICKET INFORMATION
Western Golf Association
1 Brian Road
Golf, IL 60029

COURSE
Cog Hill Country Club,
Dubsdread Course

ACCESS
Open to the public

COURSE RATING

Tees	Pro	Member
Yardage	7073	6366
Rating	75.4	71.4
Slope	142	138

GREEN FEES
$80, including cart
For more information:
(708) 257-5872

PRO-AM
Spots open to the public? Yes
Handicap: Maximum of 21
Format: Best ball of team
Entry fee: $800 Monday,
$2000 Wednesday
For more information:
(708) 724-4600

Local Knowledge

TEACH YOURSELF SAND SAVVY

If you get a chance to play Dubsdread, it's a safe bet that you'll hit a few of the 111 bunkers before the round's over. Here, as on any course that is heavily bunkered, you need confidence in sand.

One of the best things you can do for your game is to spend an hour in a practice bunker, teaching yourself. Experimentation will teach you the best way to alter the distance of your bunker shots. There are three basic ways, and you should determine the one that works best for you.

1) Vary the length of your swing: Just as with wedge shots from the fairway, you can control the distance of your sand shots by shortening and lengthening your swing.

2) Vary the pace of your swing: You may have noticed that the Tour pros occasionally make a soft, almost lazy swing in the sand. This is another way to take some distance off a shot.

3) Vary the cushion of sand: When playing most greenside bunker shots, you do not hit the ball, you hit behind it, usually an inch or two. By varying the distance between the ball and the point where your wedge penetrates the sand, you can control the flight of your shots—the more sand you take, the shorter a shot you'll hit.

Take an hour and experiment with these techniques—and to vary the trajectory of your shot, experiment with the openness of your stance and wedge. You'll be surprised at how much you'll learn just by fooling around.

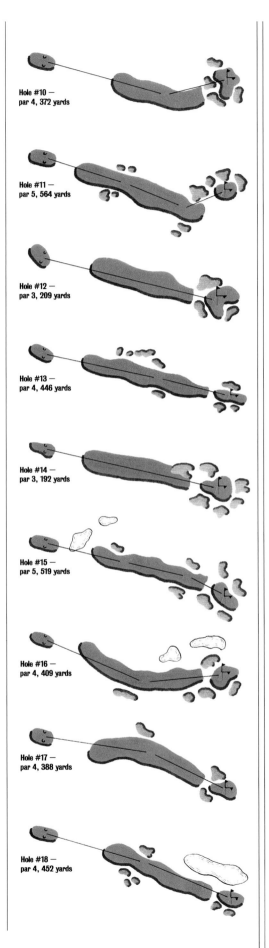

Hole #10 —
par 4, 372 yards

Hole #11 —
par 5, 564 yards

Hole #12 —
par 3, 209 yards

Hole #13 —
par 4, 446 yards

Hole #14 —
par 3, 192 yards

Hole #15 —
par 5, 519 yards

Hole #16 —
par 4, 409 yards

Hole #17 —
par 4, 388 yards

Hole #18 —
par 4, 452 yards

Anheuser-Busch Golf Classic

KINGSMILL GOLF CLUB

18th hole

Bentgrass makes for the smoothest, fastest greens in golf. Bermudagrass makes for the lushest, sternest rough. Few courses have both, but Kingsmill does. It is just north enough to sustain the cool climate for bent, and just south enough to allow bermuda alongside the fairways. Combine that with a testing design by Pete Dye, and you have the kind of course that makes you want to reach for a beer.

That's fine, since the course, the Kingsmill Golf Club, and the community in which they are situated all are owned by the Anheuser-Busch brewing company.

Amateurs who play this resort course are intimidated by the deep ravines that gape in front of several tees. But the pros will tell you that the real challenge is in the greens—first in finding them, then in getting the ball to the hole. These are not big targets, and nearly all of them are raised or elevated in some way. As a result, there is little opportunity for a running game. You must fly the ball to the putting surface—and then make it stop—a tall assignment if you happen to have caught a patch of that bermuda rough.

Once on the green, the fun has just begun. Dye dotted his modern darts-game course with Scottish-style greens, full of tiers and slopes that make them play even smaller than they are. When the bentgrass is at its fastest, putting can be an adventure.

This is a tournament where most of the

THE TV HOLES

Expect birdies:
15

Expect bogeys:
18

What to Watch For . . .

CURTIS'S STRANGE NAVY

Local boy Curtis Strange represents Kingsmill on the Tour and is a big favorite with the galleries—on water as well as land. At the 17th hole, a par three that stretches along the bank of the James, a small armada of party boats assembles on the weekend to exhort their man to victory. So far it hasn't worked—Strange's best finish here is third.

YOUTH MOVEMENT

With the exception of the tournament at Disney World, this is the favorite stop of the Tour brats. Their summer vacation includes tours of nearby Busch Gardens theme park and Historic Colonial Williamsburg, and for the competitive ones there's a Kid's Golf Classic, just like the one Dad plays. For the little ones, the A-B Classic has one of the best nurseries on the Tour.

ARTIFACTS

Remember, this is one of the most historically rich parts of the country. When developers broke ground for the course they discovered the remains of Burwell's landing, an important commercial wharf during the Revolutionary War.

HEAT

The mid-Atlantic states are famed for their humidity, and with this tournament played in the dead of summer, sweltering conditions prevail. Of course, that bodes well for the sales of title sponsor Budweiser.

Claim to Shame

Hal Sutton blew a six-stroke lead after 54 holes in 1983 when he finished with a 77 while Calvin Peete was closing with a 69. No one has ever lost a bigger 54-hole lead in any existing PGA Tour event.

Kingsmill Golf Club

Hole #1 —
par 4, 360 yards

Hole #2 —
par 3, 204 yards

Hole #3 —
par 5, 538 yards

Hole #4 —
par 4, 437 yards

Hole #5 —
par 3, 183 yards

Hole #6 —
par 4, 365 yards

Hole #7 —
par 5, 516 yards

Hole #8 —
par 4, 413 yards

Hole #9 —
par 4, 452 yards

action tends to occur in the last hour: at the 16th, a tortuous dogleg to a green surrounded by six bunkers; at the par-three 17th, where the narrow but longest green on the course can mean a different club off the tee for each of the four days; and finally, the most difficult hole on the course, a 435-yard par four that starts with a 200-yard carry over a pond and between out of bounds and water, and culminates at a small green with bunkers left and right.

In recent years, the field here has been spotty. With the date a week before the British Open, some top players opt to cross the pond a week early, either for vacation or to play in the lucrative Scottish Open at Gleneagles. Those who do play here make a Sunday-afternoon dash for their transatlantic flights.

17th hole

TOURNAMENT RATINGS

COURSE DIFFICULTY

Avg. winning score:	
14.9 under par	28th on Tour
USGA course rating:	
73.3 (2.3 over par)	23rd on Tour
Overall rating:	
Moderate	29th on Tour

PRESTIGE

Field strength (6.6)	39th on Tour
Winner quality (.460)	34th on Tour
Course difficulty (above)	29th on Tour
Plus factors: None	
Overall rating	38th on Tour

Local Knowledge

HITTING A HIGH BALL

As with many courses designed by Pete Dye, the key at Kingsmill is flying your ball to the target. Your approaches must land on the raised greens—bounce-on shots don't work.

What this calls for is an ability to hit the ball with a little more loft than usual. Fortunately, for most players this doesn't require a big adjustment. Simply take your address so that the ball is positioned a bit forward of its normal place in your stance. If you usually have it off your left heel, set up so it's off your left instep. This should ensure that you make contact with the ball just as your club begins its ascent into the finish, so the clubface will have a few degrees of extra loft. If this adjustment doesn't do the trick, try distributing your weight more on your right foot at address, and keeping it there throughout the swing. Think of staying "behind the ball" through impact. This will keep you from getting ahead of the ball at impact (which would deloft your clubface and lower your trajectory). Stay back and let your hands whip through the ball—that will give your shot plenty of loft.

Practical Matters

FOR TICKET INFORMATION
Anheuser-Busch Golf Classic
328 McLaws Circle
Williamsburg, VA 23185

COURSE
Kingsmill Golf Club

ACCESS
Open to the public

COURSE RATING

Tees	Pro	Member
Yardage	6797	6022
Rating	73.3	69.7
Slope	137	129

GREEN FEES
$105, including cart
For more information:
(804) 253-3906

PRO-AM
Spots open to the public? Yes
Handicap: Maximum of 21
Format: Best ball of team
Entry fee: $2500
For more information:
(804) 253-3985

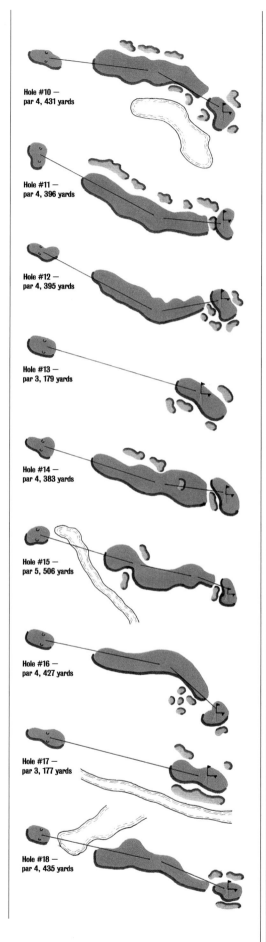

Hole #10 — par 4, 431 yards

Hole #11 — par 4, 396 yards

Hole #12 — par 4, 395 yards

Hole #13 — par 3, 179 yards

Hole #14 — par 4, 383 yards

Hole #15 — par 5, 506 yards

Hole #16 — par 4, 427 yards

Hole #17 — par 3, 177 yards

Hole #18 — par 4, 435 yards

Deposit Guaranty Golf Classic

ANNANDALE COUNTRY CLUB

A new site, a new date, and a new "officialness" make this the most improved event on the PGA Tour.

The Deposit Guaranty Golf Classic was born in 1980 and spent its formative years in total obscurity—on an unremarkable course that attracted unremarkable players—as the "other" event played during the week of The Masters. As such, it saw minimal newspaper and no television coverage.

Now, however, it is poised to blossom. In 1994 the tournament moved from the Hattiesburg Country Club, a pushover layout of less than 6500 yards (and with just 19 bunkers) to Annandale Country Club, a bruiser with a rating of 75.4. At the same time, it made a move that was even more important, being shifted on the calendar from April to July, out of the shadow of The Masters. Finally, and most important of all, with the new date came a long-awaited designation of this as an official PGA Tour event. Victory at the DGGC now brings an invitation to The Masters and Mercedes Championship along with a one-year exemption from qualifying on the PGA Tour.

Robert Morgan, the chairman of this tournament since its inception, is delighted. "For years, we had a Catch-22 problem," he says. "The Tour wouldn't designate us an official event until we attracted a strong field, we couldn't attract a

THE TV HOLES

Expect birdies:

18

Expect bogeys:

14

What to Watch For . . .

THE 3 H'S
When the DGGC moved on the calendar from early April to the dog days of summer, it became the most hazy, hot, and humid stop on the Tour. Those who want sweater weather this week should opt for the British Open.

BIGGER NUMBERS
This course is 667 yards longer than the previous venue, Hattiesburg Country Club—that's like adding a long par five. Expect the pros to post some higher scores here.

BIGGER NAMES
The list of former winners here is hardly a Who's Who in Golf, but with its designation as an official event, the DGGC can now attract a classier field.

Dreamin' Green

From 1968 through 1993, the Deposit Guaranty Classic was played the same week as The Masters. The only player to win the event and later go on to win The Masters was Craig Stadler, who won the Deposit Guaranty in 1978 and The Masters in 1982.

18th hole

Annandale Country Club

Hole #1 —
par 4, 369 yards

Hole #2 —
par 3, 213 yards

Hole #3 —
par 4, 406 yards

Hole #4 —
par 4, 465 yards

Hole #5 —
par 5, 522 yards

Hole #6 —
par 4, 398 yards

Hole #7 —
par 5, 556 yards

Hole #8 —
par 3, 209 yards

Hole #9 —
par 4, 450 yards

strong field until we got a new date, and the Tour wouldn't give us a new date. Now we have what we need."

Still, a challenge remains. The tournament now is slotted into the third week of July— opposite the British Open. But this is less stiff competition, because only a couple of dozen Americans make the trip overseas.

The course was designed by Jack Nicklaus. One of his first efforts, Annandale reflects the Golden Bear's early tendency to design holes in his own image. At 7157 yards from the back tees, it calls for booming tee shots and long towering approach shots that can settle softly on these, the first bentgrass greens in Mississippi.

The par fives are particularly rewarding to those who can pummel the ball. Number five plays just 522 yards downhill, but with the second shot over water, and to the smallest green on the course, players may well pause before pulling out the heavy artillery. Anyone who wants to get home in two at the 11th will have to clout a tee shot that carries 270 yards, over a massive bunk-

17th hole

er smack in the center of the fairway. And at the home hole, a 532-yarder, water and sand lurk on both the drive and the second shot. It is a good place for finishing birdies— and bogeys.

TOURNAMENT RATINGS

COURSE DIFFICULTY

Avg. winning score: NA*	NA*
USGA course rating: 75.4 (3.4 over par)	10th on Tour
Overall rating: Severe	10th on Tour

PRESTIGE

Field strength (0.4)	44th on Tour
Winner quality (.100)	44th on Tour
Course difficulty (above)	10th on Tour
Minus factor: Played same week as British Open	
Overall rating	44th on Tour

*New course, 1994 (when tournament rain-shortened to 36 holes)

Local Knowledge

BENT VS. BERMUDA

Most golf courses in the Deep South feature greens sown with bermuda-grass, but Annandale is an oasis of bentgrass, the predominant strain on northern greens. Locals who visit here will have to make some adjustments.

Bent greens are smoother surfaces. The difference is that the ball rolls across the bending backs of the blades of grass, whereas with bermudagrass it rolls across the tips. As such, putts on bent are less susceptible to the grain—or direction of growth—of the grass. Whereas the bristles of bermuda tend to push the ball in one direction, the bowed leaves of bent have comparatively little effect.

Each grass presents a different putting challenge. On bermuda the assignment is to read the grain and allow for it both in the pace and break of your putt: Play extra break when the slope and grain move in the same way, less break when they're opposite; hit downgrain putts more softly, against-the-grain putts harder. With bentgrass—especially well-conditioned courses—the main challenge is to control the speed, which can be very fast. For this reason, most good players raised on bent greens tend to have smooth, arm-and-shoulder strokes that glide through the ball, whereas players brought up on bermuda are more likely to use a rapping-type hit. The prevailing wisdom is that, if you can putt bermuda, you can adapt easily to bent, but it's tougher to go the other way.

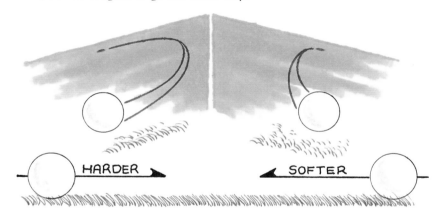

HARDER →   ← SOFTER

Practical Matters

FOR TICKET INFORMATION
Deposit Guaranty Golf Classic
837 Mannsdale Rd.
Madison, MS 39110

COURSE
Annandale Country Club

ACCESS
Private course—you must play with a member

COURSE RATING

Tees	Pro	Member
Yardage	7157	6439
Rating	75.4	71.5
Slope	134	128

GREEN FEES
$75
For more information:
(601) 856-0886

PRO-AM
Spots open to the public? Yes
Handicap: Maximum of 21
Format: Best ball of team
Entry fee: Two tiers: $750 Monday, $1000 Wednesday
For more information:
(601) 264-8113

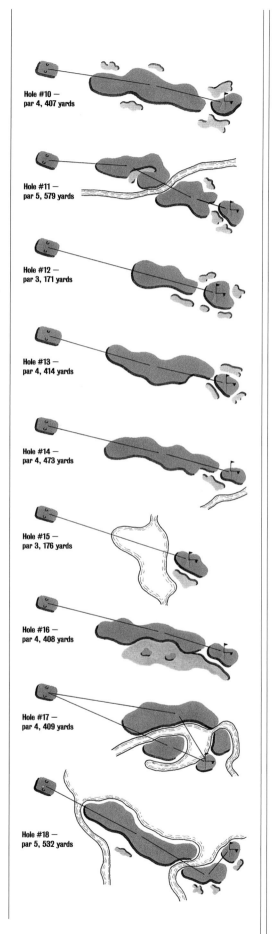

Hole #10 —
par 4, 407 yards

Hole #11 —
par 5, 579 yards

Hole #12 —
par 3, 171 yards

Hole #13 —
par 4, 414 yards

Hole #14 —
par 4, 473 yards

Hole #15 —
par 3, 176 yards

Hole #16 —
par 4, 408 yards

Hole #17 —
par 4, 409 yards

Hole #18 —
par 5, 532 yards

New England Classic

PLEASANT VALLEY COUNTRY CLUB

When you think of quaint old New England—white salt-box houses, antique shops, covered bridges, and lobster traps—think also of the Pleasant Valley Country Club and the New England Classic. As one local writer put it, "A day here is like a Sunday afternoon visit to grandma's."

The designer of this course was not Robert Trent Jones or Tom Fazio —it was Don Hoenig, a local golf pro. And in contrast to most of the stops on the Tour, this is no showcase for a corporate sponsor. In fact, there is no title sponsor at all—just a collection of local businesses that believe New England deserves a top-notch professional golf event. That, after all, was

THE TV HOLES

Expect birdies:

18

Expect bogeys:

10, 17

16th hole

What to Watch For . . .

LITTLE GREEN APPLES
Spectating at this tournament can bear fruit. Pleasant Valley was sculpted from a huge apple orchard, and not all of the trees were lopped.

SPECTATOR FRIENDLINESS
Eight holes play directly to or from the clubhouse. In fact, on more than one occasion pros have overclubbed their approach shots, and then have played *from* the clubhouse.

THE ONLY ONE THAT'S A THREE
The first hole here is a 183-yard par three, making this the only course on the PGA Tour that was designed to begin with a one-shotter.

PAAAHTISANSHIP
Boston fans are notorious for their fealty to the Celtics, the Red Sox, and the Bruins, so don't be surprised if the biggest galleries here are following New England boys Billy Andrade, Brad Faxon, and Jim Hallet.

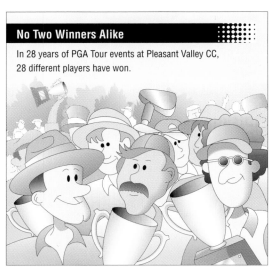

No Two Winners Alike

In 28 years of PGA Tour events at Pleasant Valley CC, 28 different players have won.

Pleasant Valley Country Club

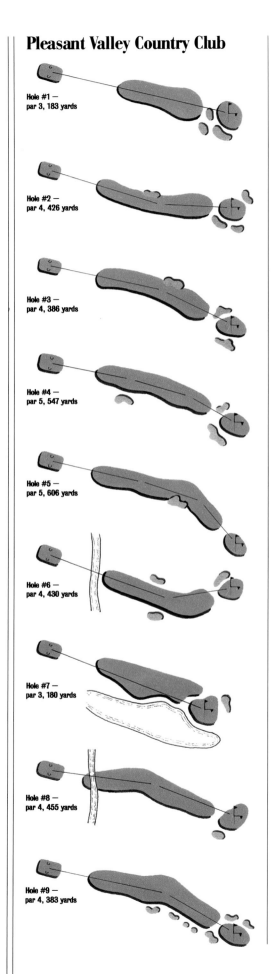

Hole #1 —
par 3, 183 yards

Hole #2 —
par 4, 426 yards

Hole #3 —
par 4, 386 yards

Hole #4 —
par 5, 547 yards

Hole #5 —
par 5, 606 yards

Hole #6 —
par 4, 430 yards

Hole #7 —
par 3, 180 yards

Hole #8 —
par 4, 455 yards

Hole #9 —
par 4, 383 yards

9th hole

the dream of Cosmo E. "Cuz" Mingolla, the contractor who bought the land, commissioned the course, and founded this event back in the early '60s. Today, his son Ted runs the family enterprise with the same loving care.

The fields at Pleasant Valley don't rival those at THE PLAYERS Championship or the U.S. Open, but there is a solid cadre of loyal players who know that tournaments such as this one are the backbone of the Tour.

The open, welcoming spirit is reflected in the course, where a feeling of expansiveness prevails—big tees, big greens, and several big holes on this par 71 of 7110 yards. This is particularly true on the back nine, which begins with a pair of par fours that stretch 467 and 480 yards, plays through a pair of "short" holes that average 215, and concludes at a finisher that measures 583.

But none of these brutes is the signature hole—that honor belongs to number 17, a picture-postcard par four that plays past a quiet pond and weatherworn covered bridge while winding downhill 412 yards through two stands of dense woods. Ray Floyd, who won here in 1977 despite a double-bogey on Sunday, calls this bucolic beauty a "monster."

TOURNAMENT RATINGS

COURSE DIFFICULTY

Avg. winning score:	
13.7 under par	22nd on Tour
USGA course rating:	
74.2 (3.2 over par)	14th on Tour
Overall rating:	
Moderate	24th on Tour

PRESTIGE

Field strength (5.0)	40th on Tour
Winner quality (.420)	35th on Tour
Course difficulty (above)	24th on Tour
Plus factors: None	
Overall rating	39th on Tour

Local Knowledge

PLAYING FROM HILLY LIES

When you play golf in the rolling hills of New England, you have to be prepared for some ups and downs.

Uphill lies are generally a bit easier to play. The key, as for downhills, is to set yourself to the ball in the correct way. This begins with your alignment, where you should attempt to set your hips parallel to the flow of the land. In other word, be sure your left hip is higher than your right. Usually, that means putting a bit of extra weight on your right foot, or adding some flex in that knee. One way to check that you've done this correctly is to hold a club across your beltline—if it isn't parallel to the ground, make the necessary adjustment in your stance. The only other key is to position the ball a bit forward of its usual point in your stance. This is because, with an uphill lie, the bottom point of your swing will occur a bit later.

The tendencies from this lie are to pull the ball to the left a bit and to hit a high shot that flies shorter than from a level lie, so in severely uphill situations, take at least one club more and aim a bit to the right.

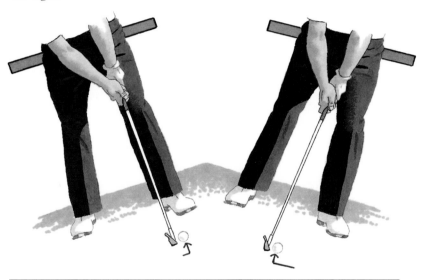

Practical Matters

FOR TICKET INFORMATION
New England Golf Classic
P.O. Box 420
Sutton, MA 01590

COURSE
Pleasant Valley Country Club

ACCESS
Private course—you must play with or be introduced by a member

COURSE RATING

Tees	Pro	Member
Yardage	7110	6507
Rating	74.2	72.0
Slope	138	133

GREEN FEES
$40 with member,
$65 unaccompanied by member
For more information:
(508) 865-5244

PRO-AM
Spots open to the public? Yes
Handicap: Maximum of 21
Format: Best ball of team
Entry fee: Two tiers: Monday $750, Wednesday $1600
For more information:
(508) 865-1491

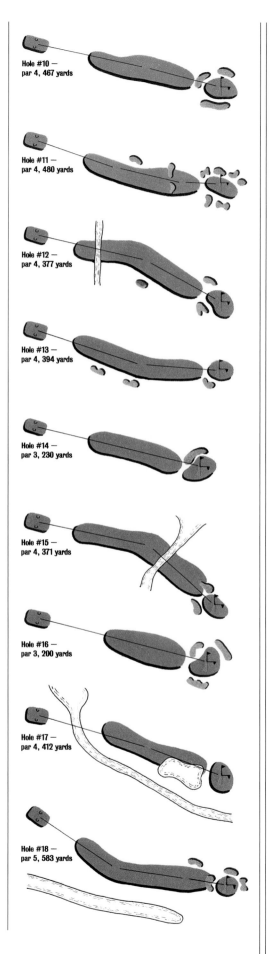

Hole #10 — par 4, 467 yards
Hole #11 — par 4, 480 yards
Hole #12 — par 4, 377 yards
Hole #13 — par 4, 394 yards
Hole #14 — par 3, 230 yards
Hole #15 — par 4, 371 yards
Hole #16 — par 3, 200 yards
Hole #17 — par 4, 412 yards
Hole #18 — par 5, 583 yards

Buick Open

WARWICK HILLS GOLF & COUNTRY CLUB

I f today's PGA Tour players had a proper sense of gratitude, they'd all be driving Buicks. The biggest and longest-standing sponsor on the Tour is the Buick Motor Division, whose name and logo are attached to four tournaments across the country with total prize money of more than $4 million.

It all began more than 35 years ago in Buick's home town, Flint, Michigan, with the Buick Open. Even then Buick was a leader, offering a princely $10,000 and a brand-new car for the winner of the 1958 Buick Open Invitational, then the richest tournament on the Tour.

Billy Casper did the deed, edging Arnold Palmer on the final hole of the Warwick Hills Golf & Country Club. His winning total was 285—three under par. Today, the Buick Open continues to be played at Warwick, but anyone with hopes of finishing first had better shoot some low scores—these days the winner needs to be about 15 under par.

Are today's pros that much better? No, but today's Warwick Hills is. In the early days, it was a course that Sam Snead described as "just a long walk," indeed the longest walk on the Tour. But in 1972, architect Joe Lee

THE TV HOLES

Expect birdies:

12, 13 14, 16

Expect bogeys:

18

17th hole

What to Watch For . . .

UNHAPPY HOOKERS
Each of the first five holes and each of the last four is bordered on the left side by out of bounds—bad news for those who hook the ball.

BUICKS
Remember the name of the tournament and, more important, remember that this is Detroit, where the first rule of the road is "buy American." Over half the cars in this lot are Buicks—many of them belonging to Buick employees who donate their time—while less than 10 percent are foreign-made. And don't even ask what the prizes are for holes-in-one.

DRAMA AT 17
The penultimate hole is a picturesque par three of 197 yards that plays to a green surrounded by four bunkers and a small pond. Also at that green is one of the most vocal grandstands on the Tour. The exuberant crowd is rarely disappointed—several Buick Opens have been settled here, and it was here in 1962 that Jerry Barber scored the first televised hole-in-one.

FRUSTRATION AT 18
Jack Nicklaus once hooked out of bounds and lost the tournament here, and no one has snatched victory from this finishing four. In the long history of the tournament, no player has come to 18 needing a birdie to win and then pulled off the feat.

Two Swings — Four Under

John Inman scored back-to-back eagles in 1993 — neither of them on par fives. In the second round, he holed a 146-yard 7-iron on the par-four 10th at Warwick Hills G&CC and on his next shot holed a 190-yard 4-iron on the par-three 11th.

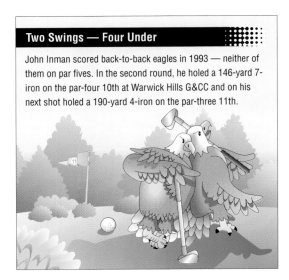

Warwick Hills Golf & Country Club

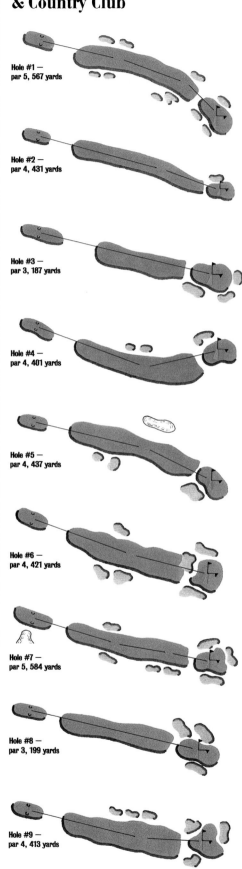

Hole #1 —
par 5, 567 yards

Hole #2 —
par 4, 431 yards

Hole #3 —
par 3, 187 yards

Hole #4 —
par 4, 401 yards

Hole #5 —
par 4, 437 yards

Hole #6 —
par 4, 421 yards

Hole #7 —
par 5, 584 yards

Hole #8 —
par 3, 199 yards

Hole #9 —
par 4, 413 yards

13th hole

came in and softened the big course, chopping 260 yards off its distance. Although he added about half of that back in the 1990s to keep pace with today's longer hitters, Warwick Hills remains a course that rewards finesse as much as brute strength. Year in and year out, it is also one of the finest-conditioned courses on the Tour, particularly its big, smooth-rolling greens. Good putters tend to do well here.

Look for charges to be mounted on the inward nine, where holes 12–14 and 16 routinely play well under par for the Tour players. At the home hole, however, they have their hands full with a lengthy par four that plays into the teeth of the prevailing wind to the shallowest target on the course.

TOURNAMENT RATINGS

COURSE DIFFICULTY

Avg. winning score:	
17.8 under par	38th on Tour
USGA course rating:	
73.9 (1.9 over par)	31st on Tour
Overall rating:	
Vulnerable	40th on Tour

PRESTIGE

Field strength (8.9)	29th on Tour
Winner quality (.278)	40th on Tour
Course difficulty (above)	40th on Tour
Plus factors: None	
Overall rating	36th on Tour

Practical Matters

FOR TICKET INFORMATION
Buick Open Marketing Office
Warwick Hills Golf & Country Club
G-8469 S. Saginaw
Grand Blanc, MI 48439

COURSE
Warwick Hills Golf & Country Club

ACCESS
Private course—you must play
with a member

COURSE RATING

Tees	Pro	Member
Yardage	7101	6489
Rating	73.9	71.3
Slope	133	127

GREEN FEES
$40
For more information:
(810) 694-9251

PRO-AM
Spots open to the public? Yes
Handicap: Maximum of 21
Format: Best ball of team
Entry fee: $3000
For more information:
(800) 878-6736

Local Knowledge

TWO TIPS TO FIGHT A NERVOUS HOOK

At Warwick Hills, out of bounds haunts the left side of the drive zone at both the first and last holes. In such tense situations, some golfers can get flustered and hit a snap hook. If you're one of those people, here are a couple of quick set-up changes that will give you some antihook insurance.

Number one, tee your ball at the extreme left side of the tee box. This will put the out of bounds more at your back and will encourage you to direct your tee shot to the right side of the fairway, away from the trouble. That way, even if you do hook the ball, you'll have a cushion.

Second, tighten your grip pressure at address, especially in the last three fingers of your left hand, and maintain that firm pressure throughout the swing. With a tighter grip pressure, you'll be less likely to turn your right hand over your left as you swing through impact, the main cause of a hook.

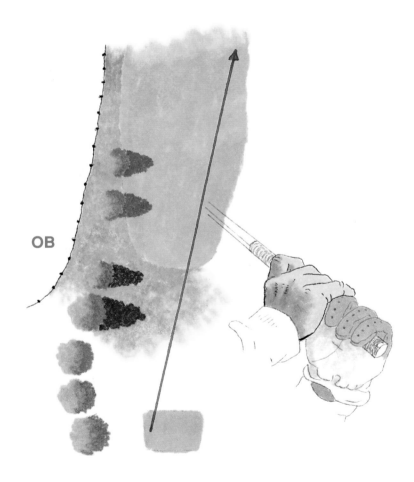

OB

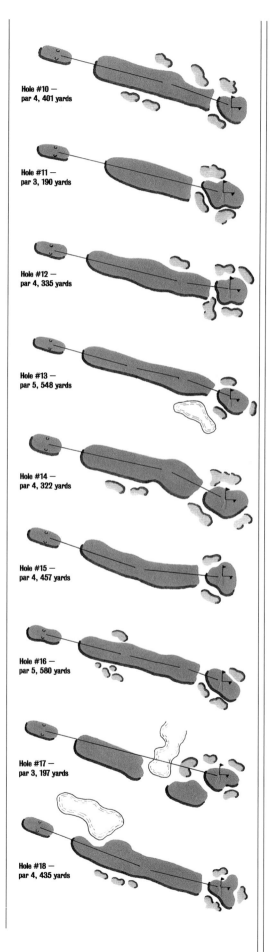

Hole #10 —
par 4, 401 yards

Hole #11 —
par 3, 190 yards

Hole #12 —
par 4, 335 yards

Hole #13 —
par 5, 548 yards

Hole #14 —
par 4, 322 yards

Hole #15 —
par 4, 457 yards

Hole #16 —
par 5, 580 yards

Hole #17 —
par 3, 197 yards

Hole #18 —
par 4, 435 yards

The Sprint International

CASTLE PINES GOLF CLUB

When your TV screen shows a scoreboard with the leading player at Plus 15, you know you've tuned in to The International. Without question, this is the most distinctive event on the Tour.

The biggest difference is its scoring system, a modified version of the Stableford method used at amateur events around the country. Instead of trying to take the fewest strokes, players try to make the most points—by making birdies and avoiding anything worse than par. In the version of the Stableford system applied at The International, points are awarded as follows: –3 points for double bogey or worse, –1 for bogey, 0 for par, 2 for birdie, 5 for eagle, and 8 for double eagle.

Difference number two derives from the playing field, a distinctive Jack Nicklaus design perched on a hill near mile-high Denver. At 7559 yards, the golf course at the Castle Pines Golf Club is by far the longest track on the Tour, with a first hole that measures 644 yards. But that distance is deceptive, because golf here is played at Rocky Mountain elevation, where the ball flies about 15 percent farther than at sea level. Thus, that opening par five plays to about 550 "normal" yards, and several players have reached it in two with middle-iron shots.

The opening hole also drops over 100 feet in elevation from tee to green and is thus a harbinger of the ups and downs that are a constant at Castle Pines. Nicklaus also put plenty of pitch and roll in the Castle Pines putting greens, and added a couple of controversial design features—

THE TV HOLES

Expect birdies:

17

Expect bogeys:

18

12th hole

What to Watch For . . .

MILKSHAKES
Any player will tell you, the best milkshakes on Tour are at The International. Thick, creamy, and made with Häagen-Dazs ice cream, they add several feet to the collective waistline of the Tour. Members of the press also get to indulge, but sadly, the shakes aren't available to spectators.

SHORTNESS OF BREATH
Castle Pines sits at an elevation of 6290 feet, where the air is thin and respiration can become labored, especially after climbing the uphill fairway of hole 17.

PRISTINE CONDITION
Castle Pines is probably the most private club on the PGA Tour—350 members, most of whom don't live in the immediate area—so the course sees only about 14,000 rounds per year. (By contrast, Pebble Beach hosts 60,000 rounds.) So expect to see the fairest fairways west of Augusta.

EARLY PLAYOFFS
The unique format calls for a cut from 144 to 72 players by Saturday morning, and to 24 by Sunday. Those on the bubble must do combat at sudden death for the last spots.

FLAGS
True to its name, The International has a diverse field of players from around the world. Since this is an invitational event it's an opportunity for budding foreign players to get their first look at the U.S. Tour and for Americans to get a look at them.

PIKE'S PEAK
On a clear day, it's in view from the course.

Long Drives Are a Must			
Longest Courses on the PGA Tour:			
Course	**Tournament**	**Yards**	**Par**
Castle Pines GC	**The Sprint International**	**7,559**	**72**
TPC at Summerlin	Las Vegas Invitational	7,243	72
Magnolia GC	Walt Disney World/ Oldsmobile Classic	7,190	72
Las Vegas CC	Las Vegas Invitational	7,164	72
Annandale GC	Deposit Guaranty Classic	7,157	72
Firestone CC	NEC World Series of Golf	7,149	70

Castle Pines Golf Club

Hole #1 —
par 5, 644 yards

Hole #2 —
par 4, 408 yards

Hole #3 —
par 4, 462 yards

Hole #4 —
par 3, 205 yards

Hole #5 —
par 4, 477 yards

Hole #6 —
par 4, 417 yards

Hole #7 —
par 3, 185 yards

Hole #8 —
par 5, 535 yards

Hole #9 —
par 4, 458 yards

18th hole

an insidious gathering bunker at 16 and a choice of fairways at 18—that have since become prevalent elements of his design work.

The play-for-points format encourages aggressive play, especially at the short par-five (492-yard) 17th hole, where the pros gun their second shots for the flag. More than once, a 5-point eagle on Sunday has raised a player from the middle of the pack onto the first page of the leaderboard. However, it was at the 8th hole in 1990 that Steve Pate scored a double eagle, sinking a 238-yard 2-iron for eight points that catapulted him from the middle of the pack into a tie for second place.

TOURNAMENT RATINGS

COURSE DIFFICULTY

Avg. winning score: NA*		NA*
USGA course rating: 75.8 (3.8 over par)		5th on Tour
Overall rating: Severe		5th on Tour

PRESTIGE

Field strength (12.0)	18th on Tour
Winner quality (.278)	40th on Tour
Course difficulty (above)	5th on Tour
Plus factors: Unique Stableford format	
Overall rating	22nd on Tour

*Stableford scoring system

Practical Matters

FOR TICKET INFORMATION
The Sprint International
1000 Hummingbird Drive
Castle Rock, CO 80104

COURSE
Castle Pines Golf Club

ACCESS
Private course—you must play with a member

COURSE RATING

Tees	Pro	Member
Yardage	7559	6834
Rating	75.8	72.4
Slope	145	140

GREEN FEES
Guest fee: $100
For more information:
(303) 688-6000

PRO-AM
Spots open to the public? Yes
Handicap: Maximum of 21
Format: Best ball of four, Stableford scoring system
Entry fee: $2500
For more information:
(303) 660-8000

Local Knowledge

HANDLING RARE AIR

When the pros get to Castle Pines, they have to deal with an additional element on every approach shot—the mile-high air. In the Colorado Rockies—or anywhere in the world where the elevation is a mile or more—the ball flies appreciably farther than at sea level.

How much farther? It's not a matter of yards, it's a percentage. The higher you are in elevation, the greater percentage you should add to your shots. Also, you should expect more yardage on your highflying shots than on the clubs that produce a lower, more boring trajectory. At Castle Pines, the increase is generally agreed to be 10 to 15 percent. Thus, if you normally hit a 5-iron 160 yards, you should expect to hit up to 184. Your 240-yard drive probably won't go the full 15 percent—276 yards—since drives tend to fly less than irons, but don't be surprised if you pick up at least 25 yards.

It takes a bit of experience to determine how your shots will react, but you can be sure of one thing—everyone picks up power in Denver.

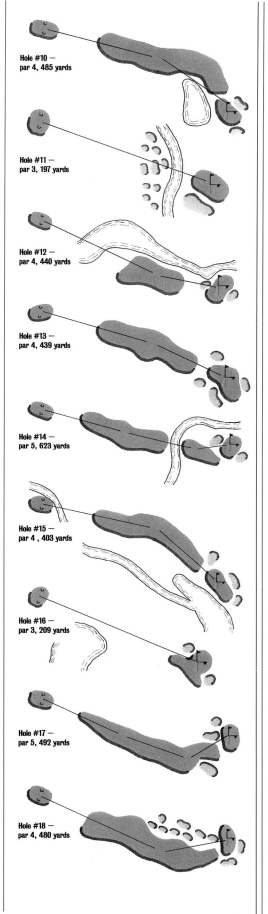

Hole #10 —
par 4, 485 yards

Hole #11 —
par 3, 197 yards

Hole #12 —
par 4, 440 yards

Hole #13 —
par 4, 439 yards

Hole #14 —
par 5, 623 yards

Hole #15 —
par 4 , 403 yards

Hole #16 —
par 3, 209 yards

Hole #17 —
par 5, 492 yards

Hole #18 —
par 4, 480 yards

NEC World Series of Golf

FIRESTONE COUNTRY CLUB
[SOUTH COURSE]

What is the most respected course on the PGA Tour? This one. Year in and year out, no layout produces higher scores from the pros while receiving higher praise. The reason: It is eminently honest and straightforward—its critics would say too straightforward, as a dozen of Firestone's fairways head monotonously back and forth, parallel to one another.

Be that as it may, this is a course that, despite its length and difficulty, wants its assailants to play well. There is nothing tricky or unfair—all the challenges are in plain sight. The holes at Firestone seem to say to the player, "Here we are—let's see what you can do to us."

This is not only a long course but a big one, largely the work of Robert Trent Jones, who refashioned the original 1929 design in the late 1950s, adding 50 bunkers and two ponds, doubling the size of the greens, and stretching the course to 7173 yards while lowering its par from 72 to 70. Even the tees here are big, averaging 3000 square feet in area, almost as spacious as some of the greens at Pebble Beach and Harbour Town.

When it began in 1962 the World Series field was to include four golfers— the winners of that year's Masters, U.S. Open, British Open, and PGA Championship. In fact, in '62 only three men competed—the Big Three—Jack Nicklaus, Arnold Palmer, and Gary Player, since

THE TV HOLES

Expect birdies:

Nowhere

Expect bogeys:

13, 18

18th hole

What to Watch For . . .

BOGEYS
At most Tour courses, the average 18-hole score by the pros is a bit under par. Here, it is two strokes over. No course yields fewer birdies.

GRIDIRON GREATNESS
A good rainy-day diversion is the Football Hall of Fame, also located in the city of Akron.

BEAR TRACKS
Jack Nicklaus has won seven tournaments at Firestone—five World Series, one American Golf Classic, and the 1975 PGA Championship. On top of that, he is the most recent architect to redesign the course. In 1986, Nicklaus's company reworked several greens and added a few mounds for improved spectating.

FOREIGN FLAIR
Although the format and qualification requirements for this event have changed over the years, it retains the international character its name implies. Wednesday's festivities include an opening ceremony wherein the competitors take part in a brief parade and the flags of their countries are displayed.

PRIZED SWING
The trophy—a unique design that features an elliptical swath of metal—is meant to suggest the golf swing of Sam Snead.

He Did Everything Except...

José Maria Olazabal's 72-hole total of 262 in 1990 is the tournament record by five strokes. He claimed a clean sweep of tournament records for 18, 36, 54, and 72 holes (61, 128, 195, 262), and for the largest lead after 18, 36, 54, and 72 holes (four, nine, eight and 12 strokes).

Firestone Country Club– South Course

Hole #1 —
par 4, 399 yards

Hole #2 —
par 5, 497 yards

Hole #3 —
par 4, 442 yards

Hole #4 —
par 4, 458 yards

Hole #5 —
par 3, 210 yards

Hole #6 —
par 4, 469 yards

Hole #7 —
par 3, 219 yards

Hole #8 —
par 4, 450 yards

Hole #9 —
par 4, 470 yards

Practical Matters

FOR TICKET INFORMATION
Firestone Country Club
452 East Warner Road
Akron, Ohio 44319

COURSE
Firestone Country Club

ACCESS
Private course—you must play
with a member

COURSE RATING

Tees	Pro	Member
Yardage	7173	6379
Rating	75.1	71.2
Slope	128	122

GREEN FEES
$70
For more information:
(216) 644-8441

PRO-AM
Spots open to the public? Yes
Handicap: Maximum of 21
Format: Best ball of five
two two-player teams) plus pro
Entry fee: $5500 per two-player team
For more information:
(216) 644-2299

Palmer had won both The Masters and British Open. But over the years the format has undergone several changes, and today invitations go to anyone who has won one of 70 qualifying tournaments around the world.

Don't expect to see too many fast starts here—the second hole is a par five of less than 500 yards. But that may be the last legitimate birdie opportunity. The next succession of holes includes three par fours averaging over 450 yards and a pair of threes averaging 210. But the biggest bruiser on the course lurks on the back nine: Firestone's signature hole is the mammoth par-five 16th, which tumbles 625 yards to a green guarded closely by a pond.

TOURNAMENT RATINGS

COURSE DIFFICULTY

Avg. winning score: 7.2 under par	2nd on Tour
USGA course rating: 75.1 (5.1 over par)	1st on Tour
Overall rating: Severe	2nd on Tour

PRESTIGE

Field strength (15.2)	10th on Tour
Winner quality (.711)	22nd on Tour
Course difficulty (above)	2nd on Tour

Plus factors: Course rated
47th in U.S., large purse,
10-year exemption to winner,
winners-only field

Overall rating	10th on Tour

16th hole

Local Knowledge

FAIRWAY WOODS MADE EASY

On a course as long and tough as Firestone, even the pros occasionally have to haul out their fairway woods. For amateurs, of course, these clubs see duty virtually every day.

The era of the metal wood has made these clubs easier to hit, as the lower center of gravity of the metal clubs eases the golfer's ability to get the ball airborne. At the same time, the higher-lofted woods—5, 6, 7, and even the 9—have become popular weapons for their ability to extricate the ball from thick rough and difficult bunkers.

All wood shots should not be hit the same way. When playing from the fairways with the steeper-faced clubs (2-wood through 4-wood), you should use basically the same swing as on your tee shots, a sweeping motion that you initiate with a one-piece takeaway that keeps the club low to the ground going back, low coming into impact.

However, for recovery shots with the more lofted woods, a slightly difficult technique is required. This time, you need an impact that is closer in nature to a middle iron—a more downward hit on the ball. To preprogram that type of hit, position the ball a bit farther back in your stance, and if you're in thick rough, a bit closer to your body as well. These changes will set you up for a more vertical impact that will gouge the ball out of a difficult lie.

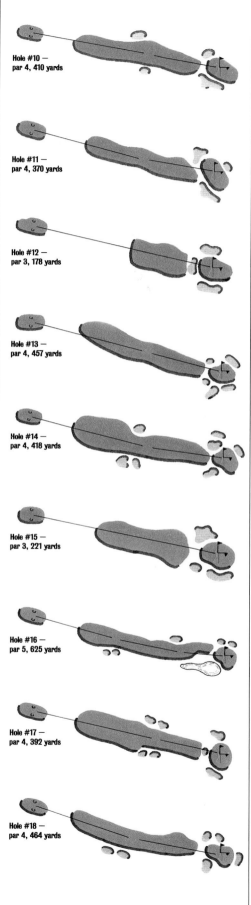

Hole #10 —
par 4, 410 yards

Hole #11 —
par 4, 370 yards

Hole #12 —
par 3, 178 yards

Hole #13 —
par 4, 457 yards

Hole #14 —
par 4, 418 yards

Hole #15 —
par 3, 221 yards

Hole #16 —
par 5, 625 yards

Hole #17 —
par 4, 392 yards

Hole #18 —
par 4, 464 yards

Greater Milwaukee Open

BROWN DEER PARK GOLF CLUB

After a 21-year run at the Tuckaway Country Club, the Greater Milwaukee Open pulled up stakes in 1994 and moved across town to a course with the unlikely name of Brown Deer Park.

The contrasts are marked. Tuckaway was a private course, Brown Deer is public. Tuckaway was designed in 1967, Brown Deer goes back to 1929. Tuckaway was long, hilly, and relatively open, Brown Deer is shortish and flattish—but it is tight.

When the pros stray from these fairways, they find themselves in stands of mature maples, oaks, and black walnuts—fine habitat for brown deer but less propitious for golfers. They will also find some of the longest, lushest rough on the Tour. And once they get to the greens, they will find some fierce, fast surfaces. The greens at Brown Deer were designed back in the days of hand mowing—well before the era of triple cutting and rolling—and as such they have some major bumps and rolls. A few greens were so steeply contoured that they were flattened out as part of the preparation for the Tour.

Most of the tougher holes appear on the front nine, led by number four, a par five for the daily-fee players that converts to a 485-yard par four for the pros. On the stretch run, however, water comes into play in the form of a small river that runs through the course.

At the 18th tee, the

THE TV HOLES

Expect birdies:

15, 18

Expect bogeys:

10

15th hole

What to Watch For . . .

BILLBOARD SCOREBOARDS
The GMO keeps its fans abreast of the action by posting daily leaders on billboards along the major highways.

GUSTS
Bring a sweater, and put some extra glue on your toupee before spectating here. By Labor Day, the fall winds begin to kick up off Lake Michigan, adding difficulty to the Brown Deer course.

ANDY NORTH
These days, the two-time U.S. Open champion is seen more frequently as an on-course reporter for ESPN than he is in the thick of competition, but he has a presence at this event. North, a Wisconsin native, was involved in the refurbishing of the Brown Deer course for its 1994 Tour debut.

Hosts With the Most

PGA Tour Courses Which Have Hosted Multiple USGA Events:

Course	Events
Pebble Beach GL	1972-82-92 U.S. Open; 1940-48 U.S. Women's Amateur; 1929 U.S. Amateur
Brown Deer GC	**1951-65-77 U.S. Public Links**
Muirfield Village GC	1986 U.S. Junior, 1992 U.S. Amateur
Cog Hill CC	1987 U.S. Women's Public Links, 1989 U.S. Public Links
Atlanta CC	1968 U.S. Senior, 1971 U.S. Women's Amateur
Colonial CC	1941 U.S. Open, 1991 U.S. Women's Open

Brown Deer Park

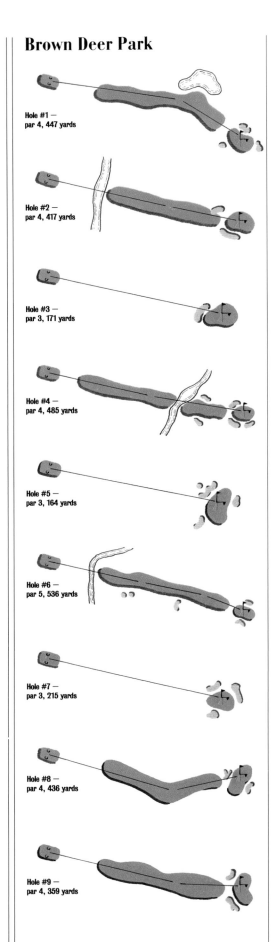

Hole #1 —
par 4, 447 yards

Hole #2 —
par 4, 417 yards

Hole #3 —
par 3, 171 yards

Hole #4 —
par 4, 485 yards

Hole #5 —
par 3, 164 yards

Hole #6 —
par 5, 536 yards

Hole #7 —
par 3, 215 yards

Hole #8 —
par 4, 436 yards

Hole #9 —
par 4, 359 yards

4th hole

toughest opponent can be Mother Nature. It's a short par five, where the only real difficulty is the tee shot, which must carry 200 yards to clear the river. On most days, that's not heavy lifting for a Tour pro, but should the prevailing west wind kick up, this will be a place where players either gamble boldly or lay up in frustration.

Over the last several years at Tuckaway, the winning GMO scores averaged about 270. The expectation is that in the next few years at Brown Deer, 270 will usually be good enough to win. The difference is that at Tuckaway the par was 72; here it's 70.

TOURNAMENT RATINGS

COURSE DIFFICULTY

Avg. winning score: 16.0 under par	30th on Tour
USGA course rating: 72.4 (1.4 over par)	36th on Tour
Overall rating: Vulnerable	36th on Tour

PRESTIGE

Field strength (7.1)	37th on Tour
Winner quality (.120)	43rd on Tour
Course difficulty (above)	36th on Tour
Plus factors: None	
Overall rating	41st on Tour

Practical Matters

FOR TICKET INFORMATION
Brown Deer Park Golf Club
4000 West Brown Deer Rd.
Milwaukee, WI 53209

COURSE
Brown Deer Park

ACCESS
Public course

COURSE RATING

Tees	Pro	Member
Yardage	6763	6470
Rating	72.4	70.9
Slope	130	127

GREEN FEES
$40 weekend, $36 weekday
For more information:
(414) 352-8080

PRO-AM
Spots open to the public? Yes
Handicap: Maximum of 21
Format: Best ball of team
Entry fee: Monday $1100;
Wednesday: $2750
For more information:
Best ball of team

Local Knowledge

READING THE ROUGH

At courses that have rough as thick as at Brown Deer, you need a combination of firmness and finesse. More often than not, a strong swing is required to extricate the ball, but of even greater importance is an ability to evaluate the lie. Whereas all lies in the fairway are fairly similar, no two lies in the rough are alike.

Fundamentally, however, there are three types of lies, which we'll call the flicker, the flyer, and the floater. The flicker (A) is a ball that is perched on top of the blades of grass—it is a lie that is almost too good. You can't bash down on it as you would most lies in the rough, because your club will slide under the ball, producing a high, weak shot, perhaps even a whiff. Instead, the best technique—no matter what club you use—is to make a driverlike swing, with a long, low takeaway. This will help you to hit the ball on a shallow angle of attack, flicking it cleanly off its perch.

The most common lie in rough is a flyer, where the ball sits down in two- to four-inch grass. You can get the club on it easily enough, but not without allowing some grass to get between your clubface and the ball. That means you'll produce a shot with less backspin—a ball that will fly higher, bounce more actively, and roll farther than a shot from the fairway. In these situations, take at least one less club than you would from the fairway, and play the ball a bit farther back in your stance to encourage a downward impact that will minimize intervention of the grass (B).

The floater is a ball that sits well down in deep rough (C). Your only option here is to take your wedge and cut your losses by slashing the ball out as best you can, using much the same technique you'd use on a sand shot. Don't try for too much distance, because the ball will not jump out of this lie, but will float lazily.

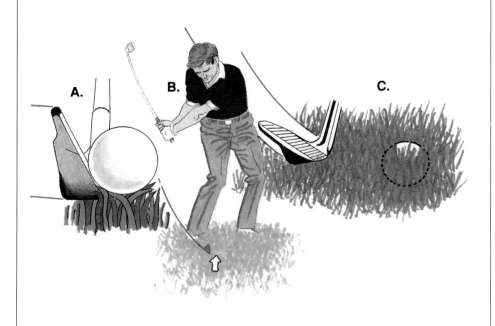

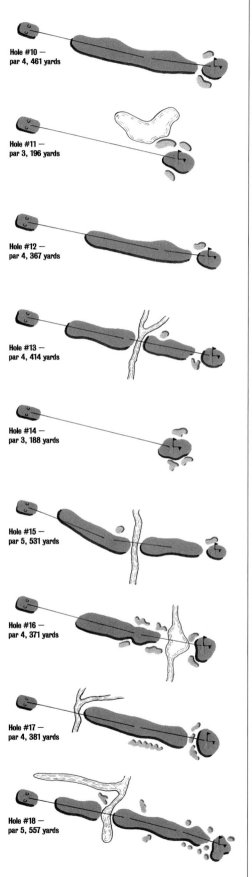

Hole #10 —
par 4, 461 yards

Hole #11 —
par 3, 196 yards

Hole #12 —
par 4, 367 yards

Hole #13 —
par 4, 414 yards

Hole #14 —
par 3, 188 yards

Hole #15 —
par 5, 531 yards

Hole #16 —
par 4, 371 yards

Hole #17 —
par 4, 381 yards

Hole #18 —
par 5, 557 yards

Bell Canadian Open

GLEN ABBEY GOLF CLUB

Welcome to the only National Championship on the PGA Tour. With a rich history that dates back to 1904, the Canadian Open is second only to the Western Open in longevity and ranks securely among the most sought-after victories on the pro circuit. Just ask Jack Nicklaus. This is unquestionably the most important tournament he never won. Despite four decades of trying, Nicklaus could do no better than second place—and he did that an incredible seven times.

Jack can't blame his failure here on the golf course. Since 1974, the Canadian has been played at the Glen Abbey Golf Club, a Nicklaus design whose long, broad rightward-bending fairways and tightly bunkered, heavily contoured greens favor his game.

Water is in play on 11 of the 18 holes here, most menacingly in the middle of the round, where the Valley Holes (11 through 15) have killed the championship hopes of Nicklaus as well as lesser mortals. Most players like to emerge from the 15th green no worse vis-à-vis par than they were when they teed up at 11, but in 1991 Nick Price birdied his way through the five

THE TV HOLES

Expect birdies:
16, 18

Expect bogeys:
14, 17

14th hole

What to Watch For . . .

HISTORY
Glen Abbey is the home of the Royal Canadian Golf Association, and the headquarters include a museum, library, and the Canadian Golf Hall of Fame.

CANADIANS
This is the one event where you can expect perfect attendance from the likes of Dave Barr, Dan Halldorson, Jim Nelford, and Richard Zokol.

AIRBORNE PUTTS
The green at the 17th hole is horseshoe-shaped with a bunker in the middle of the U. Tour players who find the wrong arm of the green occasionally will wedge across the sand to the pin. Imagine the predicament if architect Nicklaus had had his original wish—a tree separating the two sectors of green.

SWEATERS
Formerly a midsummer event, the Canadian has moved to September, when the cool Canadian air prevails.

BRUCE LIETZKE & OTHER FADERS
Ironically, this homebody who prefers fishing and coaching his kids to playing pro golf may have more rounds at Glen Abbey than any American player. For his efforts, he has two victories and several strong showings. One reason may be that this course favors Lietzke's left-to-right ball flight. Another famous fader, Lee Trevino, has won twice here, and Curtis Strange, who favors a fade, also has two victories.

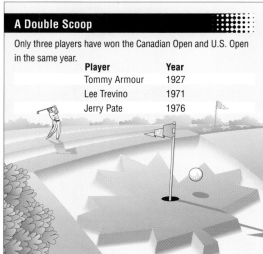

A Double Scoop

Only three players have won the Canadian Open and U.S. Open in the same year.

Player	Year
Tommy Armour	1927
Lee Trevino	1971
Jerry Pate	1976

Glen Abbey Golf Club

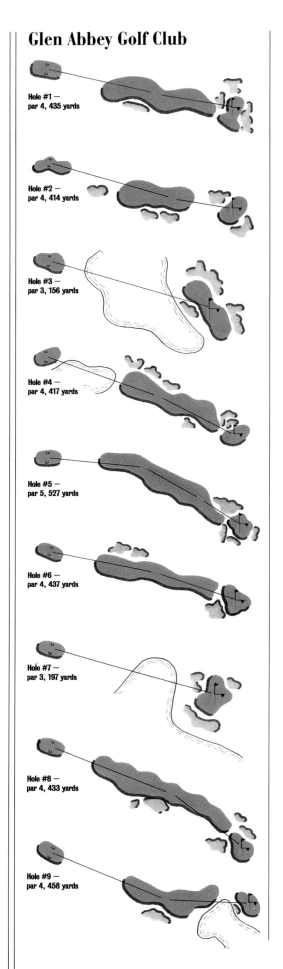

Hole #1 —
par 4, 435 yards

Hole #2 —
par 4, 414 yards

Hole #3 —
par 3, 156 yards

Hole #4 —
par 4, 417 yards

Hole #5 —
par 5, 527 yards

Hole #6 —
par 4, 437 yards

Hole #7 —
par 3, 197 yards

Hole #8 —
par 4, 433 yards

Hole #9 —
par 4, 458 yards

16th hole

holes en route to victory. The hardest hole on the course is number 14, a 426-yard dogleg that calls for a daring tee shot across the main waterway, 16-Mile Creek.

Once out of the Valley, however, the Tour players count on a fast finish, with two reachable par fives on the last three holes. Number 16, at 516 yards, is particularly vulnerable. Back in 1984, long-hitting John Adams double-eagled it, hitting his second shot into the cup with an 8-iron. Eighteen is even shorter, just 508 yards, although the second shot for the green must hurdle a sizable lake, making this a good hole on which to win—or lose—a national championship.

TOURNAMENT RATINGS

COURSE DIFFICULTY

Avg. winning score:	
11.4 under par	12th on Tour
USGA course rating: NA*	NA*
Overall rating:	
Moderate	13th

PRESTIGE

Field strength (9.2)	26th on Tour
Winner quality (.800)	15th on Tour
Course difficulty (above)	13th on Tour
Plus factors: National championship, history (event started in 1904)	
Overall rating	19th on Tour

*Course not rated

Practical Matters

FOR TICKET INFORMATION
Glen Abbey Golf Club
1333 Dorval Dr.
Oakville, Ontario, L6J 4Z3
Canada

COURSE
Glen Abbey Golf Course

ACCESS
Open to the public

COURSE RATING

Tees	Pro	Member
Yardage	7112	6509
Rating	N/A	N/A
Slope	N/A	N/A

GREEN FEES
$95 weekdays, $100 weekends
For more information:
(416) 849-9700

PRO-AM
Spots open to the public? Yes
Format: Best ball of team
Handicap: Maximum of 21
Entry Fee: $2000
For more information:
(905) 844-1800

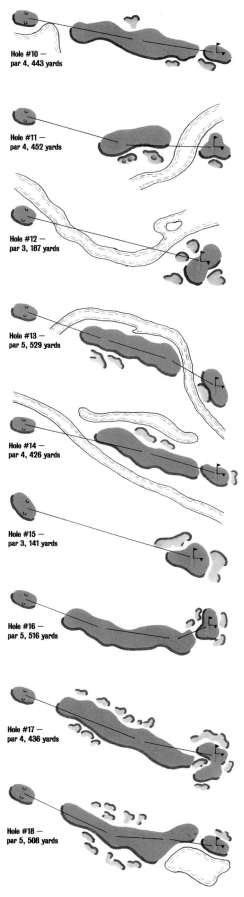

Hole #10 —
par 4, 443 yards

Hole #11 —
par 4, 452 yards

Hole #12 —
par 3, 187 yards

Hole #13 —
par 5, 529 yards

Hole #14 —
par 4, 426 yards

Hole #15 —
par 3, 141 yards

Hole #16 —
par 5, 516 yards

Hole #17 —
par 4, 436 yards

Hole #18 —
par 5, 508 yards

Local Knowledge

ON GOLF'S TOUGHEST SHOT

The long greenside bunker shot is regarded universally as the toughest shot in the game. Not an explosion, yet not a clean pick, it calls for very precise execution.

If you play on a course such as Glen Abbey, with large, well-bunkered greens, you'll often face this daunting assignment. Before you even address this shot, do yourself a favor and be sure you're properly armed. Don't ever play a long bunker shot with a third or lofted wedge; in fact, the best club is a pitching wedge or, ideally, a "strong" sand wedge with relatively little loft—something under 55 degrees. This will give you a lower trajectory shot instead of the pop-up you get from many of the more lofted newer wedges.

As for technique, don't get too complicated. Assuming you have a reasonable (not buried) lie, simply address this shot with a less open stance than you would a short bunker shot, while keeping the clubface slightly open as you should for most bunker shots. This stance will encourage a less downward swing, which will help you propel the ball forward. On extra-long shots, you'll have to make another adjustment. Unless you're very confident in the sand, however, don't try to play this shot by hitting closer to the ball or picking it clean—the consequences of even a slight mishit are too dire.
The safest way to add distance is simply to put a bit more length and power in your swing. Above all, be sure to swing upward into a full follow-through.

B.C. Open

EN-JOIE
GOLF CLUB

I t's unlikely that you've seen the B.C. Open on TV, and even less likely you've seen it in person—for most people, getting to Endicott, New York, requires at least two plane connections. But that doesn't mean you shouldn't check it out. This is a tournament that says a lot about small-town values and the joy of golf.

It began in 1973 as a one-day pro-am offering a total purse of $10,000. In those days it was called the Broome County Open, and despite its modest proportions it was one of the biggest sporting events ever to hit New York's rural southern tier. Nowadays, the B.C. Open is *the* biggest show in these parts, a million-dollar tournament that annually attracts many of the Tour's biggest names.

They come out of a sense of loyalty and gratitude. There is nothing fancy here—the players' parking lot has potholes and the stucco clubhouse is a far cry from those at Riviera and Westchester. But the folks at the B.C. offer the pros a sense of comfort and warmth that no other tournament can match. As Lee Trevino once said, "Most tournaments on the Tour cater to three or four big guns. At the B.C., a rookie gets the same treatment as a star."

Even the golf club—the En-Joie Golf Club—is the kind of place where you'd expect to see Jimmy Stewart behind the counter. It was founded in 1927 by a benevolent man named George Johnson, chairman of the Endicott Johnson shoe company, purely as a place for his factory workers

T H E
TV
H O L E S

Expect birdies:
12
Expect bogeys:
11,12,13

18th hole

What to Watch For . . .

INITIAL CONFUSION
"B.C." does not stand for Broome County. The tournament is named in honor of one of Endicott's local heroes, cartoonist and golf nut Johnny Hart, whose B.C. comic strip has long been syndicated in newspapers across the country.

NICE PRICES
Chiseled into the stone arch above Endicott's Main Street are the words: "Home of the Square Deal." This is one Tour town where you can still get a hotel room for $50 and a nourishing dinner for $10. Best of all, the green fee at En-Joie is $20, lowest of any course on the PGA Tour.

700 SPONSORS
The B.C. has never had a title sponsor, probably never will. A small, remote market virtually insures that. But its remote coziness has also bred a loyal community. Virtually every business becomes involved in the B.C., contributing anywhere from $200 to $40,000 to the tournament.

THE JOHNNY HART "THE KING IS A FINK" SHORTSHOT CONTEST
In one of the more bizarre sideshows of the Tour year, seven cartoonists pair up with seven pros for a series of mini-shootouts—pitch shot, bunker shot, putt—at the 18th green.

CADDIE CODDLING
Historically, no tournament has been more considerate of the bag toters. For years there was a nighttime baseball game between the caddies and players. That has been discontinued, but the annual Tour Caddie Golf Championship remains a fixture on the Monday after the tournament, with the winner getting an amateur-status-ending first prize of $1000.

Hurricane Andy Rips Through
In 1975, Andy North matched the PGA Tour's nine-hole record with a 27 on the par-34 back nine of En-Joie GC in the first round. Despite shooting a 63 that day, he finished tied for 20th. The only other 27 recorded on the PGA Tour was by Mike Souchak on the par-35 back nine of Brackenridge Park GC in the first round of the 1955 Texas Open.

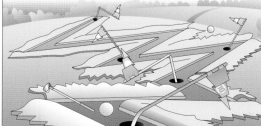

Hole #1 —
par 4, 388 yards

Hole #2 —
par 4, 363 yards

Hole #3 —
par 5, 554 yards

Hole #4 —
par 3, 175 yards

Hole #5 —
par 5, 565 yards

Hole #6 —
par 4, 433 yards

Hole #7 —
par 3, 200 yards

Hole #8 —
par 5, 553 yards

Hole #9 —
par 4, 425 yards

2nd hole

to get some recreation—the first corporate golf course in the country. Even today, many of the members are shoemakers.

The course has changed, thanks to suggestions made by Pete Dye and 1979 B.C. Champion Howard Twitty, but it remains a quirky one. Par on the front side is 37, but on the way in it's 34, because three of the last five holes are par threes. Despite the fact that Fred Couples and John Daly are two recent champions, this is not a course that favors long hitters. Its narrow fairways are lined with trees, and water comes into play on several holes—most menacingly at the 15th, a 457-yard par four that plays along the edge of a lake. Set among par threes at 14, 16, and 17, it stands out like King Kong in a kindergarten.

TOURNAMENT RATINGS

COURSE DIFFICULTY

Avg. winning score: 15.7 under par	29th on Tour
USGA course rating: 73.0 (2.0 over par)	28th on Tour
Overall rating: Vulnerable	32nd on Tour

PRESTIGE

Field strength (3.8)	43rd on Tour
Winner quality (.205)	41st on Tour
Course difficulty (above)	32nd on Tour
Plus factors: None	
Overall rating	43rd on Tour

Practical Matters

FOR TICKET INFORMATION
B.C. Open
P.O. Box 5571
Endicott, NY 13763

COURSE
En-Joie Golf Club

ACCESS
Course is open to the public

COURSE RATING

Tees	Pro	Member
Yardage	6920	6500
Rating	73.0	71.1
Slope	125	123

GREEN FEES
$18 weekdays, $20 weekends
For more information:
(607) 785-1661

PRO-AM
Spots open to the public? Yes
Format: Best ball of team
Handicap: Maximum of 21
Entry Fee: Two tiers: Monday $1500; Wednesday $2750
For more information:
(607) 754-2482

Local Knowledge

COPING WITH COLD

By late September, the climate in upstate New York can become pretty brisk, especially for those facing early-morning tee times. The B.C. locals know how to deal with a short season, but if you play most of your golf in more southerly climes, you should prepare for the challenges of cold weather.

The first rule is to stay warm but limber. Several thin layers of clothing will be better than one thick sweater or coat. The new "wind shirts" are especially good at cutting down on the chill. But the most important thing is to keep your hands warm—keep your hands in your pockets, wear gloves, use hand warmers—do anything you must to keep the feel in your fingers.

As on rainy days, you can expect to lose some distance in the cold, so remember two things: Take a long club and a short swing. Use at least one club longer than you would from the same distance in warm weather, and keep your swing compact, because on cold days your body tends to stiffen up and there is no percentage in swinging all out. Besides, if the ground is cold and hard, you'll get plenty of distance—the ball will bounce and roll a long way.

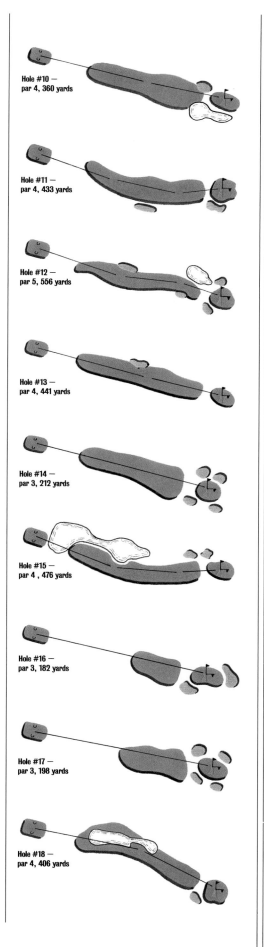

Hole #10 —
par 4, 360 yards

Hole #11 —
par 4, 433 yards

Hole #12 —
par 5, 556 yards

Hole #13 —
par 4, 441 yards

Hole #14 —
par 3, 212 yards

Hole #15 —
par 4 , 476 yards

Hole #16 —
par 3, 182 yards

Hole #17 —
par 3, 198 yards

Hole #18 —
par 4, 406 yards

Quad City Classic

OAKWOOD COUNTRY CLUB

When you think of Pete Dye golf courses, you think of the TPC at Sawgrass or the Stadium Course at PGA West. You think of the Ocean Course on Kiawah Island or Casa de Campo or Crooked Stick or Harbour Town. However, one course you most certainly do not think of is the one at Oakwood Country Club in Coal Valley, Illinois.

And yet, this one was there before all the others. Completed in 1963, Oakwood predates the architect's first trip to Scotland and thus lacks the undulating fairways, pot bunkers, railroad ties, and native grasses that influenced Dye and mark most of his later designs.

The greens here are generous, averaging about 6500 square feet, and with less than three dozen bunkers on the entire course, most of these targets are easily accessible with bounce-on approaches as well as high-flying darts. As such, the pros have posted some low scores here, most notably Fuzzy Zoeller, who in his rookie year (1976) played the first ten holes in even par and then birdied each of his last eight, a streak that still stands as a PGA Tour record.

The tournament began in 1972, when soon-to-be-Commissioner Deane Beman nosed out an unknown rookie

THE TV HOLES

Expect birdies:

10

Expect bogeys:

Nowhere

4th hole

What to Watch For . . .

THE BEST SANDWICH ON TOUR

Players, media, and fans alike look forward to the one-third-pound butterfly pork chop sandwiches sold at the Oakwood concession stands.

LOVE IN BLOOM

Coal Valley, Illinois, may not seem like the romance capital of America, but Tour players Roger Maltbie, Bobby Clampett, and Dan Halldorson all met their wives at this event.

METEOROLOGICAL SCHIZOPHRENIA

Since 1990, when the Classic shifted to a mid-September date, the weather has been unpredictable—bitter cold one day, steaming hot the next. It's little wonder the hottest hand here (with victories in 1992 and 1993) has been David Frost.

DRIVING THE ROCK

On Thursday night, the tournament throws a cookout for the players and their families, the highlight of which is a competition in which the pros—using old drivers and X-out golf balls, try to drive across the Rock River, a carry of about 250 yards, to a flag set on the opposite bank. Closest to the pin is worth $100.

AN 18 THAT IS 9

Oakwood is one of a handful of courses on the Tour that flip-flops its front and back nines for the Tour players. One of the results is that number 18 is a comparatively pedestrian par four of 391 yards.

A FLOATING CRAP GAME

This is the only tournament where one of the evening activities is riverboat gambling on paddlewheelers.

Like a Fine Wine

In 1979, Sam Snead became the first player to shoot his age or better on the PGA Tour. At age 67, he shot a 67 in the second round and then bettered his age with a 66 in the fourth round.

Oakwood Country Club

Hole #1 —
par 4, 413 yards

Hole #2 —
par 4, 400 yards

Hole #3 —
par 4, 435 yards

Hole #4 —
par 4, 495 yards

Hole #5 —
par 3, 169 yards

Hole #6 —
par 5, 515 yards

Hole #7 —
par 4, 350 yards

Hole #8 —
par 3, 183 yards

Hole #9 —
par 4, 436 yards

12th hole

named Tom Watson. For the next decade and a half it languished in semi-obscurity, played during the same week as the British Open, when many of the top stars were abroad. But the late '80s brought corporate sponsorship and then a shift to a mid-September date where the field has been bolstered by players gunning for a spot in the top-30 money winners (good for invitations to the lucrative year-ending TOUR Championship and the following year's Masters). It has also become a sort of last summertime hurrah for the friendly folks who live on the Illinois/Iowa border and come out for a few final days of sunshine before the first snow flies.

TOURNAMENT RATINGS

COURSE DIFFICULTY

Avg. winning score: 14.6 under par	27th on Tour
USGA course rating: 72.2 (2.2 over par)	25th on Tour
Overall rating: Moderate	28th on Tour

PRESTIGE

Field strength (4.5)	41st on Tour
Winner quality (.136)	42nd on Tour
Course difficulty (above)	28th on Tour
Plus factors: None	
Overall rating:	42nd on Tour

Practical Matters

FOR TICKET INFORMATION
Quad City Classic
P.O. Box 387
Moline, IL 61266

COURSE
Oakwood Country Club

ACCESS
Private course—you must play with a member

COURSE RATING

Tees	Pro	Member
Yardage	6796	6152
Rating	72.2 (par 70)	69.7 (par 71)
Slope	126	120

GREEN FEES
Guest fee: $30
For more information:
(309) 799-5558

PRO-AM
Spots open to the public? Yes
Format: Best ball of team
Handicap: Maximum of 21
Entry fee: $1350
For more information:
(800) 336-4655

Local Knowledge

INTO THE WIND

The Oakwood course is set on a bluff, and like much of Illinois in the late summer and early fall, it can get windy. One of the best weapons you can have when the wind blows is a calm attitude. Look at the wind as your friend. When it's at your back, clearly it helps you, not only by lengthening your shots but by straightening them, as a following wind reduces any sidespin you put on the ball.

Less obvious is the fact that a wind in your face can help. In fact, most pros would rather have a bit of headwind than tailwind. The reason is that it enables them to play aggressively toward the flag, to hit shots that will come straight down with little roll (as opposed to the bounding shots that result from a tailwind). So rule number one is to view the wind as your friend.

Number two, think control. Even when you're hitting downwind, keep your swing compact and smooth—don't try to kill the ball. By swinging smoothly, you'll improve your chance of making the solid contact that enables you to ride the following breeze. Into the wind, add some control by widening your stance an inch or two—this will do two things: 1) restrict your backswing turn and thereby keep you stable, and 2) lower your center of gravity a bit, creating a shallower angle of attack to the ball which will help produce the lower-trajectory, boring shot that is vital when hitting into a headwind.

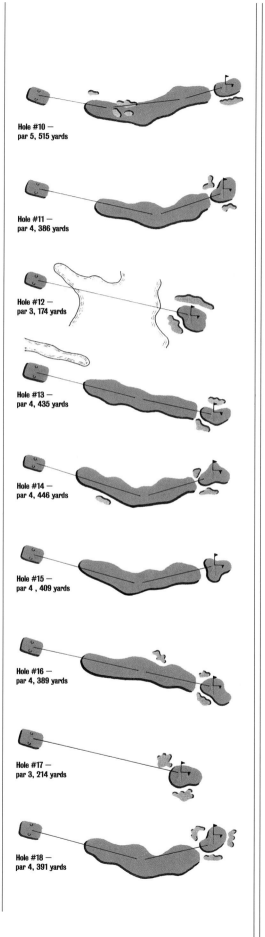

Hole #10 —
par 5, 515 yards

Hole #11 —
par 4, 386 yards

Hole #12 —
par 3, 174 yards

Hole #13 —
par 4, 435 yards

Hole #14 —
par 4, 446 yards

Hole #15 —
par 4 , 409 yards

Hole #16 —
par 4, 389 yards

Hole #17 —
par 3, 214 yards

Hole #18 —
par 4, 391 yards

Buick Challenge

CALLAWAY GARDENS
[MOUNTAIN VIEW COURSE]

Mark Twain called golf "a good walk spoiled," but he never played Callaway Gardens. The courses of this Georgia resort are set amid a 12,000-acre botanical park with hundreds of different flowers, plants, trees, and shrubs—a trove of florabundance that no amount of golf can tarnish. Not even the PGA Tour, which brought the Buick Challenge to Callaway's Mountain View course in 1991, after a 21-year run at the Green Island Country Club in nearby Columbus.

The name Callaway should be familiar to anyone who has swung a Big Bertha driver, and this is the same family—Cason and Ida Callaway, the founders of the Gardens, are first cousins of phenomenally successful club manufacturer Ely. What's more, among the Tour players their course is almost as popular as Ely's clubs are with 15-handicappers. In a recent survey, the pros called Mountain View the second-best-conditioned course of the nearly 50 sites on the Tour, while also ranking it fifth in difficulty. The course rating on this par 72 of barely 7000 yards is a hefty 74.1.

That toughness stems in part from the terrain on which this Joe Lee/Dick Wilson design is stamped. The Mountain View Course is aptly named, as several holes meander up and down hills. Moreover, its narrow fairways are lined with thick rough and shaded by stands of pine trees, so a straight ball is important. This is particularly true because of the deep greenside bunkers that call for an all-carry approach at most greens.

15th hole

What to Watch For . . .

TEEMING LEPIDOPTERA
This is an event that could lend credence to P. G. Wodehouse's remark about the neurotic golfer whose composure was so fragile he could be disturbed by "the roar of butterflies in the adjoining meadow." A major attraction at Callaway Gardens is the Cecil B. Day Butterfly Center, a tent that houses dozens of different species from around the world.

SMOKED HAM, PORK SAUSAGE, AND GRITS
This is the Deep South, and in this particular area, at the foot of the Appalachians, you'll find plenty of down-home country cooking, especially at breakfast.

SPARSE CROWDS
Although the Gardens get over 750,000 visitors each year, the tournament is one of the quieter ones on the Tour, since Callaway is about two hours from Atlanta and almost an hour from Columbus. So for those who do show, the spectating is easy.

First Steps

Twelve of the 24 winners have made the Buick Challenge their first win on the PGA Tour.

Year	Player	Year	Player
1971	Johnny Miller	1985	Tim Simpson
1974	Forrest Fezler	1986	Fred Wadsworth
1979	Ed Fiori	1987	Ken Brown
1980	Mike Sullivan	1988	David Frost
1982	Bobby Clampett	1989	Ted Shulz
1983	Ronnie Black	1991	David Peoples

Callaway Gardens – Mountain View Course

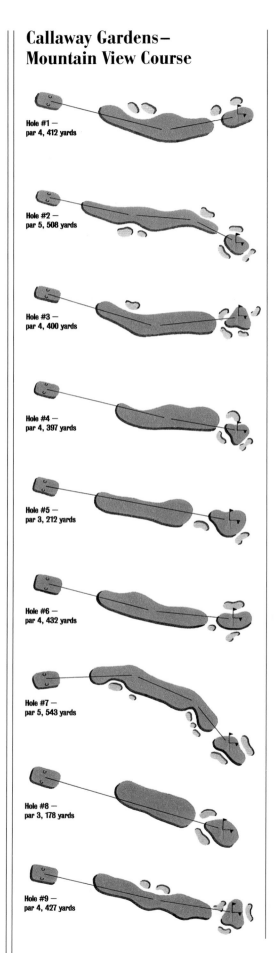

Hole #1 —
par 4, 412 yards

Hole #2 —
par 5, 508 yards

Hole #3 —
par 4, 400 yards

Hole #4 —
par 4, 397 yards

Hole #5 —
par 3, 212 yards

Hole #6 —
par 4, 432 yards

Hole #7 —
par 5, 543 yards

Hole #8 —
par 3, 178 yards

Hole #9 —
par 4, 427 yards

TOURNAMENT RATINGS

COURSE DIFFICULTY

Avg. winning score: 12.0 under par	14th on Tour
USGA course rating: 74.1 (2.1 over par)	27th on Tour
Overall rating: Moderate	22nd

PRESTIGE

Field strength (4.4)	42nd on Tour
Winner quality (.340)	39th on Tour
Course difficulty (above)	22nd on Tour
Plus factors: None	
Overall rating	40th on Tour

Curiously, despite an abundance of lakes throughout the property, water comes into play on only two holes, but at number 15 it presents itself in the formidable form of a 17-acre lake that lurks down the right side and then pokes its nose in front of the green. To make matters worse, the fairway at this par five slopes toward the water all the way. The hole is only 539 yards, but it is one of the more testing three-shotters on the Tour.

10th hole

Practical Matters

FOR TICKET INFORMATION:
Buick Challenge
P.O. Box 2056
Columbus, GA 31902

COURSE
Callaway Gardens –
Mountain View Course

ACCESS
Resort course, open to the public

COURSE RATING

Tees	Pro	Member
Yardage	7057	6630
Rating	74.1	72.3
Slope	138	129

GREEN FEES
$80
For more information:
(706) 663-2281

PRO-AM
Spots open to the public? Yes
Handicap: Maximum of 21
Format: Best ball of four
Entry fee: Monday: $600 per person; Wednesday: $9000 for four spots
For more information:
(706) 324-0411

Local Knowledge

FROM SIDEHILL LIES

The Mountain View Course, as its name implies, is full of hilly lies. The most vexing are those where the ball is either well above or well below your feet.

With a sidehill lie where the ball is above your feet, your tendency will be to pull the shot left. You should allow for this by aiming a bit right of your target. (In the case of a severe slope, open the face of your club a bit to counteract the closing of the clubface that occurs with a pull.) The ball also will be closer to your hands than with a level fairway lie, so you should adjust by gripping down a bit on the club—this may also mean that you'll have to take one club more than for a shot from a level lie.

When the ball is below your feet, everything is just the opposite. Expect a push to the right and compensate by aiming a bit left of your target. (On a severe lie, address the ball with a slightly closed clubface.) Be aware that the ball is farther from your hands than usual, and adjust by putting some extra flex into your knees to lower your hands.

No matter which type of lie you have, keep your swing "quiet" and compact. With an awkward stance, you must stay centered over the ball to insure solid contact.

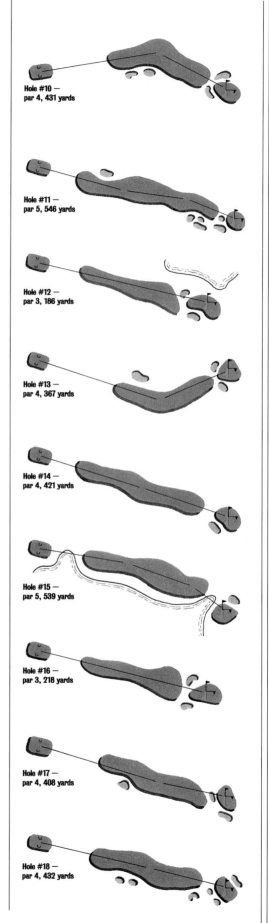

Hole #10 —
par 4, 431 yards

Hole #11 —
par 5, 546 yards

Hole #12 —
par 3, 186 yards

Hole #13 —
par 4, 367 yards

Hole #14 —
par 4, 421 yards

Hole #15 —
par 5, 539 yards

Hole #16 —
par 3, 218 yards

Hole #17 —
par 4, 408 yards

Hole #18 —
par 4, 432 yards

The Walt Disney World/ Oldsmobile Classic

MAGNOLIA, PALM, LAKE BUENA VISTA

THE TV HOLES

Expect birdies:

10, 11, 14
at Magnolia

10, 13, 14
at Palm

13, 16, 17, 18
at Lake Buena Vista

Expect bogeys:

10, 18
at Palm

Nowhere
at Magnolia,
Lake Buena Vista

12th hole
at Magnolia

S omewhere between Fantasyland and Epcot Village lie 54 holes of championship golf—a Magic Linkdom within Walt Disney World's Magic Kingdom. For 51 weeks a year, these three courses—the Magnolia, the Palm, and Lake Buena Vista— cater to the legions of tourists who visit Walt Disney World, each hosting roughly 60,000 rounds of golf. But for one week each October they become home to the PGA Tour.

You may have played them, but it's unlikely that you've seen the layouts that confront the pros. Each of these courses plays much longer for the pros—about 500 yards longer in the cases of the Magnolia and Palm—and all three are rated about two strokes tougher from the championship tees than from the men's. They are not Mickey Mouse tracks.

What to Watch For . . .

TOUR BRATS
This is one event where you'll see a plethora of kids wearing badges that say "Competitor Family." No tournament is more popular with the sons and daughters of the pros than this one. While Dad earns a living, Mom and the kids shake hands with Goofy, and get splashed by Shamu, and speed down Space Mountain.

MONORAILS
Visible from several holes is Walt Disney World's main mode of transportation. If you choose to stay at any of the theme park hotels, you can bypass the parking lot and glide to the tournament by monorail.

STROKES AND STRIKES
Truth be told, the golf tournament is a mere sideshow for some players—the main event being the Hummingbird Bass and Golf Contest that teams 16 pros with 16 bass fishermen. The twosomes play the back nine of the Palm Course (the golfers hitting from tee to green and the fishermen putting), after which they do their fishing. Each stroke in golf is subtracted from the total catch-weight of the fish.

THE OLD ONE–TWO–ONE
In each of the first three years (1971–73), Jack Nicklaus won. After that, two men were needed to fill the Bear's spike marks, with a two-man team taking the trophy in each of the eight ensuing years. Since 1982, single players have been the victors again.

Good News and Bad News
Chip Beck shot 25-under par in 1988 and lost a playoff to Bob Lohr. It's the most anyone has ever finished under par in a 72-hole PGA Tour event and not won.

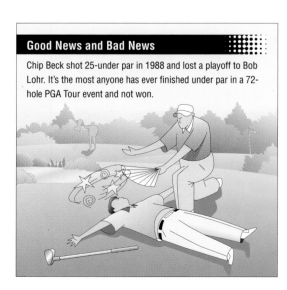

Magnolia

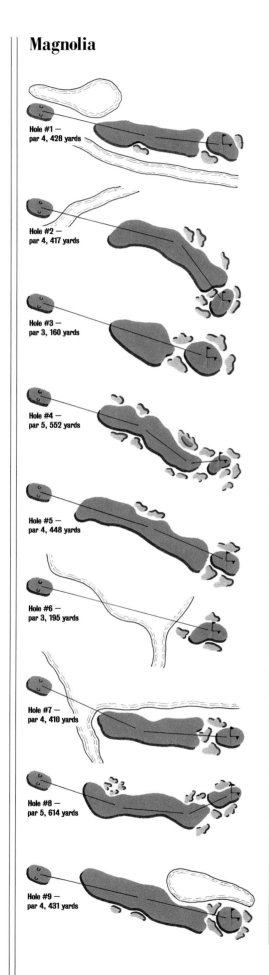

Hole #1 —
par 4, 428 yards

Hole #2 —
par 4, 417 yards

Hole #3 —
par 3, 160 yards

Hole #4 —
par 5, 552 yards

Hole #5 —
par 4, 448 yards

Hole #6 —
par 3, 195 yards

Hole #7 —
par 4, 410 yards

Hole #8 —
par 5, 614 yards

Hole #9 —
par 4, 431 yards

Still, birdies come relatively easily for the pros. In recent years the winning score at the Oldsmobile Classic has averaged more than 20 under par, and in 1992 John Huston fired a 26-under 262, one of the lowest totals in Tour history.

When seen from the blimp camera, these courses are almost as blue-and-white as green. Together, their fairways are dotted with 300 bunkers and 23 lakes and streams. At Magnolia's fourth hole alone there are 14 bunkers—and yet one year this 552-yard par five taxed the pros for only two bogeys while yielding 115 birdies and 10 eagles.

After one round on each of the three courses, the pros who survive the cut return to the Magnolia on Sunday, and the outcome of the tournament often hinges on the last hole. As at the Palm and Lake Buena Vista courses, this is the longest par four on the course. At 455 yards, it is also the longest four in the tournament. Anyone who can come down the stretch in the last group on Sunday and finish with a birdie here will have earned his victory.

TOURNAMENT RATINGS

COURSE DIFFICULTY

Avg. winning score: 20.8 under par	41st on Tour
USGA course rating: 73.4 (1.4 over par)*	36th on Tour
Overall rating: Vulnerable	43rd on Tour

PRESTIGE

Field strength (9.8)	23rd on Tour
Winner quality (.692)	23rd on Tour
Course difficulty (above)	43rd on Tour
Plus factors: None	
Overall rating	28th on Tour

*Composite of two rounds at Magnolia Course, one round each at Palm and Lake Buena Vista Courses

Practical Matters

FOR TICKET INFORMATION
The Walt Disney World/Oldsmobile Classic
P.O. Box 10000
Lake Buena Vista, FL 32830

COURSES
Magnolia, Palm, and Lake Buena Vista

ACCESS
All three are resort courses, open to the public

COURSE RATING

MAGNOLIA			PALM			LAKE BUENA VISTA		
Tees	Pro	Member	Tees	Pro	Member	Tees	Pro	Member
Yardage	7190	6642	Yardage	6957	6461	Yardage	6655	6345
Rating	73.9	71.6	Rating	73.0	70.7	Rating	72.7	70.1
Slope	133	128	Slope	133	129	Slope	128	123

GREEN FEES
$95; $45 after 2 p.m.
For more information: (407) 824-2270

PRO-AM
Spots open to the public? Yes
Handicap: Maximum of 21
Format: Three days (Thursday through Saturday) with three-man amateur teams partnering a different pro on a different course each day
Entry fee: $4900
For more information: (407) 824-2250

Local Knowledge

THE PRO SPLASH

In the course of playing the Magnolia, Palm, and Lake Buena Vista courses the pros must navigate a total of nearly 300 bunkers. If you've watched closely when a Tour player hits from sand, you've undoubtedly noticed that he makes less an explosion than a splash, with the ball riding out on a thin, wispy cushion of sand. This allows him to apply more spin to the ball, thereby enhancing control, particularly when he has relatively little green between bunker and pin.

This splash technique is a bit more demanding than the thumping-down into the sand that characterizes a traditional explosion shot. Essentially, the idea is to take a shallower divot of sand behind and under the ball.

If you'd like to develop this method, try two things: 1) Open the blade of your sand wedge as wide as you can—it should be so open and laid back that you could place a full glass of water on it without losing a drop; and 2) In playing the shot, instead of taking the club straight back and abruptly upward on the backswing, make a flatter swing, taking the club a bit to the inside. This will encourage a flatter, less steep angle of attack and, combined with the open face at impact, will produce a softer, wispier cloud of sand, and a shot that will stop quickly after it hits the green. Just be aware: This one takes some practice.

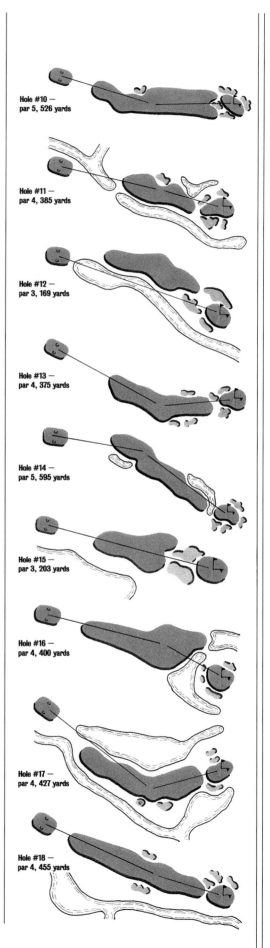

Hole #10 —
par 5, 526 yards

Hole #11 —
par 4, 385 yards

Hole #12 —
par 3, 169 yards

Hole #13 —
par 4, 375 yards

Hole #14 —
par 5, 595 yards

Hole #15 —
par 3, 203 yards

Hole #16 —
par 4, 400 yards

Hole #17 —
par 4, 427 yards

Hole #18 —
par 4, 455 yards

157

Las Vegas Invitational

LAS VEGAS COUNTRY CLUB

DESERT INN COUNTRY CLUB

TPC AT SUMMERLIN

THE TV HOLES

Expect birdies:

10, 18
at Las Vegas

10, 15
at Desert Inn

16
at Summerlin

Expect bogeys:

Nowhere

16th hole at Desert Inn

If you like watching the pros make daring shots and gun for birdie putts, check out the Las Vegas Invitational. Except perhaps for the Bob Hope Chrysler Classic, more low scores are posted here than anywhere on the PGA Tour, and it was at this tournament a few years back that Chip Beck shot 59.

Las Vegas is of course the gambling capital of America, so it's altogether fitting and proper that the three courses used to stage this event are chock full of gambler's par fives. Each of the nines at the Las Vegas Country Club concludes with a short but water-guarded five, each of the nines at the Desert Inn Country Club begins with a short but bunker-bound five, and at the host venue, the TPC at Summerlin, the tournament can hinge on hole 16, a

What to Watch For . . .

A COMPLEX PRO-AM
On day one, three amateurs team up with a pro. On day two, the three ams split up, each becoming part of a different three-man team and playing with a new pro. The same thing happens on day three, after which there is a cut—the 30 amateurs whose three teams have taken them the most under par proceed to day four along with the low 70 pros. For the final round, it's pros only.

CARTOON CRITTERS
Roadrunners are among the desert denizens you're likely to encounter while spectating at Summerlin, and you can also expect to see rabbits, squirrels, quail, fox, hawks, snakes, and scorpions.

CARPENTERS AND PLUMBERS
The TPC at Summerlin is the centerpiece of the largest planned community in America, a 22,000-acre project that is expected to be home for 150,000 by the end of the century. In the meantime, those houses are being built, many of them alongside the golf course.

A GAME WITHIN THE GAME
This event traditionally takes place only a week or two before THE TOUR Championship, the lucrative season-ending event that is limited to the year's top 30 money winners. Just qualifying for that tournament guarantees players about $50,000, and first prize is $540,000. Thus, the field at Vegas usually includes every player ranked from 25–35, scratching it out for the last few qualifying spots.

GOLD CHAINS AND LOUD VOICES
Remember, this is Las Vegas.

Chip Puts on a Show in Vegas

PGA Tour 18-Hole Scoring Record:

Score	Player	Year	Tournament/Course	Finish
59	Al Geiberger	1977	Memphis Classic/ Colonial CC	First
59	Chip Beck	1991	Las Vegas Invitational/ Sunrise CC	Third

Geiberger won in Memphis, but Beck's low score only earned him a tie for third with rounds of 65, 72, 59, 68, 67 – 331.

TPC at Summerlin

Hole #1 —
par 4, 408 yards

Hole #2 —
par 4, 469 yards

Hole #3 —
par 5, 492 yards

Hole #4 —
par 4, 450 yards

Hole #5 —
par 3, 197 yards

Hole #6 —
par 4, 430 yards

Hole #7 —
par 4, 382 yards

Hole #8 —
par 3, 239 yards

Hole #9 —
par 5, 563 yards

560-yarder that taunts its assailants to find its green, at the far side of a lake.

This is a five-day event, with the first three days of play spread over the three courses and Summerlin as the exclusive weekend venue for those who make the cut. In contrast to the two other layouts, which are not far from the Vegas Strip, Summerlin is a desert course, 20 minutes removed from the hotels and casinos. It was designed in 1991 by PGA Tour agronomist Bobby Weed with consultation from Fuzzy Zoeller, whose stated goal is to build courses that are fun to play.

The fairways are broad and treeless, the greens large, quietly contoured, and accessible to a bounce-on approach. As such, this is a course that the pros have greeted warmly. In the first year it was used as the tournament's home, John Cook blistered it for a 62, which propelled him to a two-stroke victory.

16th hole at TPC at Summerlin

Local Knowledge

ONE CLUB OR SEVERAL?

Most of Summerlin's greens are unprotected in the front. All of them are large—7200 square feet on average. On a course such as this, the pitch-and-run shot is a valuable weapon.

The technique is uncomplicated—just a long, rhythmic chip shot. More complex is the question of club selection—whether to try to play all your pitches with one club—say an 8-iron—or to use a gamut of clubs from the 5-iron through the wedges. To a great extent, this is a personal thing, but one way to choose your overall strategy is to consider your strengths.

Do you chip better than you putt? If you do, you're probably wise to take one club and use your native touch and hand-eye coordination to adapt to the demands of the various shots you face. If, however, you putt better than you chip, then vary your pitching clubs and keep your technique constant. You should rely on your putting method as your pitch-shot technique—hit every pitch with the same type of stroke—and alter the loft and run on the shot by choosing the club that best does the job.

Practical Matters

FOR TICKET INFORMATION

Las Vegas Invitational
801 South Rancho Dr., Suite C-3
Las Vegas, NV 89106

COURSES

TPC at Summerlin, Las Vegas, Desert Inn

ACCESS

All three courses are private. Guests are welcome at Summerlin; you must play with a member at Las Vegas and Desert Inn

COURSE RATINGS

SUMMERLIN			LAS VEGAS			DESERT INN		
Tees	Pro	Member	Tees	Pro	Member	Tees	Pro	Member
Yardage	7243	6866	Yardage	7164	6718	Yardage	7066	6685
Rating	74.3	72.4	Rating	72.9	70.8	Rating	74.4	72.0
Slope	139	127	Slope	128	123	Slope	134	129

GREEN FEES

Summerlin: $135; Las Vegas: $80 weekday, $90 weekend; Desert Inn: confidential
For more information: (702) 382-6616

PRO-AM

Spots open to the public? Yes
Handicap: Maximum of 21
Format: See "What to Watch For"
Entry fee: $3500
For more information: (702) 382-6616

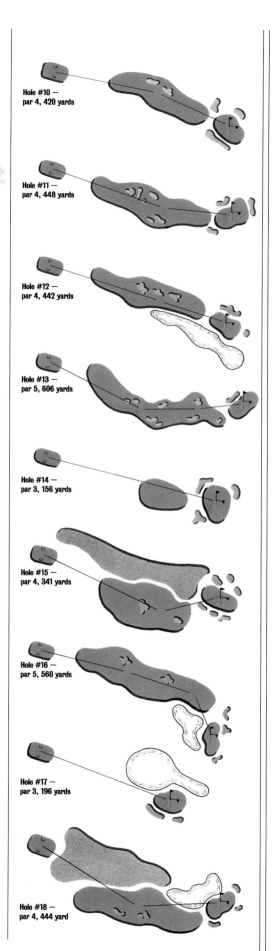

Hole #10 — par 4, 420 yards

Hole #11 — par 4, 448 yards

Hole #12 — par 4, 442 yards

Hole #13 — par 5, 606 yards

Hole #14 — par 3, 156 yards

Hole #15 — par 4, 341 yards

Hole #16 — par 5, 560 yards

Hole #17 — par 3, 196 yards

Hole #18 — par 4, 444 yard

Texas Open

OAK HILLS COUNTRY CLUB

Oak Hills Country Club refutes the myth that everything Texan is big. Just 6650 yards from its championship tees, this is one of the coziest courses on the Tour. The history of this tournament, however, is as long and mighty as the Rio Grande. Originally known as the Alamo Open, it dates back to 1922, when a Scotsman named Bob Mac-Donald sank a putt on the final hole to beat Cyril Walker by a stroke with a score of 281, then an American competitive record for 72 holes. Since then it has been won by a Hall of Fame full of stars including Hagen, Hogan, Nelson, Snead, Palmer, Watson, and Trevino. The Texas Open is a victory that every player wants to add to his credentials.

To do so requires finesse more than muscle. "Oak Hills is not an overpowering course," says 1973 and 1986 champion Ben Crenshaw, "but neither is it the kind of golf course that can be overpowered. Its strength, I believe, is its short par fours, some of the best I've ever seen."

THE
TV
HOLES

Expect birdies:
15

Expect bogeys:
13

13th hole

What to Watch For . . .

THE DASH FOR 125

Since this is traditionally the last full-field event of the season, it's the final chance for players to make the top 125 on the money list, and thereby keep their playing privileges for the next year's Tour. Thus, the tournament always gets perfect attendance from the players ranking from about 120 to 130.

A SENSE OF HISTORY

This is the fifth–oldest tournament on the PGA Tour and no state is prouder of its golf heritage than Texas, which spawned Messrs. Hogan, Nelson, Demaret, Kite, and Crenshaw, among others.

SCORING

This old A. W. Tillinghast course—the only Tillinghast design on the Tour—has been reworked over the years, but has been lengthened relatively little. It's not often that the Tour pros get to attack so short a course, and when they do, they invariably take advantage of it. But this tournament has a history of low scores. It was in the Texas Open—although a different course (Brackenridge Park, then regarded as one of the top three public courses in the country)—that Mike Souchak set a mark that has never been beaten: 257 for 72 holes—27 under par.

MONTEZUMA'S REVENGE

San Antonio is as close as Americans get to authentic Mexican food north of the border. Don't fail to sample all those burritos, fajitas, and enchiladas, but be ready for some next-day indigestion. The good news is that the water is perfectly potable.

FIELD & STREAM

For the Tour players, outdoor life comes to the fore, as the tournament arranges bass fishing and dove shooting excursions. Thirty minutes from Oak Hills, the pros can be in a bass boat or a field stalking birds.

That There's Mighty Fine Shootin'

PGA Tour 72-hole scoring record:

Score	Player	Year	Tournament	Score Below Par
257	**Mike Souchak**	**1955**	**Texas Open**	27
258	**Donnie Hammond**	**1989**	**Texas Open**	22
259	Byron Nelson	1945	Seattle Open	21
259	**Chandler Harper**	**1954**	**Texas Open**	25
259	Tim Norris	1982	Greater Hartford Open	25
259	**Corey Pavin**	**1988**	**Texas Open**	21
259	David Frost	1993	Hardee's Classic	21

Oak Hills Country Club

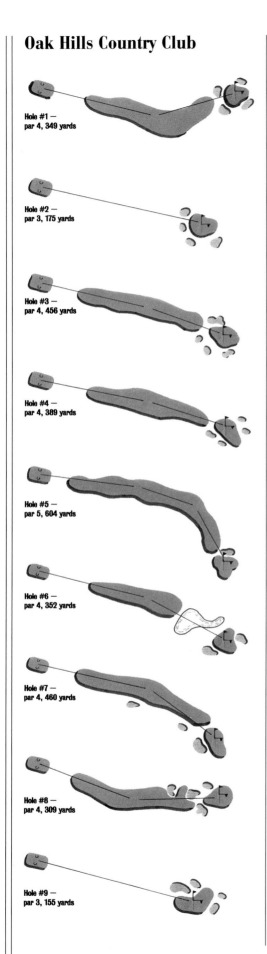

Hole #1 —
par 4, 349 yards

Hole #2 —
par 3, 175 yards

Hole #3 —
par 4, 456 yards

Hole #4 —
par 4, 389 yards

Hole #5 —
par 5, 604 yards

Hole #6 —
par 4, 352 yards

Hole #7 —
par 4, 460 yards

Hole #8 —
par 4, 309 yards

Hole #9 —
par 3, 155 yards

Five of the par fours average barely 350 yards in length, but most are lined with mesquite trees and play to small, bunker-choked, severely canted greens. Played in the incessant Texas wind, they constitute a tall assignment.

But don't get the wrong impression—there is plenty of length in them thar hills. Three other par fours average over 450 yards, one par three weighs in at 220, and there is a par five that measures 604. Granted, most of these holes play with the prevailing wind—but catch them on a day when the breeze has reversed its course, and you'll have a long, hard slog.

One aspect sets Oak Hills apart from every other course on the Tour—and 99 percent of the courses in the world: Each of its nines ends with a par three. For spectators at 18, this is a treat, as they're able to witness firsthand the tee-to-green climax of the tournament. In 1987, they got their money's worth when

18th hole

Tom Watson birdied the hole to win the $360,000 first prize in the Nabisco Championships (progenitor to THE TOUR Championship). It was Watson's last victory on the U.S. Tour.

Local Knowledge

HANDLING TWEENERS

On a course such as Oak Hills, where both nines end with par threes, it pays to know how to handle a "tweener," a tee shot where the distance falls smack between your capabilities with two clubs—a bit too long for one, a bit too short for the other.

How do you handle it? The key is to know yourself. If you're a Type A personality who likes to play aggressive, hard-hitting golf, take the shorter club and give it all you've got. If, on the other hand, you're laid back by nature, you probably have an evenly paced swing. Your wisest strategy is to take the longer club, grip down a hair, and make your usual smooth pass at the ball, letting the club do the work.

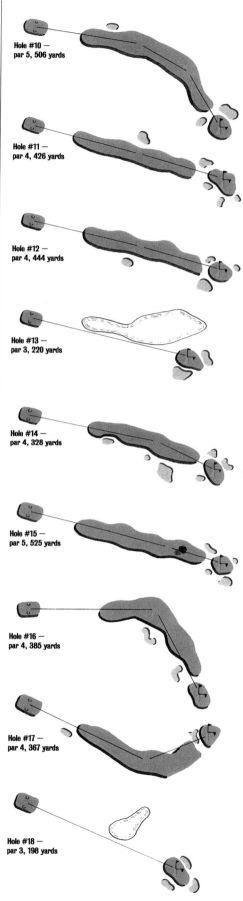

Hole #10 —
par 5, 506 yards

Hole #11 —
par 4, 426 yards

Hole #12 —
par 4, 444 yards

Hole #13 —
par 3, 220 yards

Hole #14 —
par 4, 328 yards

Hole #15 —
par 5, 525 yards

Hole #16 —
par 4, 385 yards

Hole #17 —
par 4, 367 yards

Hole #18 —
par 3, 198 yards

Practical Matters

FOR TICKET INFORMATION
Texas Open
70 N.E. Loop 410, Suite 370
San Antonio, TX 78216

COURSE
Oak Hills Country Club

ACCESS
Private course—
you must play with a member

COURSE RATING

Tees	Pro	Member
Yardage	6650	6125
Rating	71.8	69.0
Slope	128	123

GREEN FEES
$40
For more information:
(210) 349-6354

PRO-AM
Spots open to the public? Yes
Handicap: Maximum of 21
Format: Best ball
Entry fee: $2250
For more information:
(210) 341-0823

THE TOUR Championship

VARIOUS COURSES

Professional golf may not have an analog to the World Series or Super Bowl, but with THE TOUR Championship they've created something that's close, a significant tournament to end the PGA Tour calendar.

It began in 1986, with an infusion of $5 million from Nabisco Brands, Inc., in the form of something called the Nabisco Grand Prix of Golf. A three-part program, byzantine in its complexity, it included 1) an individual competition with players accumulating bonus points—and money—based on their play throughout the year ($1 million was available, with the high point-earner getting $175,000); 2) a "team-charity" competition in which foursomes of Tour players were drafted to represent the various events on the PGA Tour—$2 million was available for this part of the program with $500,000 going to the charity of the tournament whose four players accumulated the most points; and 3) The Nabisco Championships of Golf, a $2 million two-events-in-one that combined a season finale for the top money winners with a competition among representative players from the top eight point-earning teams.

Almost no one understood this maze, and the few who did objected to the idea of so much money revolving around just one tournament. After a few years it was abandoned. Today the Tour Championship is purely an individual event, bringing together the 30 top money winners for a 72-hole season-ending shootout.

All official documents from the PGA Tour refer to this event as THE TOUR Championship and the PGA Tour has taken great pains to infuse it with prominence, beginning with a purse that is, by decree, the highest on the Tour: $3 million. The winner receives a

What to Watch For . . .

SOUTHERN EXPOSURE
The Tour would undoubtedly love to play this event at Winged Foot or Shinnecock or Medinah or Oakland Hills, but don't count on it. With a late-October date, it's unlikely that the Tour Championship will migrate north of the Mason-Dixon line.

HAPPY FACES
Check out the practice tee of this event, especially during the early part of the week. There is a light-hearted feeling among the players, and why not? They've all had great years, they're about to get a two-month vacation (or make tons of money in tournaments abroad), and no matter how badly they play this week, they'll go home a lot richer.

GRINDING
By Sunday, things get serious. Besides the $540,000 first prize, other things are usually at stake, such as year-end honors for Player of the Year, leading money winner, and Vardon Trophy winner. There's also a ten-year exemption from qualifying for anyone who wins here—ample reasons to put on one's game face.

NERVOUS CADDIES
The big money is even more important to the caddies who collect 5 percent of their player's winnings, 10 percent for a victory. For many of them, this is the last big opportunity of the year.

Left: 18th hole at the Olympic Club, host of THE TOUR Championship in 1993 and 1994

Right: 17th hole at Southern Hills, host of THE TOUR Championship in 1995 and 1996

Rollercoaster Ride to Victory

In 1993, Jim Gallagher opened a five-stroke lead after the first round with a 63 at the Olympic Club. He ended up winning, but had to come from three strokes behind after 54 holes to do it.

TOURNAMENT RATINGS

COURSE DIFFICULTY

Avg. winning score:
8.8 under par   5th on Tour

USGA course rating:
73.7 (2.7 over par)*   20th on Tour

Overall rating:
Severe   8th on Tour

PRESTIGE

Field strength (19.9)   6th on Tour**

Winner quality (.813)   14th on Tour

Course difficulty (above)   8th on Tour

Plus factors: Largest purse,
season-ending event,
year's top 30 players

Overall rating   7th on Tour

*Average of courses played, 1987-94
**Rated behind major championships and
Players Championships based on Sony Ranking

whopping $540,000 (not to mention a 10-year exemption from qualifying), and the last-place finisher collects $48,000 just for showing up.

Also, after a two-year stint at the comparatively mundane Oak Hills Country Club, the Tour has rotated the event through a series of top-flight championship courses: Pebble Beach (1988), Harbour Town (1989), Champions (1990), Pinehurst #2 (1991–92), Olympic (1993–94), and Southern Hills (1995–96).

As a result, the game's marquee players take this event seriously, and that's good news for many of the Tour's late-season tournaments, as their fields are bolstered by these stars. However, the ultimate beneficiary has been THE TOUR Championship itself, which has produced a series of dramatic battles among the game's best players.

5th hole at Pinehurst #2 Course, host of THE TOUR Championship in 1991 and 1992

Practical Matters

FOR TICKET INFORMATION
PGA Tour
Sawgrass
Ponte Vedra Beach, FL 32082

Local Knowledge

PERFORMING UNDER PRESSURE

In an event such as THE TOUR Championship, where many thousands of dollars hinge on a single stroke, the level of pressure ratchets up a notch. But pressure afflicts all of us, even if it's in the fifth flight of the club championship. Suddenly, shots that seemed simple become difficult, and our mind races in a million unproductive directions.

The best way to counteract pressure is to keep that mind focused positively, and that focus begins before you even arrive at the course. Prepare yourself with a game plan for your course—chart your "personal par" for each hole and then play each hole mentally. Determine where you want to place each of your drives and approach shots.

Once you're on the course, stick with your game plan, and then narrow your focus to each shot. Visualize that ideal shot in your mind—try to see the desired path and trajectory of the ball—and keep that picture firmly in mind as you proceed through your setup and swing.

By focusing on the positives you'll leave less room for negative thoughts, less room for pressure.

The Major Championships & The Ryder Cup

The Masters

AUGUSTA NATIONAL GOLF CLUB

The U.S. pro tour may start in January, but for most of the world the golf season doesn't really begin until the playing of The Masters in the second week of April.

This is not a national championship, like the U.S. Open or British Open. It is not the championship of an association, like the PGA. It is not, in fact, the championship of anything. And yet, The Masters is unquestionably a major championship.

Why? Two reasons. The first is tradition. This is the tournament begun by Bobby Jones, launched to prominence by Gene Sarazen's double eagle, and won by virtually every important player of the modern era.

The second is the golf course, a masterpiece of strategic design unfurled across a tract of dramatic land that originally was an immense nursery. Fruitlands was its name when Bobby Jones and a consortium of investors led by Wall Street financier Clifford Roberts bought the property from a Belgian nobleman in 1931.

A year earlier, Jones had captured the Grand Slam (winning the Open and Amateur Championships of America and Great Britain in the same year), and then almost immediately announced his retirement from the pressures of competitive

THE TV HOLES

Expect birdies:

13, 15

Expect bogeys:

10, 12

Right: 13th hole

What to Watch For . . .

LITTLE FRONT BUT A BIG BACK

For years, there was no TV coverage of the first nine holes. Recently, things have loosened up a bit, but mostly what you'll see is taped highlights. That's okay, however, because The Masters doesn't truly begin until the final nine holes on Sunday. The pivotal point is invariably Amen Corner—the water-guarded trio of holes at 11, 12, and 13—but the ultimate center of triumph and tragedy may be 15, the eminently reachable but pond-fronted par five where Sarazen holed his 4-wood shot for double-eagle in 1935.

A WEAK FIELD

Most tournaments have starting fields of at least 144 players. The Masters, however, is an invitational, and although there are 15 ways to qualify, the starting field here averages about 90 players, including two dozen or so former champions (many of them too old to be competitive), a handful of amateurs, and a dozen or more "rookies" competing at Augusta for the first time. As a result, critics claim that only a third of the field is capable of winning.

GREENERY

Novelist John Updike said it best: "Green grass, green grandstands, green concession stalls, green paper cups, green folding chairs and visors for sale, green ropes, green-topped Georgia pines, a prevalence of green in the slacks and jerseys of the gallery . . . if justice were poetic, Hubert Green would win every year."

CABINS

Hard by the 18th green is a string of simple white cabins that serve as accommodations for members of the Augusta National Golf Club. One is named after President Dwight D. Eisenhower, a club member during the 1950s, and another after Bobby Jones. The Butler Cabin is where CBS anchors its coverage and the winner receives the symbol of victory, a green jacket.

Mister Masters

Jack Nicklaus not only holds the Masters record for most victories, with six, he has the most top-five, top-10 and top-24 finishes, and has completed 72 holes the most times. He's tied for first in runner-up finishes.

Victories	6
Runner-up finishes	4
Top-five finishes	15
Top-10 finishes	21
Top-24 finishes	28
Completed 72 holes	32

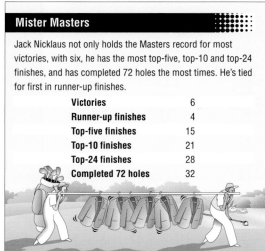

TOURNAMENT RATINGS

COURSE DIFFICULTY

Avg. winning score:	
8.4 under par	3rd on Tour
USGA course rating: NA*	NA*
Overall rating:	
Severe	3rd on Tour

PRESTIGE

Field strength (26.4**)	4th on Tour
Winner quality (1.180)	3rd on Tour
Course difficulty (above)	3rd on Tour
Plus factors: Tradition, legacy of Bobby Jones, course rated 4th in U.S., international field, 10-year exemption to winner	
Overall rating	2nd on Tour

*Course not rated
**Players in top 30 in Sony Ranking

golf. With no more worlds to conquer, he had a different golf ambition—to build a course where he and his cohorts could play friendly rounds in serene isolation.

To help him, Jones drafted Alister Mackenzie, a Yorkshireman of Scottish ancestry. The paradisiacal playing field in Jones's mind had a distinctly Scottish flavor, with broad, rolling fairways, large, undulant greens, and a minimum of rough and bunkers. His favorite course, after all, was the Old Course at St. Andrews, where he had won both a British Open and a British Amateur. So on his land in Augusta, Georgia, he hoped to import some of the strategy and mystery of that timelessly challenging links.

Mackenzie did the routing as Jones played hundreds of experimental shots from intended tees to intended fairways, intended fairways to intended greens. In the end, Bobby got what he wanted—a glorious playground for himself and his friends. Over the years, the Augusta National has undergone numerous tweaks, changes, and minor alterations, but essentially it remains exactly what Jones and Mackenzie created—a superb examination in strategic golf, perhaps the finest thinking man's

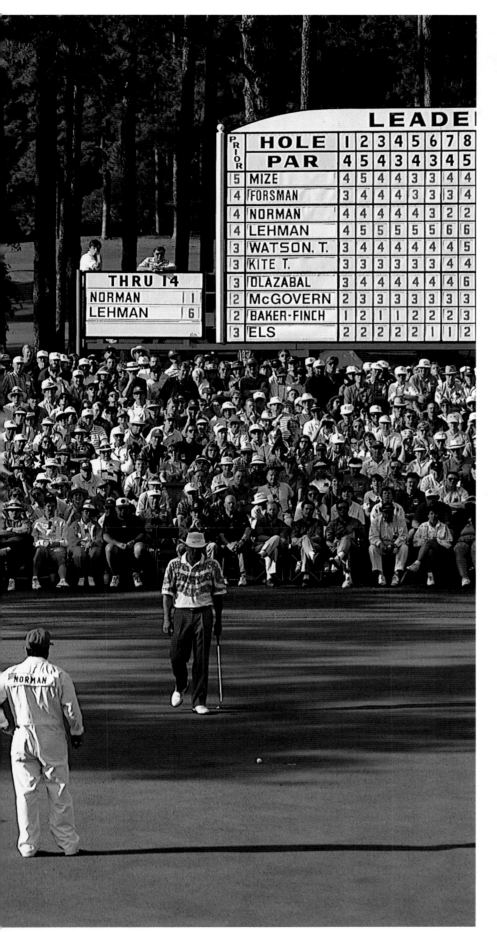

15th hole

What to Watch For . . .

NONE OF THE FOLLOWING

Periscopes, stepladders, coolers, electronic score-boards, commercial signage, hamburgers, hot dogs, parking fees, photographers inside the ropes, beverage cans, divots, mentions of attendance figures or prize money.

REDBUD, GOLDEN BELL, AND 16 OTHERS

Each of the 18 holes is named for a different tree or flowering shrub in evidence along its fairway.

THE PAR-3 JINX

There is no pro-am at The Masters, but on Wednesday afternoon a minitournament takes place at the Augusta National's nine-hole Par-3 course. Since the tournament started in 1960, no player has won the Par-3 Contest and gone on to victory on the big course that week.

STAR STARTERS

Part of Masters tradition is Thursday's opening festivities at the first tee, where the legendary Gene Sarazen, Byron Nelson, and Sam Snead hit the ceremonial first tee shots. At some point in the future, their roles surely will be assumed by four-time Masters champion Arnold Palmer and six-time champion Jack Nicklaus. Until then, however, Arnie and Jack can be seen each year in the regular field.

GLASS WITH CLASS

A pair of Waterford crystal goblets is awarded to anyone who scores an eagle during the four days of competition. Crystal vases go to those who shoot the lowest score for each round.

FREE READING MATTER

Masters galleryites—or patrons, as they are known—may avail themselves of free booklets showing the location of rest rooms and picnic areas and offering suggestions on smart spectating from the immortal Bobby Jones himself.

RULES MISCUES

The one comparatively weak area of The Masters is administration of the Rules. In contrast to regular Tour events, where rules situations are handled by a staff of full-time paid officials, many rulings at The Masters are made by volunteers—businessmen golfers who serve on various committees of the United States Golf Association and the Royal & Ancient Golf Club of St. Andrews—and other calls are made by members of the Augusta National Golf Club. Each year they make a mistake or two.

Hole #1 —
par 4, 400 yards

Hole #2 —
par 5, 555 yards

Hole #3 —
par 4, 360 yards

Hole #4 —
par 3, 205 yards

Hole #5 —
par 4, 435 yards

Hole #6 —
par 3, 180 yards

Hole #7 —
par 4, 360 yards

Hole #8 —
par 5, 535 yards

Hole #9 —
par 4, 435 yards

18th hole

course this side of St. Andrews.

But in the Augusta National Bobby Jones also wrought something much bigger than a private preserve. Within months of the course's completion, one of the club's members suggested

Practical Matters

FOR TICKET INFORMATION
Augusta National Golf Club
P.O. Box 2086
Augusta, GA 30913

COURSE
Augusta National Golf Club

ACCESS
Private—you must play with
a member

COURSE RATING

Tees	Pro	Member
Yardage	6925	6240
Rating	Not Rated	
Slope	Not Rated	

GREEN FEES
Confidential

PRO-AM
None

For more information:
(706) 667-6000

that the club host a U.S. Open. The idea got nowhere—largely because the Open is played in June, and by that late in the year Augusta is too hot and humid to host much of anything—but Clifford Roberts recognized an opportunity and proposed that the club invent an event of its own. Thus in 1934 was born the Augusta National Invitation Tournament, an event which lasted one year under that name before being rechristened The Masters. During the ensuing six decades it has earned a reputation as golf's greatest show.

Like most aspects of The Masters, the television coverage (on TBS Thursday and Friday, CBS Saturday and Sunday) is something special. Through an agreement with the event's three sponsors (Cadillac, IBM, and Traveler's Insurance), commercial interruption is kept to a minimum. That's the good news. The bad news is that television is the only way most people will ever see The Masters. Although officials will release no numbers, attendance at the tournament is limited, and tickets are restricted to longtime "patrons," most of whom have had the weeklong passes in their families for decades. For a while there was a waiting list, but that was cut off 20 years ago, with several thousand golf fans awaiting the call.

Local Knowledge

STRATEGY IS CHESS, BILLIARDS, AND BOWLING

In assessing the challenge of the Augusta National, Bobby Jones wrote: "There is not a hole out there that can't be birdied if you just think; and there is not a hole out there that can't be double-bogeyed if you stop thinking."

With its wide fairways and generous greens, this is the kind of course that can lull its assailants to sleep. It points up the need to focus not simply on playing to fairways and greens but on positioning one's shots in anticipation of the shots that will ensue, as in a game of chess or billiards.

The best way to do that is to play each hole backwards in your mind. Start at the green: If, for instance, the pin is on the right side of the green, or if there is big trouble to the left, you'll have the best chance of success if you approach from the left side of the fairway, keeping the trouble more or less at your back. Likewise, to get your drive to that left side, you should tee the ball up on the right side of the green, so that you can hit directly away from the less desirable right side. In this sense, the technique is similar to bowling. To pick up a spare on the ten pin, you approach from the left and roll the ball across the alley; to get the seven pin, you attack from the right.

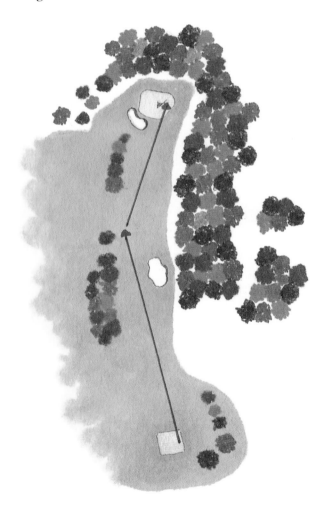

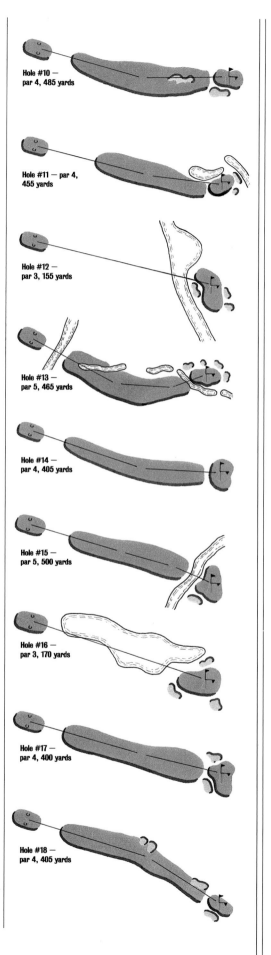

Hole #10 — par 4, 485 yards

Hole #11 — par 4, 455 yards

Hole #12 — par 3, 155 yards

Hole #13 — par 5, 465 yards

Hole #14 — par 4, 405 yards

Hole #15 — par 5, 500 yards

Hole #16 — par 3, 170 yards

Hole #17 — par 4, 400 yards

Hole #18 — par 4, 405 yards

The U.S. Open

VARIOUS COURSES

I n the year 2000, at Pebble Beach, the U.S. Open will be played for the 100th time. This is the tournament that remains the ultimate test of golf.

It started as an afterthought. When the first Open was played at the Newport Country Club in 1895, it was little more than a sideshow. Back then, attention centered on the inaugural U.S. Amateur. The pros—mostly Scottish emigres—were viewed largely as employees; their tournament, a one-day event played the day after the three-day-long Amateur, was little more than an opportunity for the gentry to place a few wagers on their working-class horses.

Ten professionals competed, along with one amateur (the Open, after all, was and is "open" to everyone), and first prize was won by Horace Rawlins. Rawlins's prizes were a $50 gold medal and $150 in cash. (Today's U.S. Open champion receives more than $300,000.)

Since Rawlins, our national championship has been won by every significant player of the 20th century, with one exception. Only Sam Snead has failed to take the title—but not for lack of trying. He finished second four times, and in an interview on the occasion of the USGA's Centennial, he claimed there hasn't been a night of his

2nd hole at Medinah Country Club

What to Watch For . . .

STIMPMETERS

These are the instruments used by the USGA to measure the speed of greens. Actually, a Stimpmeter is nothing more than a metal ramp. The USGA official lets a ball roll down the ramp and measures the distance it rolls on a flat green. For the Open, the USGA likes to see a roll of about 11 feet—at most PGA Tour events it's between nine and 10.

THREES OF A KIND

During the 1960s and '70s, then USGA Director Frank Hannigan decided to amuse himself when setting the threesomes for the Thursday and Friday starting times. In the case of a dozen or so threesomes, he grouped birds of a feather, e.g., "three Ohio State dropouts," "three fat U.S. Amateur champions." His successors have kept the tradition alive, and it has become a minor sport among insiders to detect each Open's "Hannigan-shenanigan" groups.

ENTRIES

Each year more than 5000 hopefuls—amateurs as well as pros—compete for the 150 or so places in the starting field. About 50 players are exempt because of recent playing records. Everyone else must go through at least one, usually two, qualifying rounds.

NOSTALGIA

Each year the USGA doles out a few "special exemptions" to players who have little or no chance of winning but who have forged a distinguished career or have some link to the Open course (e.g., a winner of a prior Open there). In 1994, for example, Larry Nelson, Johnny Miller, and 64-year-old Arnold Palmer were granted exemptions to play at Oakmont. Nelson and Miller were previous Open winners there and Palmer, who grew up in the Pittsburgh area, had been named by the club as the honorary chairman of the event.

Persistence Pays Off	
Most Times Entered Before Finally Winning the U.S. Open:	
Ray Floyd	**22**
Tom Kite	21
Craig Wood	15
David Graham	12
Tom Watson	11

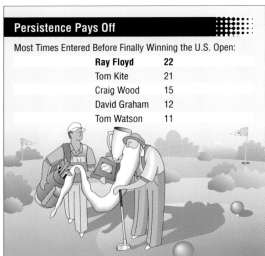

TOURNAMENT RATINGS

COURSE DIFFICULTY

Avg. winning score: 4.7 under par	1st on Tour
USGA course rating: 75.0 (4.2 over par)*	2nd on Tour
Overall rating: Severe	1st on Tour

PRESTIGE

Field strength (26.6**)	3rd on Tour
Winner quality (1.040)	6th on Tour
Course difficulty (above)	1st on Tour
Plus factors: Tradition, national championship, played on courses with average rank of 20th in U.S. (1985-94), international field, 10-year exemption to winner	
Overall rating	3rd on Tour

*Average of courses played, 1985-94
**Players in top 30 in Sony Ranking

life when he hasn't gone to sleep thinking about his missed opportunities in the U.S. Open.

USGA officials revel in making this the game's ultimate examination. Accuracy has always been more important than distance in conquering Open courses, and there are those who claim that this favors an unaggressive, plodding style of play (as played by Messrs. Kite and Strange) while discouraging the more flamboyant style of Messrs. Norman, Daly, and Couples.

The standard Open setup includes fairways narrowed to about 30 yards in width; a collar of two-inch primary rough bordered by secondary rough that ranges from four inches to knee height; and greens that roll at about 11 on the Stimpmeter (whereas PGA Tour greens average 10 or less). In 1976, the severe conditions prompted one player to ask: "What are you trying to do, humiliate the greatest players in the world?"

"No," said USGA President Sandy Tatum, "we're trying to identify them."

Right: 16th hole at Shinnecock Hills Golf Club

Inset: 16th hole at Baltusrol Golf Club (Lower Course)

What to Watch For . . .

SLOW PLAY
The USGA has a poor record on disciplining slow players. On Thursday and Friday, groups of three players take between five and five and a half hours. The ultra fast greens and the pressure of a major championship are contributing factors, but the fundamental problem is that slow-play guidelines and penalties have not been enforced.

VENERABLE VENUES
Don't expect to see a U.S. Open played on any course whose name begins with TPC. The USGA remains a conservative association that returns time and again to classic country clubs with courses designed a half century or more ago. The USGA's favorite architect is Donald Ross, whose courses have hosted more than 100 USGA championships. Ross died in 1948.

AMATEURS
The Open is just that—open to all (or at least anyone with a USGA Handicap Index of 2.4 or better). The reigning U.S. Amateur Champion is exempt from the local and sectional qualifying rounds, and each year a handful of other amateurs qualify for the starting field.

MARATHON COVERAGE
This is the one tournament of the year where, on both Saturday and Sunday, you can watch the leaders tee off at number one and follow the play all the way to their final putts at 18. Over the four days, NBC and ESPN air roughly 30 hours of live and taped coverage.

MONDAY FINISHES
The Open is the only tournament to retain an 18-hole playoff. (Most events, including The Masters and PGA Championship, use sudden death, while the British Open employs a four-hole-total format.) In the Open, if there is still a tie after 90 holes, sudden death kicks in.

SCOWLS
Check out the faces of the players. At the first tee, they are simply tense, but by the 36th green, two-thirds have suffered some combination of fatigue, frustration, and pain.

ONE-DAY WONDERS
It is a quasi-tradition for the first round of the U.S. Open to be led by a player who is less than a household name. Examples: Alvin Krueger, Bob Gajda, Lee Mackey, Dick Knight, Bobby Brue, Marty Fleckman, Pat Fitzsimons, T. C. Chen, and Rives McBee. Thursday's leaders have hung on to win only 14 of the first 95 Opens.

Current U.S. Open Sites

COURSE	HOST CITY	TIMES HOSTED	LAST TIME	NEXT TIME
Seven Regulars				
Baltusrol	Springfield, NJ	7	1993	
Oakmont	Oakmont, PA	7	1994	
Oakland Hills	Birmingham, MI	6	1996	
Shinnecock Hills	Southampton, NY	3	1995	
Pebble Beach	Pebble Beach, CA	3	1992	2000
Oak Hill	Rochester, NY	3	1989	
Olympic	San Francisco, CA	3	1987	1998
Seven Occasionals				
Winged Foot	Mamaroneck, NY	4	1984	
Inverness	Toledo, OH	4	1979	
Medinah	Medinah, IL	3	1990	
The Country Club	Brookline, MA	3	1988	
Southern Hills	Tulsa, OK	2	1977	
Hazeltine	Hazeltine, MN	2	1991	2001
Congressional	Bethesda, MD	1	1964	1997

How Hard is an Open Course?

COURSE	YARDAGE	PAR	RATING	SLOPE
Oakmont	6966	71	75.7	145
Oakland Hills	7105	70	75.5	137
Pebble Beach	6799	72	75.0	144
Baltusrol	7138	70	74.7	140
Shinnecock Hills	6813	70	74.6	144
Olympic	6812	70	74.0	135
Oak Hill	6902	70	73.8	139

Local Knowledge

HOW TO PUTT U.S. OPEN GREENS

Few courses have greens that putt as fast as those at Oakmont or Olympic, but from time to time we all encounter extra-slippery surfaces. On such occasions, there's a simple way to adjust without changing your stroke: Hit your putts off the toe of the putter.

When you strike a putt off the toe of the putter, you can expect a much softer impact than when you strike it smack on the sweetspot. A putt that would normally roll 30 feet will roll anywhere from 20 to 27 feet, depending on the model of putter you use. (Putters with heel-toe weighting will have less distance loss.) This softer, slower impact will enable you to adjust to hard, fast greens without having to alter your stroke.

What to Watch For . . .

HOME-BRED HEROES

When South Africa's Ernie Els took the title in 1994, he became only the fourth foreign champion since World War II, and the first since David Graham 13 years earlier. In contrast, international stars have dominated both the British Open and Masters during the last two decades.

AT OAKLAND HILLS: A TOUGH FINISH

Holes 16, 17, and 18 are probably the sternest closing stretch on any Open course. Don't count on anyone to steal the title with a string of late birdies.

AT PEBBLE BEACH: UNQUESTIONABLE CHAMPIONS

The three Opens held here were won by Jack Nicklaus (the best player in the 1972 field), Tom Watson (the best player in the 1982 field), and in 1992, Tom Kite (the game's all-time leading money winner).

AT SHINNECOCK: WEATHER

At the eastern tip of Long Island—as at the British Open—"if there is nae wind, there is nae golf." The breezes off the Long Island Sound and the Atlantic Ocean can reach 30 miles per hour or more.

AT OLYMPIC: GIANT KILLERS

It was here that Jack Fleck beat Ben Hogan, that Billy Casper beat Arnold Palmer, and that Scott Simpson beat Tom Watson.

AT OAK HILL: REPEATERS

Each of the four champions here—Cary Middlecoff, Lee Trevino, Jack Nicklaus, and Curtis Strange—has won at least one other U.S. Open.

AT BALTUSROL: DARK HORSES AND 4-TIMERS

Four of the six champions at Baltusrol are men who were not expected to contend: Jerry Travers, Tony Manero, Ed Furgol, and Lee Janzen. However, the two others are among the four players who have won the title a record four times: Willie Anderson and Jack Nicklaus.

AT OAKMONT: SQUEAKERS

It usually comes down to the wire in Pittsburgh. Three times there have been playoffs, twice the victory was by one stroke, and once the margin was two. Only in 1953 was it not close, when Ben Hogan lapped the field by six strokes.

Practical Matters

FOR TICKET INFORMATION
USGA
Golf House
P.O. Box 708
Far Hills, NJ 07931

The British Open

A ROTATION OF EIGHT COURSES

I n 1860—more than 130 years before the prime of Nick Faldo, Greg Norman, and Fred Couples—eight bearded men in baggy trousers and seafaring caps assembled at the 12-hole course of the Prestwick Golf Club and played it three times for the sake of winning a belt. Thus was born the British Open Championship, the oldest—and in the minds of many, most prestigious—golf tournament in the world.

Above: The British Open Trophy at the Old Course, St. Andrews

Right: 12th hole at Royal St. George's

What to Watch For . . .

STEP LADDERS AND MILK CRATES
There is none of the lawn-party atmosphere that exists at U.S. tournaments. The fans here—all of them—are dedicated golfers, and they come to watch and to appreciate the action. For the wee souls in the crowd, that can mean dragging along something that will insure a decent view over their six-deep brethren.

FOREIGNERS
The British Open is golf's world heavyweight championship. It has been won by representatives of 12 different countries, and at any moment the leaderboard might display players from a half dozen or more nations.

CARTGATE, BLAW WEARIE, THE KITCHEN, AND TEL-EL-KEBIR
British quaintness finds its expression on the scorecards of most Open courses, where the holes have not only numbers but obscure names.

TRULY GRANDSTANDS
Long before American golf was a popular spectator sport, the British Open was drawing big crowds. The bleachers surrounding the last few holes are capable of holding tens of thousands.

THE 2–1 ROTATION
Roughly speaking, for every time the British Open is held in England, it is held twice in Scotland. Never has it been held back-to-back on English soil, and only once—in 1951—was it held in Ireland. The current R&A policy is to bring the championship to its most venerable site, the Old Course at St. Andrews, every five years.

Jolly Good Scores

Progressive 72-Hole Scoring Record at the British Open:

Score	Player	Year	Score	Player	Year
305	Harold Hilton	1892	279	Bobby Locke	1950
300	Harry Vardon	1903	278	Peter Thomson	1958
296	Jack White	1904	276	Arnold Palmer	1962
291	James Braid	1908	268	Tom Watson	1977
285	Bobby Jones	1927	267	Greg Norman	1993
283	Gene Sarazen	1932			

TOURNAMENT RATINGS

COURSE DIFFICULTY

Avg. winning score:
9.0 under par	6th on Tour

USGA course rating: NA*   NA*

Overall rating:
Severe	6th on Tour

PRESTIGE

Field strength (28.0**)	1st on Tour
Winner quality (1.500)	1st on Tour
Course difficulty (above)	6th on Tour

Plus factors: Oldest championship (began 1860), most international field, played on courses ranked an average of 22nd in the world (1985-94), 10-year exemption to winner

Overall rating	1st on Tour

*Courses not rated

**Players in top 30 in Sony Ranking

What began as the Prestwick club championship has become the most international of all events, conducted by the Royal & Ancient Golf Club of St. Andrews, Scotland, the organization that is analogous to America's USGA and administers the rules for the rest of the world of golf.

Currently, The Open, as it is known to all Brits, rotates among eight courses, five of them in Scotland, three in England, all of them genuine links, stretched across sandy, undulating terrain within a few hundred yards of the sea. Weird bounces are the norm, as is thick, tangly rough in the form of heather, bracken, whins, and gorse. The greens are by far the slowest of any of the major championships—slower, in fact, than at 90 percent of the tournaments on the U.S. Tour—and that slowness is owing in part to the other element that characterizes this championship—weather. Wind and rain are normal playing conditions at the British Open.

The stature of this championship has never been in doubt among the citizens of the United Kingdom and Europe. In America, however, it has gone through stages. Certainly, when Bobby Jones was in his prime, atten-

What to Watch For . . .

LONG DAYS
In July, sunlight can prevail for as much as 18 hours each day (particularly in more northern Scotland). Thus, on Thursday and Friday, the starting times begin before 7:00 a.m. and the last group finishes after 7:00 p.m.

DRINKS ALL AROUND
This is the only major championship where the fans can step up and avail themselves of not only beer but wine, champagne, and hard liquor. By late in the day, the collective bibulousness evidences itself in the throaty roars that greet all shots played by Scottish and English players.

THE TENTED VILLAGE
Within steps of the first tee is an exhibition tent that houses purveyors of everything from British Open beer mugs to vacations in Spain. Golf clubs and apparel account for most of the trade, and the busiest booth is Pringle knitwear, which offers 40 percent discounts to the players and press. Early in the week, look for the wives of American Tour pros to carry away several thousand dollars' worth of cashmeres.

BOOKIES
Gambling is not only legal throughout Great Britain, it is tantamount to the national pastime. At the Open, you can speculate on the winner, the low American, the "top Scot," and endless other options. In 1983, Andy Bean bet on himself to win-place-show, tied for second, and won almost as much money at the betting parlor as he did on the 72nd green.

76 HOLES (SOMETIMES 77)
In 1985, the Brits adopted a compromise between the USGA's 18-hole playoff and the sudden death that prevails at most other events. Those tied after 72 holes battle for four or five more holes (depending on the configuration of the course), after which the player with the low total becomes the champion. If a tie persists, sudden death kicks in.

A MOVEABLE FEAST
Parked around the exhibition tent is a caravan of trailers bearing an assortment of foods. The soft ice cream man, the hard candy man, the baked potato man, and the fish-and-chips man all stand ready to grant your gustatory wishes.

Left: 9th hole at Turnberry
Inset: 11th hole at Muirfield

Double green: the 7th and 11th holes at the Old Course, St. Andrews

tion was focused on both the Amateur and Open championships across the pond. However, once Jones retired, interest declined among both fans and players. Ben Hogan played in only one British Open, the one he won at Carnoustie in 1953, and when Sam Snead took the title at St. Andrews in 1946, he was one of the few prominent Americans in the field. It was Arnold Palmer who revived American interest in the tournament—and gave birth to the notion of the modern Grand Slam—when he came to St. Andrews in 1960 after winning both The Masters and the U.S. Open. Arnie finished second that year but won in each of the next two, and since that time the British Open's stature has been assured.

In fact, the quality of the recent champions is unquestionably higher than in the other three majors. In addition to Palmer's two victories, the British Open has been won by Jack Nicklaus three times (along with seven runner-up finishes), by Tom Watson five times, Gary Player, Seve Ballesteros, and Nick Faldo three times each, and Lee Trevino and Greg Norman twice each.

The Current British Open Courses

COURSE	FOUNDED	TIMES HOSTED	LAST TIME	NEXT TIME
Old Course, St. Andrews	16th c.	25	1995	2000
Muirfield	1891	14	1992	1998
Royal St. George's	1887	12	1993	
Royal Lytham & St. Annes	1886	8	1988	1996
Royal Birkdale	1889	7	1991	
Royal Troon	1878	6	1989	1997
Carnoustie	1839	5	1975	1999
Turnberry	1947	3	1994	

Practical Matters

FOR TICKET INFORMATION
The Royal & Ancient Golf Club
St. Andrews, KY16 9JD
Fife, Scotland

Local Knowledge

ESTABLISH YOUR GROUND GAME

The windy seaside courses of the British Open lend themselves to golf's ground game, the low, running shots that bounce and roll onto the greens. If you get a chance to play these courses, you should be armed with a pitch-and-run shot.

Basically, this is a shot that stays under the wind (be it a headwind, tailwind, or crosswind) and bumps its way to the target. To play it, you need to give the ball a slightly downward hit, which you can preprogram at address by positioning the ball a bit to the rear of its usual position in your stance—midway between the feet works well for most players.

You can play the shot with a range of clubs, from the 5-iron through the wedges, but the 7-iron might be the best overall choice. The key to the technique is minimalism. Minimize the length of the club by gripping down on the shaft a couple of inches. Minimize the backspin (and therefore the loft) you put on the shot by keeping both your backswing and follow-through short. (Think of your ball as sitting at 6 o'clock, then swing back no farther than 9 o'clock and forward to only 3.) And as a final key, minimize the speed of your swing. It's better to hit a soft shot with a 6-iron, letting the clubface produce the bounce and forward roll, than to try to manufacture a shot by hitting more vigorously with a 9-iron.

What to Watch For . . .

AT ST. ANDREWS: A MIRROR IMAGE
This is the only championship venue—and one of the few courses in the world—where the scorecard reads the same way forward and backward. The pars of holes one through 18 (or 18 through one) are: 4-4-4-4-5-4-4-3-4 4-3-4-4-5-4-4-4-4.

AT MUIRFIELD: SUFFERING IN SAND
The British Open's most notorious bunkers live at Muirfield, where the steep faces are revetted with layers of turf so that any ball that rolls near the lip will be drawn into the pit.

AT ROYAL BIRKDALE: MULTIPLE CHAMPIONS
Five of the six men who have won at Birkdale have won at least one other major championship. Among them, Peter Thomson, Arnold Palmer, Lee Trevino, Johnny Miller, and Tom Watson have amassed 14 British Opens, six Masters, six U.S. Opens, and two PGA Championships.

AT ROYAL LYTHAM & ST. ANNES: U.S. FRUSTRATION
Bobby Jones won the first British Open played here, in 1926, but since then the victors have come from South Africa, Australia, New Zealand, England, and Spain. This is the only current British Open site where no American professional has ever won.

AT ROYAL ST. GEORGE'S: ELEPHANT BURIAL GROUNDS
The fairways at Sandwich have more humps and hollows than any British Open course since the first one, Prestwick. Former PGA Tour Commissioner Deane Beman, who won the 1959 British Amateur here, claims he didn't have one flat lie during the entire tournament: "I'd hit a shot perfectly but moments later I'd be standing on my ear to play my second."

AT ROYAL TROON: TRAINS
Many of the original Scottish courses were plotted along railways, and at Troon the trains still run. The par-five 11th hole runs alongside the tracks.

AT TURNBERRY: AILSA CRAIG
The most dominant feature of the course is ten miles removed, a massive volcanic rock that sits out in the usually fog-shrouded Atlantic. There's a saying at Turnberry: "If you can see Ailsa Craig, it's about to rain; if you can't see Ailsa Craig, it is raining."

AT CARNOUSTIE: THE BURN
A meandering stream, the Barry Burn, crosses the 17th and 18th fairways several times, making for the most menacing finish in the British Open rotation.

The PGA Championship

VARIOUS COURSES

Above: 3rd hole at Bellerive

Right: 18th hole at Crooked Stick

O rganized golf in America is general-ly agreed to have begun with the founding of the St. Andrew's Golf Club in 1888. In those days, there was only one important kind of competition—amateur golf. Golf professionals—most of them immigrants from Scotland and England—were looked upon as second-class citizens, employees of the club — like waiters or charwomen — their only purpose to serve the members.

In January of 1916, however, steps were taken to improve the club pros' lot. At a meeting at the Taplow Club at the Hotel Martinique in New York City, the Professional Golfers Association of Ameri-ca was founded. The guiding light was Rodman Wanamaker, heir to the depart-ment store fortune, who realized that the pro had to be taken seriously if the game was to grow.

To get the ball rolling, Wanamaker proposed an annual tournament—for pros

What to Watch For . . .

ALL PROS

This is the only one of the four major championships where every player in the 150-man field is a professional. Thus, in most years, the PGA can claim to have the strongest field of the four major championships.

A RYDER CUP SUBPLOT

In odd-numbered years, the PGA is the final event in which American players may earn points that qualify them for that year's Ryder Cup Team, and often the competition comes down to the wire. In 1985, for example, Tom Watson needed a bogey at the 72nd hole at Cherry Hills to earn enough points for the last spot, and missed when he made double-bogey 6.

UNKNOWNS

Roughly a quarter of the field is made up of PGA club professionals (the top 40 finishers from the PGA Club Professional Championship). Virtually every year at least one of them ranks among the Thursday and Friday leaders, then folds under the weekend pressure.

Not Too Lonely at the Top

There was a nine-way tie for the lead after the first round of the PGA Championship in both 1959 and 1969 – a record for a major championship. On both occasions, the leading score was 69.

Year	Players
1959	Jerry Barber, Jackson Bradley, Walter Burkemo, Billy Casper, Dick Hart, Chuck Klein, Mike Krak, Gene Littler, Mike Souchak
1969	Ray Floyd, Larry Ziegler, Charles Coody, Bunky Henry, Larry Mowry, Johnny Pott, Tom Shaw, Bob Lunn, Al Geiberger

only—and put up $2500 in prizes and medals for the winners. The first PGA Championship was played later that year at the Siwanoy Country Club in Bronxville, New York, just north of New York City. A match-play elimination event, it came down to a 36-hole final between two British professionals, Jock Hutchison and Jim Barnes, who had finished second and third, respectively, in that year's U.S. Open won by amateur Chick Evans. In a seesaw battle, Barnes prevailed, 1 up.

World War I put the championship on hold for two years, and when it returned in 1919, Barnes took the title a second time. In the more than three-quarters of a century since, over 60 of the world's greatest golf professionals have been crowned PGA Champions. It remains the ultimate pros-only tournament, and one of golf's four major championships.

And yet, by unanimous agreement, the PGA is the least prestigious of the four majors. Why? For one thing, poor timing. Chronologically, it is fourth on the calendar, played in early to mid–August of each year. The August date also brings uncomfortably hot weather in most years, an unpleasant contrast to the rite of spring that is The Masters. Critics have consistently advocated a date shift to May, which

TOURNAMENT RATINGS

COURSE DIFFICULTY

Avg. winning score: 8.6 under par	4th on Tour
USGA course rating: 74.9 (3.6 over par)*	7th on Tour
Overall rating: Severe	4th on Tour

PRESTIGE

Field strength (27.6**)	2nd on Tour
Winner quality (1.080)	4th on Tour
Course difficulty (above)	4th on Tour
Plus factors: Tradition, played on courses with average rank of 56th in U.S. (1985-94), international field, 10-year exemption to winner.	
Overall rating	4th on Tour

*Average of courses played, 1985-94
**Players in top 30 in Sony Ranking

10th hole at Inverness

What to Watch For . . .

YANKEE SI, EUROPE NON
Despite the strength of European Tour players during the past two decades, the last pro from "across the pond" to win the PGA was Scotsman Tommy Armour in 1930.

GEOGRAPHIC DIVERSITY
One of the stated purposes of the PGA of America is to expose its championship to golf fans all over the country. In contrast to the U.S. and British Opens, which return repeatedly to the same tried-and-true sites, the PGA shifts around, rarely hitting the same course twice in less than a decade. In 1998 it will be played at Sahalee Country Club near Seattle, Washington, bringing major championship golf to the Pacific Northwest for the first time in over half a century.

HEAT
No one seems able to answer the question, "Why, when the PGA is played in mid-August, do they ever hold it in places like Tulsa, Birmingham, and Los Angeles?" Normal weather conditions for this championship include 90-degree-plus temperatures and 80-percent-plus humidity, and in some years, much worse.

A SUPERLESSON
A PGA Championship tradition is the Champions' Clinic, held at the practice tee on Tuesday afternoon of tournament week. The gallery is treated to a series of brief lessons from past PGA champions, each of them demonstrating a different club. The best show: John Daly on the driver.

would put the four majors in neat monthly succession: April (Masters), May (PGA), June (U.S. Open), and July (British Open).

Another reason: the format. This championship, which originated as a match-play event, is now contested at stroke play. The change was instituted in 1958, largely to make the tournament more appealing to television (and thus more lucrative), and while this was undeniably a sound business decision, it did little to enhance the event's image. Today, the PGA Championship is no longer distinct in format from the other four majors. There is nothing "special" about it except its field, which remains composed exclusively of professional golfers.

A final liability in recent years has been the quality of the courses on which the PGA has played. Certainly, the tournament has been contested on some fine and venerable sites, such as Oakmont, Oakland Hills, and Riviera. But it has also been held at a number of questionable venues—new and unproved courses without the breeding and tradition expected of a major championship venue.

Despite its image problems, however, the PGA will surely retain its status as one of golf's four major championships, if for no other reason than that it is one of the four tournaments the world's best players most want to win. Arnold Palmer strove for decades to add a PGA crown to his titles in The Masters, U.S. Open, and British Open, and as Tom Watson approaches age 50, he, too, thirsts after a PGA Championship to complete his conquest of the modern grand slam.

16th at Cherry Hills

Practical Matters

FOR TICKET INFORMATION
The PGA of America
P.O. Box 109601
Palm Beach Gardens, FL 33418

Local Knowledge

THE HEAT OF COMPETITION

Anyone who has watched a few PGA Championships on television knows that this tournament gives new meaning to "the heat of competition." Here's what the players do, and what you should do when the heat is on.

Keep dry: Carry a towel to mop up perspiration, particularly on your hands. It's also smart to take your glove off between shots so that it won't become slippery. An extra glove for the back nine will give you confidence the minute you slip it on.

Keep cool: Wear light-colored, loose-fitting clothing, and by all means wear a hat, both for shade and to reduce the risk of getting skin cancer.

Keep hydrated: Don't pass up any water fountains, and if you're on a course where the opportunities are few and far between, consider taking along some bottled water of your own. One good trick to keep it cold is to freeze the water overnight, so it begins the day as a solid block of ice, then melts into cold water as you play.

As far as playing strategy, remember that your muscles will be loose and elastic, the ball will be warm and resilient, and the ground will likely be hard and dry. These factors combine to suggest two things: You won't need to swing hard to get plenty of distance, and you won't need as much club as on a cool day.

The Ryder Cup

VARIOUS COURSES

Professional golf has only four major championships. The Ryder Cup is not one of them—it is something different entirely and, in the minds of a growing majority, something better.

Why better? Because the Ryder Cup is an event for teams, not individuals; because it's contested at match play, not medal; because it's staged not annually but every two years; and most important, because it is played not for money but for national pride. During the past two decades, in particular, this has been

Above: One of the most potent partnerships in the Ryder Cup—Seve Ballesteros and José Maria Olazabal—celebrate a victory

Right: Bernard Langer misses a putt to hand over victory to the American team during the 1991 competition at Kiawah Island

What to Watch For . . .

FIRST-TEE JITTERS

Even the most hardened PGA Tour pro will admit to sweaty palms and shaky knees before the opening tee shot in a Ryder Cup. It may have something to do with the introduction: "Now playing for the United States of America . . ."

UNIFORMS

This is the one week in the year when the big-name stars do not honor their apparel-endorsement contracts. The Ryder Cup Team is outfitted with a half dozen or so changes of clothing—some more tasteful than others—and a week-long dress code, so that on each day all team members look exactly the same. The only concession: Payne Stewart gets to wear plus-fours.

WIFE PACKS

It's easy to spot the American players' wives. Like their husbands, they're decked out in matching (usually red-white-and-blue) windbreakers, and when play is in progress they tend to walk the sidelines in groups, for moral support.

GIMMES

This is the only major event in golf where you see a player pick up his ball before putting out. In match play, you may concede your opponent his putt if it's clear that the hole has been decided. The most famous (and controversial) such incident was in 1969 at Royal Birkdale, when Jack Nicklaus graciously conceded Tony Jacklin a three-footer on the final hole of the final singles match, enabling that Ryder Cup to be halved.

Jack Fell Down, But We Kept the Crown

Brian Barnes pulled off a shocker when he defeated Jack Nicklaus twice in one day during the 1975 Ryder Cup Matches for the Great Britain and Ireland team. Barnes won the morning match by a 4 and 2 margin, then took the afternoon match, 2 and 1 — this in a year when Nicklaus had won two major championships. Nonetheless, the United States won handily, 21–11, at Laurel Valley CC in Ligonier, Pa.

the hottest event in golf.

It's unlikely that British seed merchant Samuel Ryder envisioned the current level of international interest when, in 1927, he commissioned a small gold trophy and spearheaded the first Ryder Cup Match, in Worcester, Massachusetts. That encounter was expected to be a rout. A year earlier, in the exhibition match that was Ryder's inspiration, the Brits had drubbed a team of visiting Americans, 13½ to 1½, and they came to America expecting to repeat. Well, the match was indeed a rout—9½ to 2½—but the victors were the Yanks, and their one-sided triumph ignited 60 years of Ryder Cup domination by America. Although Great Britain & Ireland won the return Matches in 1929 and traded victories over the next two encounters, they would take the Cup only one more time in the ensuing half century.

The Brits kept a stiff upper lip. However, on the U.S. side, the biennial slaughters became so routine that both players and fans lost interest in the Matches. By the 1970s, it was clear something had to be done. That something came from Jack Nicklaus, who suggested that the British side expand to include all of Europe (including the charismatic Spaniard Seve Ballesteros, then the best player outside the United States).

The change took effect in 1979, and it wrought the desired result—a rebirth of competitiveness from across the pond. In the five Matches since 1985, two have been won by Great Britain and Europe, two by the U.S., and one has been tied, with each encounter a neck-and-neck race to the finish. In 1987, the Americans lost for the first time ever on U.S. soil. Appropriately, perhaps, the site was Muirfield Village in Ohio, the course built by Jack Nicklaus.

More important, the highly competitive foreign teams, led by Ballesteros and his world-class comrades Nick Faldo, Bernhard Langer, Sandy Lyle, José Maria Olazabal, and Ian Woosnam—have rekindled America's nationalistic interest to the point that the Ryder Cup is second

Right: Christy O'Conner's victory putt during the 1989 Ryder Cup at The Belfry

Far right: British fans display their colors

What to Watch For . . .

ROVING CAPTAINS
The guy ripping around the course in a golf car with a walkie-talkie in his hand and a look of apprehension on his face is the Ryder Cup captain. Frankly, once play begins there's not much he can do, and with up to 12 matches in progress simultaneously he'd get a better grip on things by camping in the TV production trailer and watching the monitors. But that, as the Brits say, would be poor-class stuff.

THE GOLDEN ABE
The Ryder Cup trophy is cast in gold and the figure on the top is a depiction of British professional Abe Mitchell, a close friend of Samuel Ryder.

CHAUVINISM
The look, feel, and sound of a Ryder Cup gallery is unlike any other in golf. Miniature British and American flags are waved everywhere; throaty, partisan roars of approval greet not only good shots by the good guys but bad shots by the bad guys; and rabid nationalism occasionally rears its ugly head. Says Peter Allis: "When I beat Arnold Palmer at Atlanta in 1963, I thought I was going to get lynched."

INSCRUTABLE SCOREBOARDS
Back in the days when America routinely throttled the Brits, keeping score was not much of an issue. These days, however, you have to stay on top of the scoreboards, and since this is match play, it can be tricky, especially on Sunday when a dozen matches are in simultaneous progress. The TV folks help viewers sort things out, but if you're on site—particularly overseas—reading one of the "monsterboards" can be like trying to translate the Koran.

Local Knowledge

MATCH-PLAY TACTICS

Match play is of course the format under which most weekend golf is played. Each hole becomes the scene of a minibattle between two opponents.

Match-play strategy becomes tricky, especially when you're playing a big match such as a club championship. You don't want to become obsessed with what your opponent is doing, and yet you shouldn't ignore him. Ideally, it's best to play your game and play the course, but in some instances that's foolish. For example, if your opponent has made a birdie on a hole and you face a 60-foot putt to tie him, there's no point in lagging up close for a par. Here are some general strategies:

When you're ahead in a match, don't let up. Keep hitting the best shots you can until the match is over. Don't be conservative unless that is your nature and a conservative game is what got you on top. Above all, don't get ahead of yourself, daydreaming about your next opponent or your acceptance speech. Keep concentrating on one shot at a time.

When you're behind, don't panic, especially if it's early in the match. Stick to your game plan—don't go for hero shots. Stay calm, stay focused, and don't act as if you've already lost. Looking strong when you're down can rattle your opponent as he wonders what it takes to shake you. Above all, keep a positive frame of mind, because good things rarely happen until you think they will.

only to The Masters as the most coveted ticket in golf. Since the venues for the Matches alternate between the U.S. and Europe, they are played here only once in four years. Tickets for the 1995 Matches at Oak Hill in Rochester sold out within hours of becoming available.

Today's PGA Tour players regard membership on the Ryder Cup Team as tantamount to victory in a major championship. They earn their berths according to a point system established by the PGA of America, which runs the Matches. Points are awarded for finishes within the top ten places of PGA Tour events and the four major championships over the 24-month period preceding the Matches. (Tour events in the year immediately preceding the Ryder Cup are worth twice the points of events played two years before the Matches, and the four majors are weighted more heavily than regular tournaments.)

The top 10 point earners make the 12-man team, with the last two team members chosen by the captain, a respected veteran player appointed by the PGA. The European Team is determined in a similar way, according to points won on the European PGA Tour, with the difference that nine players earn their way and three are chosen by the captain.

The Matches run for three days, with a total of 28 points available (one point awarded for each match won, a half point for ties). On the first and second days, two-man teams square off, playing foursomes (partners hitting alternate shots on the same ball) in the morning and four-ball matches (on each hole, the lower score of the two partners counts) in the afternoon. With a total of eight matches each day, 16 points are decided before Sunday, when the two teams go at each other in a series of 12 singles matches for the last dozen points.

The victorious U.S. team at Kiawah Island in 1991

Practical Matters

FOR TICKET INFORMATION
The PGA of America
P.O. Box 109601
Palm Beach Gardens, FL 33408

LPGA Tour Events, Senior PGA Tour Events, & the U.S. Amateur

Nabisco Dinah Shore

MISSION HILLS COUNTRY CLUB

Ask a hundred golf fans to name an event on the LPGA Tour, and it's a safe bet that at least 80 of them will say "The Nabisco Dinah Shore."

Why? Consistency. As other tournaments—even major tournaments—have changed names, sponsors, dates, and courses, this one has remained constant and strong.

Since its beginning in 1972, the Dinah has been played each spring at the same golf course—the Mission Hills Country Club in Rancho Mirage, California—where the Tour brings together its top players, those who have gained a first, second, or third-place finish in the previous year. As such, it has become sort of a distaff Masters, the LPGA's annual rite of spring.

There have been only two sponsors—and they've been major ones. For its first ten years, the tournament was called the Colgate Dinah Shore Winners Circle, as then Colgate chairman David Foster poured millions of dollars into the LPGA in general and this event in particular. Then, in 1982, another golf-addicted CEO, RJR/Nabisco's Ross Johnson, stepped in and bankrolled the event. In a very visible corporate takeover, Johnson's company was conquered and divided and he was deposed—but Nabisco's commitment to the Dinah Shore has continued.

Above all, however, the key to this event has been the enduring presence of Dinah herself. More than the titular host, Dinah Shore was an integral part of the tournament. When her name went on the event, she learned the game well enough to play without disgrace in the annual pro-am. She worked hard with the sponsors, tournament organizers, and volunteers, and she became a close friend of dozens of LPGA players. Her death in 1994 was unquestionably a loss to the tournament, but to the golf world she left this major championship as her lasting legacy. This is one tournament that every LPGA player wants desperately to win.

Previous pages: 5th hole at Mission Hills

Right: 16th hole

What to Watch For . . .

A FINISH WITH A FLOURISH

The final hole is a reachable par five, but water fronts the green. Powerful players such as Laura Davies and Michelle McGann can reach this green in two, but almost everyone ends up with a wedge in hand for the third shot and then a makable birdie putt. Sometimes that birdie is needed for victory, as was the case in 1994, when Donna Andrews made a finishing 4 to edge Laura Davies by a stroke.

CELEBRATORY AQUATICS

Champions have been known to baptize their victories with a quick dip in the pond at 18. The most memorable of these came in 1991, when Amy Alcott set the tournament record of 15 under par and then joined hands with her caddie and Ms. Shore as the three of them jumped into the drink.

HOLLYWOOD TYPES

Without question, the Dinah has the glitziest pro-am in women's golf. It runs for two days and is played over two courses (the Palmer course at Mission Hills as well as the Old Course—now known as the Dinah Shore Tournament Course). The star power may not rank with the Bob Hope or the AT&T Pebble Beach Pro-Am (the big names here tend to be guys like Joe Garagiola and Dennis James), but dozens of semicelebrities show up each year. The tournament telecast usually includes a quick recap of their best and worst moments.

AMATEURS

Part of the Masters feeling comes from the amateur contingent that is annually included in the field. Only a handful take part, but that's a handful more than at just about any other LPGA event.

Practical Matters

FOR TICKET INFORMATION
Nabisco Dinah Shore
2 Racquet Club Drive
Rancho Mirage, CA 92270

U.S. Women's Open

VARIOUS COURSES

The oldest and most prestigious of the four women's major championships, the U.S. Women's Open began in 1946. Back then, it was conducted not by the USGA but by the fledgling Women's Professional Golfers Association.

Why was there no Women's Open before this time? Essentially, because there were no women professional golfers. Prior to World War II, the top players such as Patty Berg and Babe Zaharias competed as amateurs. But in that same year—1946—they formed the WPGA, and one of their premier events was the Women's Open. By 1949, however, the WPGA had been reformed as the Ladies Professional Golf Association, and in 1953 the LPGA had the wisdom to turn over the reins of the Open to the USGA.

Today, typical of the USGA's other national championships, it is the hardest of all tournaments to win. In contrast to the slowish greens the women face week in and week out, Open greens are groomed to roll at close to 10 on the Stimpmeter. The rough, while not as long and thick as for a men's Open, is longer and thicker than virtually anything the ladies see all year, and the typical Open course is also appreciably longer than those on the LPGA Tour. Until relatively recently, a four-round score of 300 was a number well earned.

The Open field numbers 150 players, about 60 of whom earn their way through their performance on the LPGA Tour. The other 90 spots are determined through sectional qualifying held at ten sites across the country. Since this is truly an Open championship, qualifying is open to any woman professional and any woman amateur with a USGA Handicap Index of 4.4 or less. In a typical year, the USGA receives close to a thousand entries for the qualifying process.

Not surprisingly, many of the names on this trophy belong to Hall of Famers, beginning with Berg and Zaharias and including Betsy Rawls, Louise Suggs, Mickey Wright (who won a record four Opens), Sandra Haynie, JoAnne Carner, Carol Mann, Pat Bradley, and Patty Sheehan.

What to Watch For . . .

JOHNNY MILLER & CO.

The Women's Open doesn't generate big television ratings, but when NBC wrested from ABC the rights to televise the lucrative U.S. Open, the Women's Open was part of the package. Thus, it gets the full treatment—all the cameras, anchormen, foot soldiers, and extended coverage—just like the men's championship.

LONG-IRON SHOTS

Most LPGA tournaments are played on courses that measure barely 6000 yards. At the Women's Open, however, the site typically stretches to at least 6300 yards or more. As a result, middle-length hitters find themselves playing lots of 3- and 4-iron approaches to par fours.

A SOFT SPOT

The USGA's sense of tradition asserts itself in the form of special invitations to compete. Typically, these are granted to former Open champions unwilling or unable to qualify.

SIDESHOWS

To boost attendance at the championship, the USGA has allowed several recent sites to set up a tented village in which golfers may test-hit golf clubs and sample a variety of products, golf-related and otherwise.

10th hole at Witch Hollow Course, Pumpkin Ridge Golf Club

Practical Matters

FOR TICKET INFORMATION

The USGA
Golf House
P.O. Box 708
Far Hills, NJ 07931

McDonald's LPGA Championship

Du Pont Country Club

The second oldest tournament on the LPGA Tour (after the U.S. Women's Open), the McDonald's LPGA Championship dates back to 1955, a decade after Patty Berg, Babe Zaharias & Co. started the women's tour. Patty and the Babe never won the LPGA, but virtually every other important women's player has taken this title. Mickey Wright won it four times between 1958 and 1963, and she has been joined by fellow Hall of Famers Louise Suggs, Betsy Rawls, Sandra Haynie, Kathy Whitworth, JoAnne Carner, Nancy Lopez, Pat Bradley, and Patty Sheehan.

In 1987, with the burgeoning Senior PGA Tour putting increasing pressure on the LPGA to compete for tournament sponsors, the association "sold" its flagship event and the LPGA Championship became the Mazda LPGA Championship until 1994, when McDonald's took over title sponsorship. McDonald's had been the sponsor of one of the most successful events on the women's tour—the McDonald's Championship at the Du Pont Country Club in Wilmington, Delaware—and they agreed to drop that event and bring the McDonald's LPGA Championship to Wilmington for an extended stay.

Extended stays have been the history of this event, which embraces neither a permanent home (like the Nabisco Dinah Shore) nor a yearly change of venue (like the

Betsy King

Women's Open). The LPGA Championship has had two runs at a pair of current PGA Tour sites (six years at the Las Vegas Country Club and seven years at Pleasant Valley Country Club), and throughout the 1980s it was at the Jack Nicklaus Golf Center in Kings Island, Ohio.

At Wilmington, however, they have a strong course, an efficient tournament administration headed by Executive Director (and 1959 LPGA Champion) Betsy Rawls, and ardent support from the local community, which is dedicated to the McDonald's Children's Charities. In this case, perhaps because of (rather than despite) corporate involvement, continued major championship status seems assured.

What to Watch For . . .

BIG MACS

Not surprisingly at a tournament whose name begins with McDonald's, the main concession stand is a "Mini-Mac," a mobile fast-food vendor where the number-one offering is two all-beef patties/special sauce/lettuce/cheese/pickles/onions on a sesame-seed bun.

CHEMISTS

Wilmington is headquarters to the Du Pont chemical company, and the Du Pont Country Club was founded as a recreational outlet for the plant workers, which it remains to this day, with over 8000 members, all of them employees or former employees. During LPGA week, the chemists give up their vacation days to work as tournament volunteers.

TOUGH FINISHES

The hardest hole at Du Pont is the last one, a lengthy par four that takes a hard left turn and moves uphill for the second shot. Look for the longer hitters to shine on this one as even the medium-length women have difficulty approaching this green.

Practical Matters

FOR TICKET INFORMATION
McDonald's LPGA Championship
P.O. Box 394
Rockland, DE 19732

du Maurier Classic

VARIOUS COURSES

The LPGA, like the Senior PGA Tour, has chosen to designate four tournaments as its major championships. Also like the Senior Tour, two of those events are unquestionably deserving of major status (the LPGA and the U.S. Women's Open are equivalent to the PGA Senior Championship and the U.S. Senior Open). However, just as the seniors' two other "majors," The Tradition and the Senior Players Championship, are lacking in patina and panache, so is the du Maurier missing something on the LPGA Tour. This is the ladies' fourth major, not just on the calendar but in the public mind.

Beyond the fact that the whole notion of "designating" majors is spurious, there is the whole question of whether a major championship can have a commercial sponsor (particularly a tobacco company). Major championship status evolves, it isn't decreed, and it evolves from the support of the players, press, and fans, not from a corporate promotion budget.

That having been said, the du Maurier is undeniably a significant tournament. For one thing, it is the only regular-season LPGA event that takes place outside the United States. This lends it an exotic difference, arguably akin to the British Open on the men's Tour. For another, it boasts a list of past champions that is as impressive as any: JoAnne Carner, Donna Caponi, Judy Rankin, Amy Alcott, Pat Bradley, Jan Stephenson, Sandra Haynie, Hollis Stacy, and Juli Inkster. Finally, like the Women's Open, the du Maurier changes its venue every year and has stopped at a collection of impressive courses in Canada. The field of players is annually among the two or three strongest of the year, and many players rank it alongside the Nabisco Dinah Shore (the LPGA's other quasi major) as the best-run event of the year.

Nancy Lopez

What to Watch For . . .

A FULL WEEK
Those who attend this event can expect seven days of action. Monday features a pro-am for women only; on Tuesday there's a free instruction clinic given by the LPGA players; Wednesday is the traditional pro-am, and the tournament runs from Thursday through Sunday.

CANADIANS
Each year, three Canadian players earn their way into the field by finishing in the top three places in "The du Maurier Series," a mini-tour of five events played throughout Canada.

FRANGLAIS
The du Maurier moves all across Canada, but about a third of the time it's played in the Montreal area, and in those years the French influence is pervasive. Players are announced at the first tee in two languages, and all printed information is in French as well as English.

SOLHEIM SENSITIVITY
This is the last tournament of the year in which American players may earn triple points in qualifying for the Solheim Cup Team. As such, in even-numbered years, the point race becomes a major subplot to the tournament.

MADEMOISELLE JOCELYNE
In its inaugural year (1973) the tournament was known as La Canadienne—and it was won by a Canadienne, Jocelyne Bourassa, who took the title at the Montreal Golf Club in her native city. Today, Bourassa is retired as a player but works full time as the Executive Director of the du Maurier.

Practical Matters

FOR TICKET INFORMATION
LPGA
2570 W. International Speedway Blvd.
Suite B
Daytona Beach, FL 32114-1118

JAL Big Apple Classic

WYKAGYL COUNTRY CLUB

Ask the LPGA players to name their favorite course on the Tour, and it's a cinch that one name will lead the list: a charmer in New York's Westchester County named Wykagyl.

That's pronounced "WIKE-a-gill," and don't ask what it means because nobody's quite sure. One guess is that the fellow who was put in charge of finding a name, a Mr. William K. Gillett, simply made creative use of his own initials. Another guess is that it's an Indian word, like Siwanoy and Mahopac, two other courses in the area. And then there are those who swear Wykagyl came from the original Dutch settlers.

Whatever its derivation, Wykagyl means great golf course to the LPGA players, and the JAL Big Apple Classic annually draws one of the strongest fields on the women's tour. This is a shotmaker's course, a par 71 of 6095 yards whose treelined fairways wend up and down hills to small, fast-rolling greens. It is a course that has been fine-tuned by both Donald Ross and A. W. Tillinghast, a course that puts a premium on position play and patience, and that makes it the perfect tune-up for the U.S. Women's Open, which follows it by one week on the LPGA schedule.

With each passing year, however, the Big Apple Classic adds to its own aura of prestige. This is the only women's tournament in the

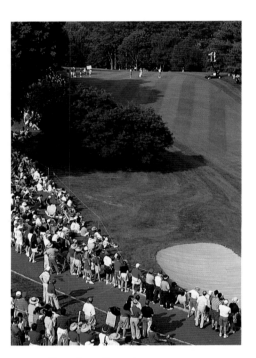

Crowds gather at the 18th hole

New York area, America's media and advertising capital, so it's an important place for a woman to be noticed. It's also one of the few LPGA events that enjoys network TV coverage, and even better, there's no direct head-to-head competition from the men's Tour since the Big Apple runs the week of the British Open, which airs live in the U.S. during the morning hours.

Moreover, those who win on this golf course join a list of champions that reads like the Who's Who of Women's Golf: Pat Bradley, JoAnne Carner, Beth Daniel (twice), Julie Inkster, Betsy King (twice), and Nancy Lopez (twice).

What to Watch For . . .

FLIP-FLOPPED NINES
The front and back nines at Wykagyl are reversed so that the tournament can end on the short par five that plays to an amphitheater green at the back steps of the clubhouse. Since the hole is reachable to the longer hitters, the winning putt is almost invariably for a birdie.

THE TOUR'S LONGEST 3
The 7th hole is a 223-yard brute that is the longest par-three hole on the LPGA Tour. All of the lady pros need woods, and some of them can't reach the green. (Wykagyl's women members play it as a par four.) However, one male who has managed to subdue it is Cincinnati Bengals coach Bruce Coslet, who aced it with a 4-wood during the pro-am in 1993.

THE TOUR'S FASTEST 3
The green at the 157-yard 16th hole slopes fiercely from back to front and is usually shaved to lightning speed. At this hole, three putting is not a possibility, it's an achievement.

FOREIGN FLAIR
GOLF Magazine, the presenting sponsor and organizer of this event, has worked hard to position the Big Apple as the "fifth major championship" on the LPGA Tour, and a major part of that effort has been to promote this as the year's most international field.

Practical Matters

FOR TICKET INFORMATION
Big Apple Classic
GOLF Magazine
2 Park Avenue
New York, NY 10022

The Tradition

THE GOLF CLUB AT DESERT MOUNTAIN
[COCHISE COURSE]

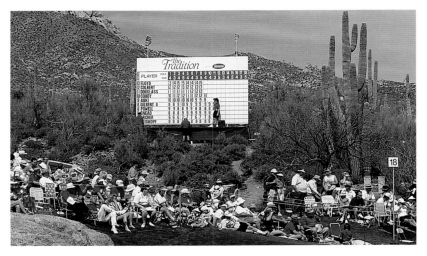

18th hole

Money can't buy immortality, but it surely can attract golf's immortals. For proof, consider The Tradition.

This tournament is the brainchild of real estate developer Lyle Anderson, a shrewd businessman who also has a genuine love and respect for the game of golf. A few years after he'd developed Desert Mountain, a three-course resort community near Scottsdale, Arizona, Anderson conceived the idea of a special senior event, both to promote his property and to honor the great players of the past. He called it The Tradition, and it was an instant hit.

One key was Anderson's ingenious generosity: He invited all the living past Masters, U.S. Open, British Open, and PGA Champions to come and enjoy the tournament as his guests, whether they competed or not. In 1989, the convocation of legends at Anderson's $13 million clubhouse was enough to give the inaugural staging of this event instant panache. A year later, when Jack Nicklaus won the tournament in his debut as a senior golfer and then returned to defend successfully in 1991, coming from an incredible 12 strokes back in the last two rounds, The Tradition actually had a bit of tradition.

Not long thereafter, Commissioner Deane Beman summarily designated it one of the four major championships on the Senior Tour. Most of the golf press scoffed at this status-by-decree, and not even Anderson would argue that his event ranks in prestige with the PGA Seniors' Championship or the U.S. Senior Open, but The Tradition's status seems in place. Certainly, the seniors have a reverence for this tournament—and the way it treats them—and if one factor influences the status of an event, it is the collective opinion of the competitors.

What to Watch For . . .

THE BEAR
It's a safe bet you'll see Jack Nicklaus playing this event as long as he can swing a club, and loyalty will have nothing to do with the fact that he has won the tournament thrice. Nicklaus is a close friend and the preferred golf course architect of Lyle Anderson. He designed all three courses at Desert Mountain.

SAM PARKS AND DOW FINSTERWALD
This is the only tournament where you're apt to shake hands consecutively with the winner of the 1936 U.S. Open, the 1958 PGA, or a score or so other near-ancient major champions who attend the tournament each year as noncompeting invitees.

PERFECT WEATHER
The Scottsdale area is one of the driest parts of the country, with barely seven inches of rain per year; in early April the mercury stays well below the 100-plus summer levels for which Arizona is notorious.

Practical Matters

FOR TICKET INFORMATION
The Golf Club at
Desert Mountain
10333 Rockaway Hills
Scottsdale, AZ 85262

PGA Seniors' Championship

PGA NATIONAL GOLF CLUB
[CHAMPION COURSE]

The oldest major championship on the senior circuit, the PGA Seniors' started not with a professional but with the game's greatest amateur, Bobby Jones.

Back in 1937, Jones suggested that a championship be started for the PGA professionals over the age of 50, to give the older guys a chance to compete with their peers. To show he was serious, Jones offered the Augusta National Golf Club as the site. And so the PGA Seniors' was born, with a total purse of $2000.

It stayed in Augusta for two years,

and then moved to Florida, where it has remained ever since. Most recently it has been held at the Champion Course of the PGA National Golf Club in Palm Beach Gardens, site of the 1983 Ryder Cup Matches and the 1987 PGA Championship.

The tournament was a 54-hole event until 1958, when it went to four rounds. In that year, Gene Sarazen took the trophy, and he has been followed by the likes of Sam Snead, Arnold Palmer, Gary Player, Jack Nicklaus, and Lee Trevino. Today, along with the U.S. Senior Open, this is the most coveted victory in senior golf. It was during this championship, in 1979, that talks began on the notion of developing a series of events for senior golfers, and the following year the Senior PGA Tour began.

17th hole

What to Watch For . . .

THE BEAR TRAP
The Champion Course was originally designed by Tom Fazio, but in 1990 Jack Nicklaus came in and stiffened the challenge. The Bear Trap refers to the water-logged stretch of holes from 15 through 17, where more than one championship has been lost.

GATORS
Like most courses in southern Florida, PGA National has its share of swamp denizens with long tails and sharp teeth. People are not in danger, but small dogs should be kept out of range.

THE PGA OF AMERICA
The group that conducts this championship is the PGA of America, the organization of 23,000 club pros and apprentices that also runs the PGA Championship and the Ryder Cup Matches. Their national headquarters are hard by the tournament site.

SAM'S HI-LO
Sam Snead has the distinction of having won this event with both the lowest and highest total scores. In 1970 he took this title at 290, two under par, and three years later on the same course he won with a total of 268, 22 strokes lower. The durable Snead won this title a record six times.

ROOKIES
On the Senior circuit, youth is a big advantage. Nearly a third of the time, the PGA Seniors' Championship has been won by a 50-year-old making his first appearance.

Practical Matters

FOR TICKET INFORMATION
The PGA of America
100 Avenue of the Champions
Box 109601
Palm Beach Gardens, FL 33410-9601

Ford Senior Players Championship

TPC OF MICHIGAN

Although the Senior PGA Tour began in 1980, it didn't reach full throttle until 1983, when 18 tournaments were added. Corporate sponsors suddenly had sensed the good business of bringing their clients together for pro-ams and schmoozing with the golf greats those clients had worshiped for years.

One of the more prominent of those 18 events was the Senior Players Championship, a tournament conceived and conducted by the PGA Tour itself and modeled after the successful Players Championship on the regular Tour.

To insure the event received proper attention, the Tour put up a purse of $750,000 (then one of the highest in senior golf) and staged the event at Canterbury Country Club in Cleveland, Ohio. This is one of *GOLF Magazine*'s Top 100 Courses in the World and site of the 1973 PGA Championship, won by Jack Nicklaus.

The first Senior Players Championship was won by Miller Barber, at that time the best player on the over-50 circuit. In subsequent years the tournament gained luster as Arnold Palmer, Chi Chi Rodriguez, Gary Player, Billy Casper, and Jack Nicklaus marched into the victory circle.

In 1991, the Tour unveiled the TPC of Michigan and brought the Championship there, now with a total purse of more than a million dollars. The course is a Jack Nicklaus design, and at 6876 yards from the back tees it is one of the longest tests on the Senior Tour. However, its bentgrass fairways and greens usually are in perfect condition, and winning scores here have averaged ten under par.

What to Watch For . . .

A TOUGH FINISH

Number 18 annually ranks as one of the two or three most difficult finishing holes on the Senior Tour. A par four of 417 yards, the tee shot must thread between a creek on the left and a tree that blocks any approach from the right. Another tough test is number 14, a 429-yard brute that taxes the old pros, who play it in an average score of about 4.5 strokes.

JEKYLL & HYDE NINES

The front nine of this course is parkland in nature, flat and treelined in the manner of many courses in the Midwest. But the back nine takes on the look of the TPC chain of spectators' courses, its relatively open holes cradled by gallery mounds to enhance viewing.

WATER

More than a dozen lakes, creeks, and marshes dot this course and come into play on ten of the holes. In the center of the lake at 17, however, is a brand-new Ford for anyone who can make a hole in one.

8th hole

Practical Matters

FOR TICKET INFORMATION

The TPC of Michigan
One Nicklaus Drive
Dearborn, MI 48120

U.S. Senior Open

VARIOUS COURSES

The U.S. Senior Open was held for the first time in 1980—and no one came to see it. Here it was, the first and only national championship for the Grecian Formula set, unfolding at venerable Winged Foot Country Club, in Mamaroneck, New York—less than an hour from the world's most exciting city—and no one seemed to care. Barely 500 people came through the turnstiles that week as the colorful Argentinian Roberto DeVicenzo took a four-stroke victory over longtime amateur star and soon-to-be USGA President Bill Campbell.

Why was there no interest? Two reasons. First, the PGA Senior Tour had barely cut its teeth. America—particularly corporate America—didn't yet appreciate what had been wrought by giving these aging stars a mulligan on their careers. Second, the USGA had made the tactical error of defining a senior golfer as anyone age 55 or over, whereas the PGA Tour had opted to set the cutoff at age 50.

The next year the USGA lowered the age to 50—and that just happened to coincide with the year Arnold Palmer became eligible. At Oakland Hills in 1981, Arnold showed, the fans showed, Arnold won, and the Senior Open suddenly took flight. Today, it is the most prestigious title in senior golf, not to mention a huge source of revenue for the USGA.

Whereas in 1980 only 631 men entered the qualifying process, current entries run well over two thousand.

Following Palmer into the victory circle have been the three best players of the Palmer and post-Palmer era: Jack Nicklaus (twice), Gary Player (twice), and Lee Trevino, each of them winning in dramatic fashion, in a playoff. Player in fact likes to include his wins here in his total victories in the four men's major championships.

The cream tends to rise to the top because the Senior Open—like the U.S. Open—is played on testing courses that have been groomed and toughened to standards set by the USGA, standards intended to separate the best from the rest.

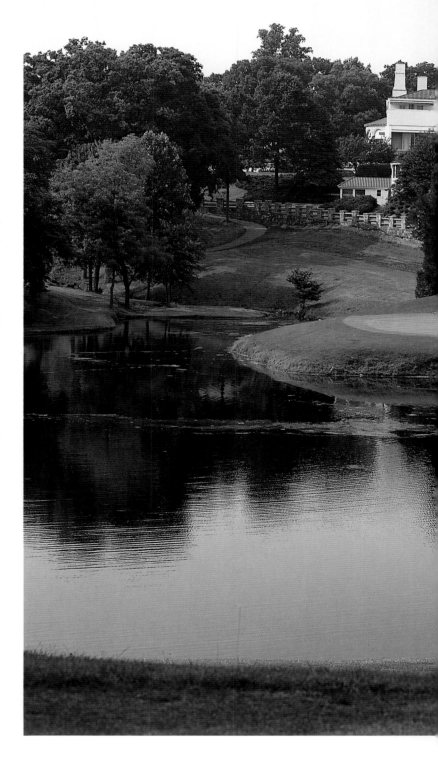

18th hole at Congressional Country Club, Bethesda, Maryland

What to Watch For . . .

LIMPING AND WHEEZING
This is the only Senior event where "automotive transportation is not permissible" during the competition. So don't be surprised if, by Sunday afternoon, a few of the older guys start showing their fatigue.

AMATEURS
The Senior Open is just that—open to any professional age 50 or older and any amateurs with a USGA Handicap Index of 5.4 or less. Each year dozens of amateurs survive the sectional qualifying rounds to make the final field of 156 players.

BENTGRASS
The USGA has a bias toward courses with bentgrass greens. This means that few courses south of the Mason-Dixon line will host national championships.

OPEN TRYOUTS
In recent years, the USGA has awarded the Senior Open to courses slated to hold the big show—the U.S. Open—a few years later. Examples include Pinehurst #2 (Senior in 1994, Open in 1999) and Congressional Country Club (Senior in 1995, Open in 1997).

MEDALS
In addition to the trophy for first prize, the champion is awarded a gold medal. The low amateur also gets a gold medal, the second-low amateur gets a silver, and any amateur who finishes 72 holes gets a bronze.

18-HOLE PLAYOFFS
As is the case with the U.S. Open, a tie for first place after 72 holes is settled with an 18-hole playoff on Monday. If a tie remains after that, the players go into sudden death until a winner emerges.

Practical Matters

FOR TICKET INFORMATION
The USGA
Golf House
P.O. Box 708
Far Hills, NJ 07931

U.S. Amateur Championship

VARIOUS COURSES

The oldest golf tournament in the United States is not the U.S. Open—it's the U.S. Amateur—by one day. The first Amateur and Open were played the same week of October, 1895, at the Newport Country Club in Rhode Island. In those days, however, the Amateur took precedence, both chronologically and in the minds of America's pilgrim golfers.

The tournament came into being as a result of a complaint lodged by the imperious Charles B. Macdonald. One of the driving forces of early golf in America, Macdonald had been the victim of narrow defeats in two invitational tournaments played in 1894—one at Newport and the other at the St. Andrew's Golf Club near Yonkers, N.Y.—and each of those clubs had proclaimed its winner the national champion. Macdonald led a storm of opposition, and called for an organizing body to conduct a true national championship.

The result was the formation of the United States Golf Association. In its first full year of operation, the USGA brought the Amateur Championship to Newport, where an immensely gratified Macdonald became the champion.

Back then, barely 100 American golf clubs existed, most of them on the East Coast, and for the gentlemen golfers who belonged to them, the U.S. Amateur was an event of great importance. (There was no such thing as organized professional golf, and most of the club pros were émigrés from Scotland and England who were expected to teach the game, tend the greens, and stay out of the way.)

The U.S. Amateur continued to grow in prominence throughout the first third of the 20th century as it became the ultimate stage for Bobby Jones, who took the title a record five times in seven years and in 1930 added it to his victories in the British Amateur and U.S. and British Opens to complete the Grand Slam.

But Jones retired later that year, and in the wake of the Depression, America's best gentleman golfers were finding themselves in need of work. More and more of them turned pro, and the U.S. Amateur began to lose its luster.

During the last half century, Arnold Palmer and Jack Nicklaus have added their names to the Havemeyer Trophy. It is still the most prestigious victory in amateur golf, but no one refers to it as a major championship.

The tournament is open to any amateur with a USGA Handicap Index of 3.4 or less. Each year over 5000 men subject themselves to 36 holes of sectional qualifying, scheduled at more than 70 sites throughout the country. This pares the field to 312 players who convene at the championship site for another hurdle—36 holes of stroke play from which the low 64 scorers emerge and move into match play. To become the champion, a player must win five straight 18-hole matches and then a 36-hole final.

17th hole at Pumpkin Ridge

What to Watch For . . .

SHORTS
Anyone watching this tournament for the first time will be startled to see that 90 percent of the competitors wear shorts. The long-pants-only dress code that prevails on the PGA Tour and in the U.S. Open does not apply here.

MASTERS TALK
The biggest perk the U.S. Amateur champion gets is an invitation to play at Augusta the following year.

COLLEGE KIDS
In contrast to the early days, when men in their 20s, 30s, and 40s dominated this event, most U.S. Amateur Champions of the modern era have been collegiate golfers en route to the PGA Tour. In fact, such was the dominance by the kids that in 1981 the USGA inaugurated a Mid-Amateur Championship, restricted to players 25 and older, to give post-college amateurs a chance for a national title.

LOGOLESSNESS
Although the USGA has no qualms about selling $150,000 corporate hospitality tents at their Open championship, they have an aversion toward commercialism at the Amateur championship, where no one plays for pay. In fact, when it comes down to the televised semifinal and final rounds, USGA officials have been known to remove the hats of players whose visors say "Titleist."

NOT MUCH SUSPENSE
Since the final match goes 36 holes, it's rarely a photo finish. Since 1980, the average victory margin has been 5-and-4, victory coming by the 14th green of the afternoon round.

Practical Matters

FOR TICKET INFORMATION
The USGA
Golf House
P.O. Box 708
Far Hills, NJ 07931

Volvo PGA Championship

WENTWORTH
[WEST COURSE]

What the Players Championship is to American professional golf, the Volvo PGA is to the European pro tour. Each year, the Tour invites all of its pros to a spectacular golf course alongside the Tour's headquarters for a springtime shootout that is tantamount to a major championship.

This event always concludes on the last weekend in May—in Britain it's known as the Whitsun bank holiday—a big sports weekend that marks the traditional transition from winter to summer. In fact, since this is a three-day weekend, the tournament begins on Friday and ends on Monday. It is also one of the few tournaments where the British television coverage extends to all four rounds.

The tournament began in 1955, and for the first dozen years entry was restricted to pros from the United Kingdom and Ireland. Now, however, it boasts the strongest field of the European year. Every major player shows up, and many of the best have won: Jacklin, Faldo, Langer, Ballesteros, and Woosnam. And in 1975, this event was won by a 45-year-old Arnold Palmer, the last important victory of Arnie's career. Since 1984, the tournament has been played at the West Course of venerable Wentworth, a heavily wooded heathland layout designed by H. S.

THE TV HOLES

Expect birdies:
11, 12, 18

Expect bogeys:
15

Colt, the man who fashioned Pine Valley.

Its first hole—a 471-yard par four that plays through two heather-lined valleys to an elevated, bunker-flanked green—is one of the tougher openers in the game. And although there are birdie holes along the way, the first nine ends with another crusher of a four, this one climbing 450 yards with out of bounds along the left side.

Wentworth's head professional, former Ryder Cup Captain Bernard Gallacher, calls the par-three 10th the best short hole in the world. It plays an all-carry 187 yards, with trees on both sides, to an awkwardly angled green.

However, most of the drama at this course nicknamed Burma Road unfolds over the last 1100 yards in the form of two par fives. Since the course first held the Ryder Cup here in 1953, these two holes have been the scene of countless triumphs and disasters, in this tournament as well as in the World Match Play championship contested here each fall. Out of bounds on the left and a blind second shot add intrigue to 17 while the reachable 18th—just 502 yards—is a hole that has produced dozens of birdies, and even a few eagles for victory.

Preceding pages: 1st hole at Wentworth
Right: 18th hole

What to Watch For . . .

ROYALTY
The European Tour promotes this event as golf's equivalent to Royal Ascot, the horse race where Britain's high society turns out in gray top hats, morning suits, and fancy frocks. Since it is set in Surrey, the stockbroker belt of southern England, it draws a large crowd of British preppies and the mood is more garden party than golf tournament. Don't be surprised if the gallery here includes Prince Andrew, the avid golfer in the royal family.

MOËT TO McDONALDS
Except for the British Open, no event stages a more elaborate sideshow than this one, where spectators may partake of a variety of food and drink.

INTERNATIONAL INCIDENTS
As at the Masters and U.S. Open, Rules decisions are made by a consortium of referees representing golf associations from around the world, including not only Great Britain, Ireland, and Europe but Australia and North America as well.

BRIEFCASES
Hard by the Wentworth course is the headquarters of the European Tour, with a staff of more than 70. Not surprisingly, this is a week when endless meetings are held with sponsors, players, and other sectors of the European golf fraternity.

Murphy's Irish Open

MOUNT JULIET

Mention Ireland to a golf aficionado, and he'll rattle off a roster of dramatic seaside links: Ballybunion, Portmarnock, Lahinch, Portrush, County Down. These are the "must" visits on every serious player's list. More and more, however, the news in Irish golf is coming not from the seacoasts of the north and west but from the parkland courses of the southeast, and it is there that the Murphy's Irish Open is played.

In 1990, Jack Nicklaus came to Ireland and designed a championship course at Mt. Juliet, a 1500-acre estate in County Kilkenny. The property had been held by a pair of ancient Norman families until 1757, when the two estates were united under the first Earl of Carrick, who built a manor house on a bank above the River Nore and named the house after his wife, Juliana. That manor is now the centerpiece of the Mt. Juliet resort, where golf, trout fishing, horseback riding, and hiking are among the activities offered to guests.

The course, which flows gracefully with the gentle contours of the land, is generally agreed to be one of Nicklaus's finest. It wanders through an open meadow, then a forest, with a couple of bucolic ponds along the way. There is good balance, with a couple of Nicklaus-sized par fours balanced by shorter holes. The driving areas are mostly generous, as are the greens, which undulate more than any at Ballybunion or Lahinch.

The finish is both scenic and testing. Number 16 pays homage to the Old Course at St. Andrews, with a putting green hard by a stone wall, and both 17 and 18 curl around the edge of a swan-dotted lake. The Irish Open likely will not stay here long—it has a rather itinerant history—but for the time being the European Tour and its players are very happy here. As Nick Faldo said in 1993 after shooting a 65 to win his third Irish Open in a row, "I like it here—nobody dies of an ulcer in Ireland."

What to Watch For . . .

HORSES
Mt. Juliet is in the heart of National Velvet country. The Ballylinch stud farm abuts the course, and thoroughbreds frolic in the nearby fields.

CROWDS
This is the only major tournament held in Ireland, and the golf-starved Irish fans come out in droves and stay until dark.

JOVIALITY
The sponsor—Murphy's—is a popular brand of Irish beer. The brewery is less than two hours away; its product flows freely throughout the tournament grounds. Not surprisingly, this has been voted the favorite event on the European circuit.

THE TV HOLES

Expect birdies:
17

Expect bogeys:
13, 18

10th hole

Bell's Scottish Open

CARNOUSTIE

Surprisingly for the country generally agreed to be the birthplace of golf, the Scottish Open is a relatively young event, having started in 1986 under the sponsorship of Bell's Scotch Whisky.

Almost from the outset, this event had two things going for it: a great site—the King's Course at the luxurious Gleneagles Hotel in Auchterarder—and a great date—one week before the British Open Championship. Today, the site has changed; after a nine-year run at Gleneagles, it has moved a couple of hours east, to Carnoustie. However, the Bell's Scottish Open retains its propitious slot in the European schedule, a week when international interest in British golf is reaching its peak.

Top players from all over the world come to play in this event as a final tuneup before "The Open," as it is known in Great Britain. And as the tournament settles in at Carnoustie, surely its popularity with the stars will grow, for Carnoustie is a course that has the respect of all. The site of five British Opens between 1931 and 1975, it was dropped from the rotation only because the tiny town of the same name lacks the hotel accommodations and other conveniences that

THE TV HOLES

Expect birdies:

12

Expect bogeys:

16, 17, 18

are vital to the administration of a modern major championship. However, a major hotel is now under development, and the R&A plans to bring back The Open to Carnoustie in 1999.

In the meantime, the Scottish Open should be a good fit. Although it draws thousands of spectators, many of them are commuters from Glasgow and Edinburgh and Dundee. As for the course, it instantly becomes the most challenging venue on the European Tour. In contrast to the parkland setting at Gleneagles, Carnoustie is a classic links, stretched along barren, windblown, rolling land near the Firth of Tay. And while the last four or five holes at the King's Course yielded barrages of birdies and eagles, the home stretch at Carnoustie has been called the most fearsome finish in golf.

It begins with the 14th, a par five that lists as only 482 yards on the scorecard but rarely plays that way. Into the prevailing breeze, this dogleg is all the challenge a professional golfer wants, with the second shot played over a pair of cavernous cross bunkers set into the face of a ridge. Despite the name of these bunkers—the Spectacles—the shot is blind. Number 15 doglegs 430 yards left through terrain that pitches the ball contrarily to

the right—again, a stiff assignment in the wind.

How tough is the par-three 16th? In the last British Open played at Carnoustie, the victor—Tom Watson—was unable to par it. In five trips through the hole, including a playoff with Jack Newton, the best Watson could do was lip-out a 40-footer. From the back tees, it plays about 250 yards to a narrow

What to Watch For . . .

AMERICANS

This event consistently draws the largest American field of any tournament on the Volvo European Tour, and for one big reason: The top five finishers, not otherwise qualified for the British Open, receive exemptions.

LATE FINISHES

In midsummer, daylight in Scotland lasts nearly 18 hours, and this tournament takes advantage of most of that time. Although the first players go off at 7:00 a.m., there have been days when the early rounds have not concluded until after 9 p.m.

FAST FINISHES

When the tournament was played at Gleneagles, it built a reputation for closing charges. The most astounding of them was the run to the clubhouse by Australian Peter O'Malley in 1992. He played the last five holes (pars of 4-4-3-4-5) in scores of 2-3-2-3-3, three birdies flanked by two eagles, to beat Colin Montgomerie by two strokes.

A SATURDAY CONCLUSION

Because this event is played the week before the British Open, it is concluded on Saturday instead of Sunday, to allow players who so desire to make their way to the qualifying rounds which begin on Sunday near the British Open course. More than one player has been known to drive through the night in order to make his starting time at the qualifying site.

green shaped like an inverted cereal bowl.

The 17th hole at Carnoustie is easiest the first time you play it. After that, you realize that the Barry Burn crosses this fairway three times, ready to engulf and drown even the slightest fade, draw, or top. At the 440-yard 18th the burn reappears, first on the left, then all the way down the right

18th hole

side before cutting in front of the green, where it swells to a width of 25 feet. Meanwhile, down the entire left side is out of bounds. There could be no more fitting send-off for the pros en route to the British Open.

European Open

EAST SUSSEX NATIONAL

Although one of the younger events on the Volvo European PGA Tour, this is an unqualified success story as the showpiece and symbol of European togetherness in golf. It was the brainchild of Sven Tumba, the great Swedish sportsman and Olympic hockey player. In 1973, Tumba had begun the Scandinavian Enterprise Open in his home country, and a few years later he wanted to expand.

In 1978 he convinced the European Tour's executive director, Ken Schofield, to take on the event with a multitude of small companies funding it, rather than one title sponsor. The tournament got a fall date on the Tour, paid several big-name players to appear, and secured as a site Walton Heath, the venerable heathland course that boasts Winston Churchill, Lloyd George, and the Duke of Windsor among its former members.

The inaugural event, played in the short days of late October—didn't come off easily. Seve Ballesteros, the number-one marquee attraction, lost his golf clubs and was never a factor, and the event was won by Bobby Wadkins (the only significant victory of his career) in a playoff over Gil Morgan and Bernard Gallacher that ended in the dark. (On the same weekend, brother Lanny won in Japan.)

The next several years saw the tournament move to Turnberry, back to Walton Heath, Royal Liverpool, and then Sunningdale for a run of five years. From 1986 to 1993 the site alternated between Sunningdale and Walton Heath. Given that heritage, the current site—East Sussex National—has a tough act to follow.

Roughly 50 miles from London and 20 miles from the south coast of England, East Sussex is hardly in an established golf area, and it will have to prove itself as a successful site. Moreover, this is an upstart of a course, especially by the standards of past European Open venues. It is the first work in Britain by Bob Cupp, the longtime associate of Jack Nicklaus who went into business for himself in the late 1980s.

Cupp's designs lean toward large, complex greens, and East Sussex is no exception, its expansive, multitiered surfaces providing plenty of pin placements and prompting lots of shot-planning on the approaches. But these greens are also among the best-conditioned and fastest-rolling on the Volvo Tour. The championship course is part of a 36-hole complex that also includes a three-hole golf academy and a 13-acre practice fairway. From the beginning, it was designed to hold a major tournament, and the holes toward the finish have the look of most American PGA Tour sites, with massive gallery mounds cradling the greens. It also has the length of most American Tour courses—a par 72 of 7138 yards.

What to Watch For . . .

MASTERS MIMICRY
The champion is presented with a (usually ill-fitting) white blazer.

ETHNIC DIVERSITY
The tournament has been won by players from eight different countries. The list includes Greg Norman, Isao Aoki, Tom Kite, Bernard Langer, Sandy Lyle, Ian Woosnam, and Nick Faldo. The only important name missing is Seve Ballesteros. This is the biggest European event the Spaniard has not won.

RUNNING WATER
Generally, British courses do not abound in water hazards, but East Sussex has two lakes and a pair of brooks that meander through roughly half the holes, in the manner of the Barry Burn and Jockey's Burn at Carnoustie.

THE TV HOLES

Expect birdies:
10, 14
Expect bogeys:
17

17th hole

Volvo Masters

VALDERRAMA

In America, some of the best-run golf clubs and finest courses have grown from the vision and vigilance of benevolent despots—men like George Crump at Pine Valley, Sam Morse at Pebble Beach, and Henry Fownes at Oakmont. Ironically, in aristocracy-steeped Europe, such one-man rule did not prevail—until a few years ago when a man named Jaime Ortiz-Patino walked onto the stage.

Patino, a Bolivian tin magnate, is the czar-in-residence at Valderrama, a Spanish course that has been called the finest on the European continent. He did not create this jewel on the Costa del Sol—Robert Trent Jones did—but in 1985 Patino bought it, remolded it, upgraded it, and converted Valderrama into a showplace so grand it was chosen to hold the 1997 Ryder Cup Matches.

Few courses across the Atlantic can rival the conditioning of those in America, but Valderrama does, with pristine fairways and big greens that roll consistently at speeds of 10 or more on the Stimpmeter—U.S. Open speeds. Credit for this goes to Patino, who schooled himself in agronomy and greenkeeping and personally supervises everything from turf condition to placement of the pins.

His course winds through stands of pine and thickly leaved cork trees, and every shot is complicated by the Mediterranean breezes. The most dramatic hole is unquestionably number 17, a one-time par four that Seve Ballesteros converted into a par five with a water-fronted green, similar to the 15th at Augusta National.

In fact, Patino has tried to mimic Augusta in many ways, so it's no accident that the tournament played here is the Volvo Masters. However, this event is closer in nature to THE TOUR Championship on the American circuit. The last official event of the season, it assembles only the season's best performers: the top 50 players off the money list plus up to four others from among the major championship winners and the European Order of Merit. Unlike our Tour Championship, however, this event has not moved from site to site—there has been no reason to leave Valderrama.

THE TV HOLES

Expect birdies:
11, 14, 17
Expect bogeys:
12, 18

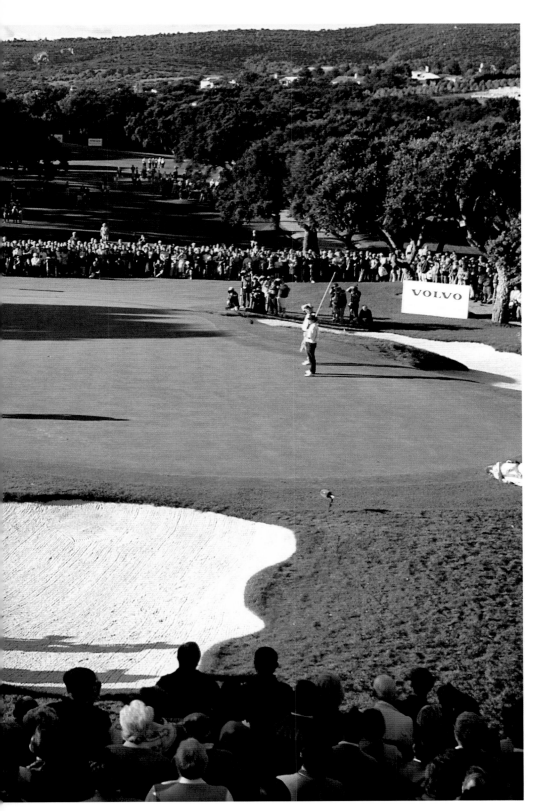

What to Watch For . . .

"SILENCIO, POR FAVOR" SIGNS

Remember, this is Spain. You can't expect the galleries to obey a sign that says "Quiet, Please."

BIG NUMBERS

Since the tournament began here in 1988, the average winning total has been 282—two under par. That's the highest of any event on the European Tour.

FROM AQUILEGIA TO CEANOTHUS

Whether or not Valderrama is the Augusta National of Europe, there is unquestionably a horticultural parallel in the variety of wildflowers and ornamental plantings that blossom throughout the property and throughout the year.

PAELLA, ETC.

Nearby Marbella is a Mediterranean seaport with an abundance of good restaurants. If you crave authentic Spanish food, this is a good place to get it.

THE METRIC SYSTEM

The American pros have to work extra hard to get accurate yardages for their approach shots at Valderrama. The scorecard lists this as a par 71 of 6353 meters.

SWEDISH MASSAGE

For tournament sponsor Volvo (which also has its name on the entire Tour), this is the most important event of the year, and they spare no expense wining, dining, and generally pampering their dealers.

OBJETS DE GOLF

Patino is a golf collector with very deep pockets, and Valderrama includes a golf museum filled with antique clubs, art, porcelain, and other collectibles.

18th hole

The Johnnie Walker World Championship

TRYALL GOLF CLUB

Give Mark McCormack's company—International Management Group—the credit (or blame, if you prefer) for creating this end-of-the-year event which claims to be the Super Bowl of Golf.

The field of players is 28, and it is comprised of the defending champion, the winners of 24 qualifying events in the U.S., Canada, Europe, and the Far East, plus the three leading players in the World Rankings not otherwise qualified. They all come to the Tryall Golf Club in Montego Bay, Jamaica, and fight it out for the largest first prize in golf: $550,000.

And when the wind blows at Tryall, it is a fight indeed. Back in 1992, Fred Couples was the only player to complete four rounds under par, and in one round John Daly shot 87.

Since even the 28th-place finisher receives a check for $50,000, player attendance is excellent. However, when a player opts not to play (or when a player wins multiple qualifying events), an international committee decides which players get to fill out the field. And you can bet that players who are clients of the superagent get extremely serious consideration.

This tournament is not a new idea—the Mercedes Championship and the World Series have been winners-only events for decades. What the JWWC has going for it, however, is timing. Played the week before Christmas, this is truly the last gasp—and the final determinant—of the golf year.

THE TV HOLES

Expect birdies:

14

Expect bogeys:

15, 17

15th hole

What to Watch For . . .

ISLAND HOPPING

This event won't stay in Jamaica forever, but its options are limited. Since it's not part of the PGA Tour, it cannot take place in the United States. Since it's played in December, it cannot take place in Europe. And since a live telecast to the States is important, it probably will not go to the Far East. Most of the course alternatives therefore lie in the Bahamas and Caribbean.

NEPOTISM

Ten of the qualifying events are in North America, and eight of them are among the most prestigious titles in golf: The Masters, U.S. Open, PGA Championship, THE PLAYERS Championship, The Memorial, Bell Canadian Open, NEC World Series of Golf, and THE TOUR Championship. The ninth, the Doral-Ryder Open, annually draws the first strong field of the PGA Tour year. However, in the case of the 10th event, the Bay Hill Invitational, we have a bit of insider trading: The event is played at the home course of Mark McCormack's longtime friend and number one client, Arnold Palmer, and is conducted by IMG.

THE SPIRIT OF COMPETITION

Clearly, the marketing moguls at the Schieffelin & Somerset Co. have determined that golf fans are prime customers for scotch. The first qualifying event for the Johnnie Walker World Championship is the Johnnie Walker Classic in Thailand. Every four weeks on the European Tour a Johnnie Walker Player of the Month is selected, and at the end of the season, a Johnnie Walker Player of the Year. There's also a Johnnie Walker Skins Game and every four years, when the Ryder Cup is played in Europe, it becomes the Johnnie Walker Ryder Cup.

GOOD PRESS

From the beginning, the IMG operatives knew that, in order to convince the world of the importance of this event, they first had to convince the international media. So they laid on the hospitality. Each year a charter flight is organized just for the press. The writers and broadcasters (and their wives) are ensconced in the villas of the Round Hill Club, where they enjoy the finer things in life. All meals are free, rounds of golf are arranged for them, and there are parties every night. As a result, you don't see much negative coverage.

VISA Taiheiyo Masters

GOTEMBA GOLF COURSE

Every so often, the notion of a world golf tour becomes topic number one in the forum of professional golf. The idea would be to combine a number of America's best events in a year-long calendar with a few tournaments from each of Great Britain, Europe, and Australasia. If it ever comes to be, count on the VISA Taiheiyo Masters to be a main event.

For most of the year, the Asian Tour proceeds virtually unnoticed by golfers in the Western Hemisphere. But when the second week of November arrives in Japan, so does a planeload of American PGA Tour stars, en route to the Gotemba Golf Course for the Taiheiyo Masters. With the end of the U.S. Tour, many of the top players head overseas, and this is one of their first and favorite stops.

Gotemba, at the foothills of Mount Fuji, has been the site of the tournament since 1977. A shotmaker's course with several water hazards, narrow, sloping fairways, and lots of white sand, it discourages the American power game but gets high praise from most who have played it. More often than not, it is the par-five final hole that decides the tournament. In 1993, Greg Norman won with an eagle after hitting a 4-iron ten feet from the hole. Had the tournament gone into sudden death, the playoff would have started at the same 18th hole. Why? To please the assembled fans. This event draws about 50,000 spectators, far more than any event that precedes it on the Asian Tour.

**T H E
TV
HOLES**

Expect birdies:
18

Expect bogeys:
Nowhere

9th hole

What to Watch For . . .

SWEATER WEATHER

November at Gotemba isn't much different from November in New York. Daytime highs don't get much above 60 degrees and at night the temperature can go below freezing. One good by-product of the cool climate: The course has bentgrass greens.

BRAND DISLOYALTY

Take a close look at some of the American players and notice they're wearing different clothing and playing different clubs than they do in the States. Your favorite player may wear Izod and play Wilsons at the Greater Greensboro Open, but at Taiheiyo he could be decked out in Fila and swinging Mizunos. Most of the big stars have separate and lucrative endorsement contracts for competition in Japan, and some of them play there each fall only to honor their contract commitment to make a yearly appearance.

CADDIES WHO AREN'T LADDIES

Few Japanese players have their own professional caddies, and even fewer Americans import their regular bagmen from the U.S. Tour. The caddie ranks at tournaments are composed of club pros, aspiring pros, students, or "house" caddies—middle-aged women who pull the clubs along on golf carts.

THE LEADING MONEY WINNER IS *NOT* CHARITY

There are no volunteers at Japanese events. Most of the usual jobs—as marshals, scorers, parking attendants—are filled by local college students, and they're all paid.

Dunlop Phoenix

PHOENIX COUNTRY CLUB

11th hole

THE TV HOLES

Expect birdies:

18

Expect bogeys:

17

Most American players who enter the VISA Taiheiyo Masters stay a second week and make their way to Miyazaki for the second of Japan's major events, the Dunlop Phoenix.

Our pros like this place, because everything is relatively Western—almost American. They check in at the modern Phoenix Sun Hotel, smack on the beach. In contrast to the cool climate at Taiheiyo, the daytime temperatures here are in the 70s—perfect golf weather. And there are no traffic hassles getting to the course — the first tee of the Phoenix Country Club is a two-minute walk from the hotel.

Phoenix is a par 72 of 7000 yards, but the sea breezes change the distance each day. Most of the fairways are lined with trees, which, in combination with the wind, create a special challenge; above the tree height, the wind gets the ball, but down on the ground, the players don't notice it. Club selection is therefore difficult, especially for first-time visitors.

The tournament often comes down to who can survive the penultimate hole, a par three that plays over water to a fiercely sloped green.

What to Watch For . . .

FOREIGN CONQUERORS
Johnny Miller won the first edition of the Dunlop Phoenix, and it has been won by several major championship winners: Tom Watson, Seve Ballesteros, Scott Simpson, Craig Stadler, Larry Mize, and Ernie Els. Curiously, however, it has been won by a Japanese player only once— Tommy Nakajima in 1985.

A DAY IN THE COUNTRY
The tournament atmosphere can resemble that of a county fair—families picnicking in the rough, kids cavorting among the trees. "It's usually pretty noisy," says Larry Nelson, who has learned to live with it. Nelson won here in 1991 and has a total of five Japanese victories, the most of any American.

BENTOH TO GO
Don't expect hot dogs and hamburgers at the concession stands. The standard fare is Bentoh, a box lunch based on rice or noodles, seafood, and tempura. The standard beverages are green tea along with Japanese beers (Sapporo, Kirin, Asahi).

CONEY ISLAND EAST
Miyazaki is a prototypical seaside resort with all the tourist trimmings. The centerpiece is a huge amusement center with an outdoor-indoor pool in which the waves from the Pacific Ocean come indoors.

Australian Open

VARIOUS COURSES

In the world of professional golf, there are three major tours—in America, Europe, and Japan. The circuit in Australia is comparatively insignificant, a string of a dozen or so events with weak fields and low purses.

However, the Australian Open is one event that stands out, not only Down Under but throughout the world. Indeed, Jack Nicklaus has called this the fifth major in international golf.

Why? For one thing, it has history—this is a tournament that dates back to 1904—only Great Britain and America have national championships that are older. For another, it is played on some of the finest courses on the planet.

Royal Melbourne, Kingston Heath, New South Wales, Huntingdale, Royal Adelaide, Victoria, The Australian, and Commonwealth all have been ranked among *GOLF Magazine*'s Top 100 Courses in the World. Finally, this championship has been won by the best players in the game. Gene Sarazen took the title in 1936, and he has been followed in the post–World War II era by Arnold Palmer, Peter Thomson, David Graham, Tom Watson, Jack Nicklaus (who has won it six times), and Gary Player (who has a record seven victories).

Today's American players see this as a long way to go for a victory, but the wiser ones know it's a trip worth taking.

1st hole

What to Watch For . . .

LIGHTNING SPEED IN THE SAND BELT
Just outside Melbourne is Australia's famed sand belt, an area similar to Surrey in England that is home to a handful of special courses. They play through corridors of firs and gum trees to greens that roll as fast and smooth as any in the world. The surfaces at Royal Melbourne and Kingston Heath in particular can roll like polished marble.

WINTER HEAT
The Australian Open is played in November, but remember, this is the other side of the world, where it's the start of summer. The fact is, the Australian Tour starts in January, runs through April, and then breaks for the May to September winter season before resuming in October.

KOOKABURRAS, KANGAROOS, AND KOALAS
Native wildlife and birds are denizens of some of the Australian Open courses.

THE ULTIMATE PLAYER
The little South African has his name all over this record book. In his 1965 victory, Gary Player set the 72-hole mark of 264—24 under par—and in doing so he shot two rounds of 62, including a nine-hole score of 28. His seven victories constitute a mark that likely will never be broken.

MARK MCCORMACK & CO.
This tournament is run by International Management Group, the conglomerate owned and operated by sports superagent McCormack, who has helped keep the quality of the field high by urging his big-name players to attend.

ALISTER MACKENZIE COURSES
The noted architect was brought here in 1926 to revise the two courses at Royal Melbourne. Before he was finished, he also designed a half dozen other courses including Victoria, Royal Queensland, and Royal Adelaide—all Australian Open sites.

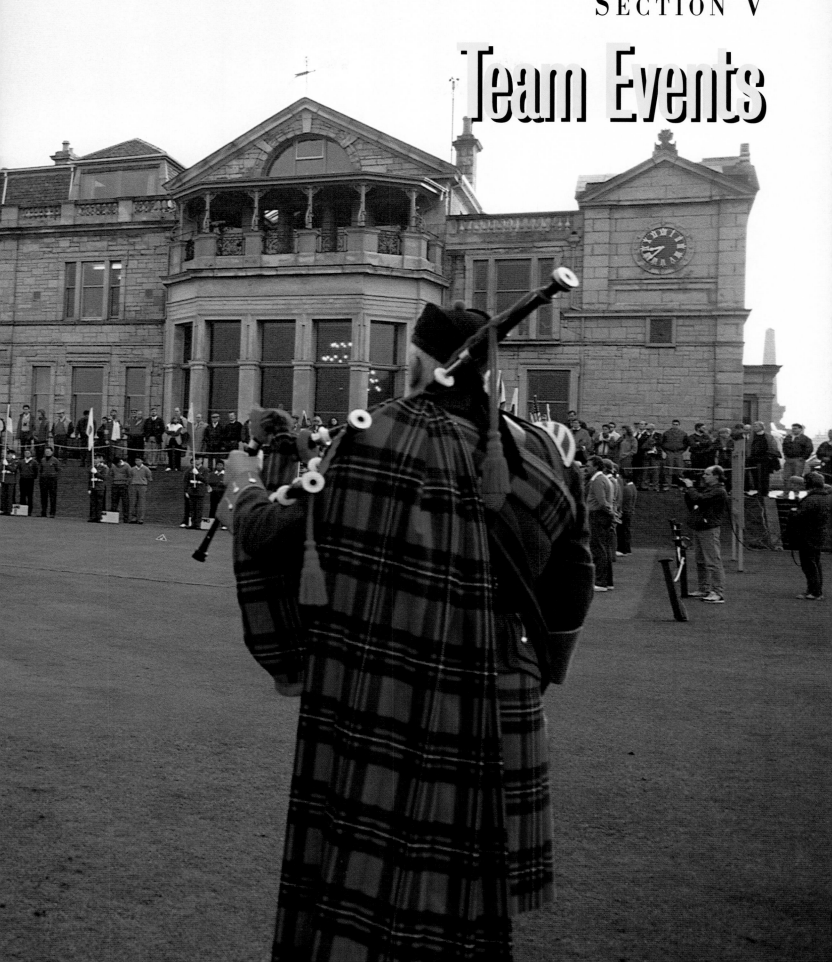

Team Events

The Walker Cup

VARIOUS COURSES

Shortly after World War I, at a time when transatlantic sea travel had become not only comfortable but chic, gentleman golfers from America and Great Britain began crossing the pond to play in each other's national championship tournaments.

At about the same time, a group of golf officials from the USGA met in St. Andrews, Scotland, with the Rules Committee from the Royal & Ancient Golf Club to discuss changes in the Rules of Golf. Out of that meeting grew the suggestion for an international competition among teams from different countries. One of the USGA officials, George Herbert Walker (grandfather of former president George Bush), so liked the notion that he donated a trophy—the International Challenge Cup—which quickly became known as the Walker Cup.

In 1921, the USGA invited the golf-playing countries of the world to compete for the Cup, but no nation accepted. A year later, however, the R&A sent a team of British golfers to compete for the first Walker Cup at the National Golf Links in Southampton, Long Island, which the Americans won by a score of 8 to 4. Since then, it has been a competition between amateur teams from the United States and Great Britain & Ireland.

The Walker Cup was played each of the next two years—at St. Andrews in 1923, then back to Long Island at the Garden City Golf Club in 1924, America winning each time. Since 1924, it

has been a biennial event, like the Ryder Cup on the professional side, and also like the Ryder Cup, the site of the Matches alternates between America and Great Britain & Ireland.

Each team consists of ten players plus a captain. The American players are selected by the USGA, the Brits by the R&A. They compete against each other for two days, with matches in both the morning and afternoon. Each morning consists of four 18-hole foursome matches, wherein partners from each team play alternate shots on the same ball. The two afternoons feature eight 18-hole singles matches. Each match is worth one point for the victory (in halved matches, each team gets one-half point).

The women's version of the Walker Cup, the Curtis Cup, is played according to the same format, between eight-member teams from America and Great Britain & Ireland. Three foursomes matches are played each of the two mornings, with six singles matches each afternoon. Like the Walker Cup, the Curtis Cup site moves back and forth across the Atlantic, every other year. It is played in even-numbered years; the Walker Cup takes place in odd-numbered years.

Preceding pages: Opening ceremonies for the Dunhill Nations Cup at the Old Course, St. Andrews

Above: The victorious 1993 American team

Right: 7th hole at Quaker Ridge

What to Watch For . . .

YANKEE SUPREMACY
Both the men's and women's matches have been one-sided. Through 1993, the United States leads the series of Walker Cup Matches with 30 victories, 3 losses, and 1 tie. In the Curtis Cup Matches, the U.S. leads 20-5-3 through 1994.

HOLDOVERS
Walker Cups held in America are scheduled one week before the U.S. Amateur Championship (often held at a nearby site) so that members of the British team may compete. Likewise, when the Matches take place in the United Kingdom, they are scheduled a week before the British Amateur.

BLUE BLAZERS
The few people who attend these matches are predominantly the officials, staff, and committee members of the USGA and R&A. Other than that, the gallery is made up of the competitors' families and friends, plus a smattering of locals.

TEENAGERS
Fewer and fewer of the world's best golfers choose to remain amateurs past their college years. This means that most Walker Cup and Curtis Cup Teams include several college students and occasionally even a high school kid or two. If you want an up-close preview of the future professional stars, this is the place to get it.

VENERABLE VENUES
The quality of the sites for the Walker Cup is higher than that of any event in golf. Many American clubs that would never dream of holding a U.S. Open are happy to host the Walker Cup because they know it doesn't attract huge galleries or require the parking facilities and other services and sacrifices attendant to big-time tournament golf. Recent U.S. sites have been Cypress Point (1981), Pine Valley (1985), Peachtree (1989), and Inter-lachen (1993), with Quaker Ridge scheduled for 1997.

Practical Matters

FOR TICKET INFORMATION
The USGA
Golf House
P.O. Box 708
Far Hills, NJ 07931

Fred Meyer Challenge

OREGON GOLF CLUB

Few people outside of Oregon know Fred Meyer, but most golf fans know Peter Jacobsen: professional golfer, television golf commentator, talented mimic, leader of Jake Trout and the Flounders, author of *Buried Lies*, pro-am partner of Jack Lemmon, and likely the PGA Tour's most lively intelligence. And despite its name, this is not Fred's tournament—it's Peter's party.

This regional event, although not sanctioned by the PGA Tour, is more successful than many official Tour events. The main reason is Jacobsen

himself, a Portland boy who has used his charm and salesmanship to gain corporate backing, the dedication of hundreds of volunteers, and loyal support from the game's marquee players.

The field here is not large—24 players in 12 two-man teams, but it's high in quality. Bring Arnold Palmer, Jack Nicklaus, Greg Norman, Fred Couples, and John Daly to town, and you have a virtual lock on success—and Jacobsen gets at least four of that fivesome every year, along with the likes of Curtis Strange, Tom Kite, Ben Crenshaw, Paul Azinger, all of whom are happy to play. Indeed, whereas many events struggle to fill their fields, it has become something of an honor to be invited to the Fred Meyer.

One of the reasons they're glad to show is that this event does not compete with any other tournament. It's played on a Monday and Tuesday—specifically, the Monday and Tuesday of World Series of Golf week. As part of the inducement to players, Jacobsen lays on a charter flight to Akron immediately following the awards ceremony on Tuesday afternoon.

Fred Meyer, by the way, is the owner of a chain of food stores.

What to Watch For . . .

AUCTION ACTION
One of the tournament highlights is the Monday night auction where the players get involved as both auctioneers and donors of items. One year, Curtis Strange auctioned off—and took off—his blue jeans, a happening that he's still trying to explain to his wife.

COMMERCIALISM
Another reason this tournament is successful is the sales team at PJP—Peter Jacobsen Productions—a company that runs everything from the Fred Meyer to riverboat races and ice shows. This is surely the only Monday/Tuesday event in golf with corporate tents, a high-priced pro-am, and commercial signage on every tee.

SPEEDY GREENS
In most climates, green superintendents are afraid to shave greens too close for fear that the sun's heat will burn them out. But that's no problem in rainy Portland, so the surfaces at the Jacobsen-designed Oregon Golf Club (indeed at most courses) are smooth and fast—at least until the rain returns.

ROWS OF ROSES
In 1994, the Oregon Golf Club won the grand prize from a nonprofit group called All-American Rose Selections, Inc. Why? Because this course is festooned with a total of 3500 rose bushes, 3000 of which appear at the 12th hole, in the form of a thorny but breathtaking hazard.

Lefty Phil Mickelson tees off at the 9th hole

Practical Matters

FOR TICKET INFORMATION
Peter Jacobsen Productions
8700 Southwest Nimbus Avenue
Suite B
Beaverton, Oregon 97005-7119

The Presidents Cup

ROBERT TRENT JONES GOLF CLUB

The recent popularity of the Ryder Cup Matches has been great for golf on both sides of the Atlantic. But if you live anywhere else, the last two decades of Ryder Cup mania haven't done much for you, except perhaps make you jealous.

Among the most envious: some of the top players in the world—led by Australia's Greg Norman and Nick Price of Zimbabwe. For years they lobbied for a Ryder Cup alternative that would pit America against the best of the rest of the world. And now they have it—the Presidents Cup.

In 1994, the PGA Tour launched these matches, despite some resistance from some of its own players. Some claimed the Presidents Cup would detract attention from the more venerable Ryder Cup; others were

concerned that the event, played in mid-September, overlapped with significant tournaments on both the U.S. and Asian Tours; and still others bristled at the prospect of playing for pride—and pride only—every year, since the Presidents Cup and Ryder Cup will be played in alternate years. That last concern generated little sympathy, since the 12-man U.S. team is comprised of the top-10 money winners from the PGA Tour while the International Team brings together the top 10 eligible players from the Sony Ranking System, with each team also getting two captain's picks. These are 24 men who can afford to take a week without pay.

To reinforce the Presidents theme, the Tour wanted these Matches to take place at venerable Congressional Country Club, in Beth-esda, Maryland, just a few miles from the White House, but when negotiations with the club failed, the site moved down the road to Gainesville, Virginia, and the brand-new Robert Trent Jones Golf Club. By game time in 1994, all hands were on deck and playing hard for their captains—Hale Irwin and Australian David Graham—as the Americans won a hard-fought contest, 20 to 12. The final score didn't indicate the closeness of the matches, which came down to the wire on Sunday. It was settled in spectacular fashion when, on the final hole of the Fred Couples–Nick Price singles match, Couples played a terrific approach shot from a fairway bunker that stopped a foot from the cup, giving him a 1-up win and locking up the Cup for the Yanks.

What to Watch For . . .

32 POINTS
The PGA Tour took pains to distinguish its event from the Ryder Cup. Although it uses the same general format—foursomes, four-balls, and singles matches—the Presidents Cup calls for five foursomes and five four-balls on each of the first two days, in contrast to the Ryder Cup's four and four. As in the Ryder Cup, the Sunday play features 12 singles matches.

NO RESTING
Another contrast with the Ryder Cup: Each player on each team is required to play at least one match each day.

HOME GAMES
Despite the fact that half of the competitors hail from outside the U.S., plans call for the Presidents Cup to be held at the Robert Trent Jones Course for at least the first few stagings of the event. Why? Because the PGA Tour invented it—in contrast to the Ryder Cup, which is run jointly by bodies on the two sides of the Atlantic. This is an all-American show. Greg Norman's reaction? "Once we win it a couple of times, there's no way it's staying in America."

A MISNOMER
No players from England, Scotland, Ireland, Northern Ireland, Wales, or any European country are eligible, because these are the nations that make up the Ryder Cup Team. Furthermore, about half of the "Internationals" make their residence in the States.

NO TIES
In contrast to the Ryder Cup, where halved matches result in ½ point for each side, singles matches which go 18 holes without a winner will go on until one player wins a full point. And if the entire match ends in a 16-16 tie, the Cup will be decided by a sudden-death playoff between two players designated in advance by the captains.

4th hole

Practical Matters
FOR TICKET INFORMATION
The PGA Tour
Sawgrass
Ponte Vedra, FL 32082

The Dunhill Nations Cup

THE OLD COURSE

Back in the mid-1980s, when the World Cup was struggling to gain its lost prominence as an international team event, sports super-agent Mark McCormack devised this competition that also brings together teams of players from countries around the world.

But this is not so much a rival to the World Cup as it is a completely different event. Whereas the World Cup involves teams from all over the world, the Dunhill includes only 16 teams. Eight get exemptions, while eight qualify in regional playoffs. Also, the Dunhill team is composed of three players in contrast to the two-man teams at the World Cup.

Another unique feature is the format. The countries play against each other in match-play brackets and according to a format similar to soccer's World Cup, where one loss does not eliminate a team from competition. Each three-man team confronts another team in a series of three one-on-one matches with one point scored for each victory. But even the format for the individual matches is different. The two players compete not on a hole-by-hole basis, but for an 18-hole score, with the lower total winning the point.

Perhaps the Dunhill's most outstanding asset is its site. While the World Cup shuttles from course to course and country to country, the Dunhill has only one home—the ultimate home of golf—the Old Course at St. Andrews. Not only is this the most revered golf course in the world, it is full of bumps and bounces, a course where good fortune can sometimes be a match for good play. As such, the medal matches are unpredictable, even when on paper one player seems to outclass another.

What to Watch For . . .

LOW NUMBERS
The medal match format can encourage aggressive play and lots of birdies. For example, in 1987 Curtis Strange beat Greg Norman with a 62, the lowest score ever shot on the Old Course. However, his victory was still worth only one point.

UPSETS
Although the winning team is always a "golf nation," the early rounds have seen some surprises. In 1993, the formidable Scottish team of Colin Montgomerie, Sam Torrance, and Gordon Brand, Jr., was upset by a three-some from Paraguay, and both the U.S. and Australia have been beaten by teams from France. If that sounds plausible, try naming any golfer from France.

LOTS OF PUTTS
The salient feature of the Old Course is its double greens. Seven of them serve 14 of the holes, and one or two are over an acre in size. Consequently, the pros tend to hit a lot of greens in regulation, but on occasion, three-putting is not simply a possibility, it's a triumph.

Opening ceremonies

Practical Matters

FOR TICKET INFORMATION
International Management Group
Pier House, Strand on the Green
Chiswick, London W4 3NN
England

The World Cup of Golf

VARIOUS COURSES

As its name implies, this is the most international golf tournament in the world. It is also one of the oldest, dating back to 1953, when American industrialist John Jay Hopkins, hoping to "promote international goodwill through golf," brought together seven nations in Montreal for a tournament then known as the Canada Cup.

A pair of Argentinians, Roberto De Vicenzo and Antonio Cerda, took the top prize in the competition based upon the total score of two-man teams. A year later it returned to Canada, and this time Australia took the title courtesy of two British Open champions, Peter Thomson and Kel Nagle.

After that the tournament began to move around the world—to nine different countries in the next nine years. By 1967, when the pairing of Arnold Palmer and Jack Nicklaus won

for the fourth time in five years (and four countries), the Canada Cup had earned a more fitting designation as the World Cup.

The 1960s, when Palmer and Nicklaus were dominating the competition, were the glory years for the World Cup. In those days, it was an honor just to be chosen to represent one's country, and no one complained that the event carried no prize money. But as big-time professional golf grew and prospered, the pros became spoiled. Many of them—notably the Americans—began to question the value of playing simply for national pride, when exhibition fees and lucrative alternative events beckoned. Less-than-stellar fields resulted.

For a decade, the International Golf Association watched its tournament decline in appeal and prestige, and wrestled with the question of whether to go commercial. When the 1981 World Cup had to be canceled for lack of interest, the course was clear. In 1982 the tournament returned, and when Manuel Pinero and José Maria Canizares won, they each brought $10,000 home to Spain. Today, the World Cup purse is over a million dollars.

Berths on the World Cup teams are earned in a variety of ways. Some nations hold qualifying events, while others select the top players from their Order of Merit list. In the U.S., the first invitations go to the winners of the Players Championship and the Masters (assuming they are Americans). Otherwise, the American representatives are selected by a panel comprised of the IGA's Executive Director, Birch Riber, former USGA President Howard Clark, golf course architect Robert Trent Jones, and former president Gerald Ford.

What to Watch For . . .

ICELANDERS, ISRAELIS, AND GREEKS
With 32 different nations represented, this is a rare chance to see the best golfers from countries not recognized as powers in the world of golf.

100-STROKE DEFICITS
Since the final score is determined by adding the 72-hole totals of both players, big numbers result. While the winners typically shoot something around 560, it's not unusual for the last-place team to be more than 100 strokes off the pace.

FAR-FLUNG FASHIONS
Past editions of the World Cup have seen teams arrive at the first tee in all manner of garb, including turbans, Bermuda shorts, grass skirts, sandals, and bare feet.

AN EVENT WITHIN AN EVENT
Simultaneous with the two-man team title there is a competition for individual low score. Players from 13 different countries have won it, including Ben Hogan, Sam Snead, Gary Player, Arnold Palmer, and Jack Nicklaus.

16th hole at La Moraleja

Practical Matters

FOR TICKET INFORMATION
International Golf Association
7442 Jager Court
Cincinnati, Ohio 45230

Franklin Funds Shark Shootout

SHERWOOD COUNTRY CLUB

Start with golf's most charismatic player. Then take a glamour course in southern California, invite 20 of the game's biggest stars, pair them up in two-man teams, and let them go at each other for three days in three different competitive formats. Those are the ingredients of the ultimate made-for-television event, the Franklin Funds Shark Shootout.

The idea started at the 1986 member-guest tournament for the Bay Hill Club in Orlando, Florida. At the time, one of Bay Hill's members was Greg Norman, and he not only entered the member-guest, he won it (with golf photographer Lawrence Levy as his partner). Greg liked the tournament format so well, he brought a similar event to the Sherwood Country Club outside Los Angeles, and invited a few of his friends from the pro tour to compete.

The first-round format of the Shark Shootout is alternate-shot (or foursomes, except that this is not match play, it's medal—each team posts its 18-hole score). On day two, it's better ball—on each hole, the lower score of the two players is used. For the finale, the twosomes play a scramble—each player hits a tee shot, then they select the better of the two and from that point each player hits an approach shot; then they select the easier third shot and both go for the hole.

This unique format encourages aggressive play from the game's best players, and that means low, low scores. The third-day scramble is where the really low scores can happen. In 1989, the first year of the tournament, after Norman teamed up with Jack Nicklaus they opened poorly with a 74 but roared back on Sunday with a 14-under-par 58 that included a 26 on the last nine holes—one par, six birdies, and two eagles. Still, it wasn't enough, as Curtis Strange and Mark O'Meara took the prize with a three-day total of 190—26 under par for 54 holes. A year later, Ray Floyd and Fred Couples posted a record 182—that's 34 under par for 54 holes!

What to Watch For . . .

L.A. LAVISH

Sherwood Country Club is a Jack Nicklaus course commissioned by Dole Pineapple magnate David Murdoch, a nongolfer who decided to build the best private country club money could buy. It's conspicuous consumption, southern California style, but no one can fault the condition of the course or the elegance of the clubhouse, which ranks alongside Denver's Castle Pines as the height of locker room luxury.

HIGH-PROFILE MEMBERS

Not surprisingly, glitzy Sherwood has attracted a high-profile membership that includes Sean Connery, Wayne Gretzky, Mark Messier, Jack Nicholson, Joe Pesci, Dennis Quaid, Tom Selleck, and Robert Wagner.

BIRDIES

On most days at most tournaments, most players follow a relatively conservative game plan, favoring accuracy over distance from the tee, giving bunkers and hazards a wide berth, and rarely attacking the pins. In this format, however, knowing they have strong partners as backups, the pros attack virtually every hole. If you've ever wondered how well a pro can play when he decides to go for broke all day, this is the place to find out.

NATURAL DISASTERS

If you choose to see this event in person, be careful. Sherwood is in the Thousand Oaks area northwest of Los Angeles that has been the center of recent forest fires, mudslides, and earthquakes.

15th hole

Practical Matters

FOR TICKET INFORMATION
Sherwood Country Club
2215 Stafford Road
Thousand Oaks, CA 91361

The Solheim Cup

VARIOUS COURSES

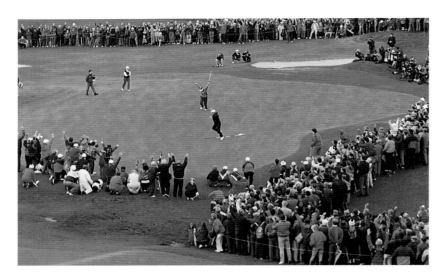

T he history of women's professional golf has shown a pattern of imitation—imitation of the men's tour. The LPGA came into being several years after the men's circuit was in full operation. The notion of four major championships took shape on the ladies' side in the 1970s, decades after the Masters, U.S. Open, British Open, and PGA had settled in as the men's Grand Slam. So when American interest in the Ryder Cup matches suddenly skyrocketed, it was only a matter of time until a women's version arose.

In 1990, it arrived in the form of the Solheim Cup, a biennial contest that pits the best women professional golfers in America against their counterparts from Europe. It is sponsored by Karsten Mfg. and named for founder, chairman, and CEO Karsten Solheim. If that seems

Victory at Dalmahoy Golf Club

commercial, remember that the Ryder Cup is named for a seed merchant.

The first Solheim Cup was held at the Lake Nona Golf Club near Orlando, Florida, and after the Americans won it by a whopping seven points, this confrontation seemed headed for a long run of U.S. domination. But in 1992, the Europeans came right back. Facing an American team that outnumbered them in victories (147–84) and major championships (23–2), the ladies from across the pond stampeded to an 11½-to-6½ victory on their home turf at Dalmahoy. In 1994, the rubber match at the Greenbrier resort in White Sulphur Springs, West Virginia, went to the Americans, 12–8. The 1996 matches will be played in Wales.

What to Watch For . . .

GRIM FACES
Usually, the players of the LPGA Tour are more lighthearted, more accessible to fans, and more gracious to their peers than are the dour-faced grinders on the PGA Tour. But not this week. Victory is everything for both squads.

INCREASED ACTION
The first three Solheim Cups featured teams of 10 players, competing at Four-ball match play (lower score of two players) for two days, followed by 10 singles matches on the final day. For 1996, however, the sides will expand to 12 and the competition format will mirror the Ryder Cup, with Four-ball matches in the morning and foursomes (alternate shot) in the afternoon on Friday and Saturday, concluding with 12 singles matches on Sunday.

ALTERNATES
In addition to the 10 players who qualify from the point standings and the two captain's picks, an alternate is designated by the captain, based on the next-qualified player from the point standings.

DECIMAL POINTS
American players qualify by gaining top-10 finishes in LPGA Tour events during the 24 months previous to the Solheim Cup: 20 points for a win, 10 for second, and then descending down to two points for 10th place, with the points doubled for the LPGA's four major championships. However, in the year in which the Cup is played, all point values are multiplied by one and a half. Thus, a third-place finish (worth 9 points in the year before the Matches) is worth 13.5 points in the year of the Cup, with the four majors offering triple points. Typically, a player needs more than 100 points to make the team.

Practical Matters

FOR TICKET INFORMATION
The LPGA
2570 International Speedway Blvd.
Daytona Beach, FL 32114

Liberty Mutual Legends of Golf

LA QUINTA RESORT

By unanimous agreement, this is the event that gave birth to the phenomenally successful Senior PGA Tour. It began with Fred Raphael, who in the 1960s had produced the popular TV series, "Shell's Wonderful World of Golf." One of the commentators on the show was Jimmy Demaret, and he and Raphael began talking about staging a tournament of their own, an unofficial affair that would bring back some of the older players in a better-ball event. Demaret, who had helped design a course at Onion Creek near Austin, suggested bringing the tournament there.

That is what they did, in 1978, with the first staging of the Liberty Mutual Legends of Golf. With NBC-TV on hand, 65-year-old Sam Snead birdied the last two holes and he and partner Gardner Dickinson tied five-time British Open Champion Peter Thomson and Kel Nagle. Then, in sudden death, Snead made a third straight birdie for victory. The show was an instant hit.

A year later, the Legends top-ped itself as the team of Julius Boros/Roberto De Vicenzo strung together a mind-boggling six consecutive birdies in sudden death, needing every one of them as Tommy Bolt and Art Wall made five in a row. The next morning, those fantastic old golfers were topic number one in every clubhouse locker room and at every office water cooler. Within months, the Senior Tour was launched. By 1984, the Legends had been joined by two dozen events, and today the senior pros play almost every week of the year, for a total purse of nearly $30 million.

Although the Legends flourished for 15 years as a team event, in 1993 it abandoned the partner format and reverted to the standard 54-hole stroke play event, with every man for himself. This proved to be an unsuccessful experiment, and in 1994 it wisely reverted to team play. In 1995, another change took place, as the event left Texas for the first time, moving to more glamorous quarters at the La Quinta Resort in Palm Springs.

What to Watch For . . .

OLD FRIENDS
The oldsters tend to gravitate toward their longtime buddies, whether or not that makes for a strong team. Dave Hill and Mike Hill are an obvious twosome, and just as obvious have been pairings such as Bob Charles and Bruce Devlin, Billy Casper and Gay Brewer, Tommy Aaron and Lou Graham, Dale Douglass and Charles Coody, and Gene Littler and Don January.

SHORT DRIVES
This event retains its sense of history, and the average age of the competitors is higher than at any other event on the senior circuit. Gene Sarazen came out of retirement to play this event, and Sam Snead competed throughout his 70s.

GOLF CARS
Players on the Senior Tour are permitted to use golf cars (although if they do, their caddies must walk—otherwise the players tend to move faster than their galleries), and with the advanced average age at the Legends, almost all contestants are riders.

SHOTMAKING
With the advent of hi-tech equipment, today's Tour players hit the ball prodigious distances, but something has been lost in the games of modern golfers: the ability to play artful shots. The Legends of Golf is one of the last showcases of shotmaking—playing gentle hooks and soft fades, shots that bump and run and shots that stop on a dime. Legends founder Jimmy Demaret may have been the best shotmaker ever, and Tommy Bolt wasn't far behind, but in this event, which encourages partners to play aggressively for the flags, you can still enjoy the handiwork of players such as Chi Chi Rodriguez, Lee Trevino, Dave Hill, Isao Aoki, and Tom Weiskopf. They're the last of a dying breed.

17th hole at
PGA West/Stadium Course

Practical Matters

FOR TICKET INFORMATION
Liberty Mutual Legends of Golf
55920 PGA Blvd.
La Quinta, CA 92253

Wendy's 3-Tour Challenge

VARIOUS COURSES

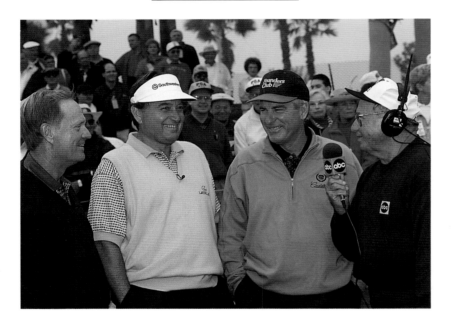

O ne of the more interesting made-for-television events, the Wendy's 3-Tour Challenge brings together teams representing the PGA Tour, the LPGA Tour, and the Senior Tour for 18-holes of head-to-head-to-head medal-play competition.

Only nine players are involved —three from each tour, grouped in three threesomes with one player from each tour in each group. The 18-hole scores for each tour's threesome are added, and the tour with the lowest total wins.

Players are selected for the Wendy's team based on their play in their tour's major championships, past as well as current. In order to maintain parity, the three tours tee off from different sets of

The 1994 Senior Tour team: Jack Nicklaus, Ray Floyd, and Dave Stockton

tees. The Senior's course is about 300 yards shorter than the one the younger guys play, while the women get roughly a 900-yard head start on their opponents from the PGA Tour. The idea is to allow the LPGA and Senior Tourists to approach greens with essentially the same clubs as the big boys use.

The event started in 1992 with a surprise victory by the LPGA team. A year later, Ray Floyd led the Senior Team to the winner's circle, and in 1994 the PGA Tour made it one win apiece.

What to Watch For . . .

NICKLAUS COURSES

This tournament is staged by Jack's Golden Bear Productions, which tends to take its tournaments to sites that show off the boss's architectural prowess. In 1992, the inaugural was held at Nicklaus's New Albany Country Club in Ohio, and in 1993 it went to Nicklaus's highly regarded Colleton River Country Club.

QUICK SHIFTS

With each team's position dependent upon three players at a time, the leaderboard can change quickly. If, for instance, all three women birdie the same par four, their collective score is 9. If all three senior players happen to bogey the same hole, their total is 15, and the one-hole swing between the women and seniors is six strokes.

HIRED HANDS

The course is set up by David Eger, Senior Director of Rules and Competition for the USGA, and officials from each of the three tours follow the action, ready to make Rules calls.

VIDEOTAPE

Occasionally, prior commitments don't allow one or more of the nine players to spend both days filming this show. However, the telecast must run on both Saturday and Sunday. The solution? They play all 18 holes on Saturday, and save the back nine on tape to show on Sunday, pretending it's live. As long as the press plays along—and the players change their clothing ensembles at the turn—no one knows any better.

Practical Matters

FOR TICKET INFORMATION
Golden Bear Productions
11780 Highway #1
North Palm Beach, FL 33408

JC Penney Classic

INNISBROOK RESORT
[COPPERHEAD COURSE]

This is the only event in golf where men and women from the PGA and LPGA Tours come together as partners. It is the modern version of the Haig & Haig Scotch Foursome, a tournament which ran during the 1960s, stopped for a decade, and returned in 1976 under the less inebriating aegis of Pepsi-Cola. Since 1978, JC Penney has been the title sponsor, and since 1990 the site has been the Copperhead Course at the Innisbrook Resort in Florida.

Innisbrook is in Tarpon Springs, on Florida's west coast, but the Copperhead is a distinctly non-Floridian golf course, with plenty of elevation changes and fairways lined with tall trees—pines rather than palms. Several holes call for carries over water, and that adds plenty of strategic interest to this tournament.

Until 1994, play was conduct-ed according to the Pinehurst format, wherein each player hits a drive, then the partners hit second shots from each other's drives. Then they proceed to the two second shots and decide which one offers the better potential for success. Once that choice is made, they take the other ball out of play and finish the hole with the selected ball, with the partners alternating shots until the ball is holed. Now, that format is used only in rounds one and four. On Saturday the partners play a scramble, choosing the better drive and playing both second shots from that point; then, in the same way, choosing the better second, the better putt, etc. On Friday, they play a better-ball format, wherein both partners complete the hole with their own balls, and the lower of the two scores is used.

The men play this par-71 course from the championship tees at 7065 yards, while the women move up to just in front of the regular men's tees—at 6394 yards.

18th hole

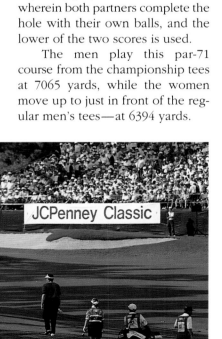

What to Watch For . . .

PAR-FIVE CONFERENCES
On Friday and Sunday, the strategy can get complicated on holes such as number 14, a reachable par five. A male pro may hit a 270-yard drive, then his female partner will add a 220-yard approach shot, straight down the middle and just short of the green. They must then weigh the promise of that position against that of their other ball, driven 240 by the woman pro and then boomed by the male pro into a greenside bunker 50 feet from the pin. For the third shot, should the man play a half-wedge shot from the fairway or should the woman try to blast it close from the bunker?

SADIE HAWKINS MENTALITY
The women players tend to enjoy this event a bit more than most of the men—partly because they're playing on television (something they do only about one week in two) and also playing for more money than in many LPGA events. Thus, most of the partnerships are formed at the invitation of the gals, and the field usually includes most of the top LPGA players but few PGA Tour stars.

WONDER WOMEN
Virtually every great woman player of the last half century has been a winner here, including Mickey Wright, Ruth Jessen, Kathy Whitworth, JoAnne Carner, Nancy Lopez, Pat Bradley, Beth Daniel, Jan Stephenson, and Hollis Stacy.

Practical Matters

FOR TICKET INFORMATION
JC Penney Classic
Innisbrook Resort, P.O. Drawer 1088
Tarpon Springs, FL 34688

Diners Club Matches

VARIOUS COURSES

The notion of a match-play event has never succeeded on the PGA Tour. Over the years it has been tried a couple of times, and abandoned. This failure is both ironic and understandable. Ironic because the game's hottest event—the Ryder Cup—is a match-play contest and because match play—a hole-by-hole battle—is the game most American golfers play every weekend of the year. Understandable because match play can make for terrible television if the final match is a rout or brings together two unappealing players.

In the Diners Club Matches, which began in 1994, there may be a solution. Instead of depending on just one Tour for the action, all three Tours play separately and simultaneously. Thus, if the PGA Tour final match turns out to be a dud, there are still the Senior Tour and LPGA to watch.

Jack Nicklaus's production company came up with this concept and the three tours embraced it immediately. A total of 64 players compete in two-player teams: 16 teams vying for the PGA Tour title and eight teams each in the Senior Tour and LPGA divisions. The first player on each team is chosen based on tournament performance, money-list standings, and—most important—marquee appeal. That player then selects a teammate. To boost interest in the inaugural event, Nicklaus participated and chose Arnold Palmer as his partner, and they nearly won. In the final match against Dave Eichelberger and Ray Floyd, Jack and Arnie came from four down to pull one up with one to go, before a pair of birdie putts by Eichelberger at 18 and the first playoff hole sank the two titans. Jeff Maggert and Jim McGovern won the PGA Tour title, while Tammie Green and Kelly Robbins were the champions in the LPGA bracket.

The first-round PGA Tour matches are televised on Thursday, the Friday show includes the second-round matches for the PGA Tour and opening matches for the seniors and ladies, and the semifinals and finals for all three tours are telecast on Saturday and Sunday, respectively.

What to Watch For . . .

FRANTIC FRIDAY
With 16 matches going on simultaneously, there's a lot to monitor, whether you're the TV producer or a viewer trying to stay on top of the action.

THE BEST SAVED FOR LAST
Neither "age before beauty" nor "ladies first" is honored when setting the tee times for the final matches. The producers simply decide which of the three matches offers the most appealing confrontation.

BEAR TRACKS
Like all Nicklaus-conceived events, the competition showcases courses designed by the Golden Bear. The first event took place at the Jack Nicklaus Resort Course at PGA West in La Quinta, California. One thing you won't see is any courses from the northern states, since this event is played in the middle of December.

1st hole at PGA West/Nicklaus Resort Course

Practical Matters

FOR TICKET INFORMATION
Golden Bear Productions
11780 Highway #1
North Palm Beach, FL 33408

The Skills Challenge

VARIOUS COURSES

Preceding pages: 14th hole at the Plantation Course at Kapalua, site of the Lincoln Mercury Kapalua Invitational

Above: Tom Weiskopf from the sand

What to Watch For . . .

A CATALYST

Since the players are chosen by NBC and SNI, entertainment value is at least as important as golf ability. The promoters like to have at least one entrant to stir things up, throw a few one-liners, and generally loosen up the other stiffs in the competition. Count on this event to include at least one and probably more of the game's clowns and sideshow attractions: Peter Jacobsen, Chi Chi Rodriguez, Fuzzy Zoeller, John Daly, etc. Jacobsen won the first two Skills Challenges while also providing most of the banter.

NO DOWN TIME

The Skills Challenge is not live, it's taped, so despite the fact that all the players wear microphones, you shouldn't expect to hear any startling revelations or breaking news stories. Also, don't look for much walking between shots. It's all hitting, chuckling, and celebrating.

This one is not only made for television, it's made by television, a joint venture between NBC and SNI Sports Network. It's not a tournament at all, except in the medieval sense of jousting. There are no pars or birdies, no holes won or lost. In fact, there are no holes of any kind.

The Skills Challenge is pretty much what it says, a matching of skills among a group of golfers who are challenged to outperform each other in a series of shotmaking tests. Eight players compete in eight events: driving for distance and accuracy, a 200-yard shot, a trouble shot, a 100-yard shot, a fairway bunker shot, a chip, a greenside bunker shot, and a putt. Each player gets three tries at each shot. (Simple multiplication will tell you that, with eight guys making three swings at eight shots each, there is a total of 192 drives, irons, blasts, chips, and putts—thus, this is a two-day telecast.) The player whose best shot finishes closest to the target wins first prize ($18,000 per event in 1994, with second-through-eighth places getting progressively less cash). At the end, the overall winner receives a bonus payment of $20,000. In all, over $400,000 is up for grabs.

Practical Matters

FOR TICKET INFORMATION
SNI Sports Network
11525 Olde Cabin Rd.
St. Louis, MO 63141

The Skins Game

VARIOUS COURSES

The king of golf's "junk events" (or more politely "made-for-television competitions") is The Skins Game, a staple of Thanksgiving weekend TV fare since it began in 1983 with the foursome of Arnold Palmer, Jack Nicklaus, Gary Player, and Tom Watson.

No one can explain the derivation of the term "skins," but everyone can understand this event. Indeed, this is a format often used by weekend golfers. Basically, it's a hole-by-hole competition in which each player competes against the rest of the field. Amateurs tend to play skins most commonly when they have a threesome, but the format can be used for four players, or, for that matter, an entire tournament. If, on a given hole, one player scores lower than everyone else, he wins the agreed-upon stake that has been anted up—it may be a quarter per hole, a dollar, or any amount. If, however, two or more players tie for low score, everyone gets a free ride to the next hole, when everyone antes again and the stakes double. Thus, if the first hole was worth a dollar, the second hole is worth two dollars. If the second is tied, the third hole becomes worth three dollars.

But when the pros play a Skins Game, there are two big differences. Number one, the money they play for is not their own—it's provided by the tournament organizers—and number two, that money is big: over a half million dollars. The payout for the PGA Tour pros is $20,000 for each of the first six holes, $30,000 for each of holes seven through 12, and $30,000 for each of the last six holes. Thus, on the off chance that each of the first 17 holes is tied, the four players go to the last tee playing one hole for $540,000—winner take all.

That never happens, but it's not uncommon for the players to tie five or six holes in a row, leaving $200,000 or more on the table for a single skin. In year two, Jack Nicklaus sank a putt on the last hole that was worth $240,000.

With that kind of cash available, The Skins is one game every Tour pro wants to play. But the selection of the four players is carefully controlled—a panel of media types chooses two of them, one is picked by the tournament organizers, and the final spot goes to the defending champion.

Critics argue that subsidized skins is something of a sham, as the players have nothing to lose, but this hasn't deterred the event from attracting consistently big ratings.

12th hole at Big Horn Golf Club

What to Watch For . . .

DEW SWEEPING
The Skins is a tape-delayed broadcast. It airs midafternoon on the East Coast but is played on the West Coast. In order for the show to be taped and edited in time for the broadcast, the competitors have to get their four balls off the tee on holes one (Saturday) and 10 (Sunday) by 8 a.m.

CHATTER
From year one, this event has exploited its made-for-television status. All four players wear remote microphones, and the TV audience listens in on their conversations.

AGGRESSIVENESS
Since every hole is a minitournament, all four players go all out all the time, firing boldly at every flagstick.

SPINOFFS
Shortly after the Skins' successful debut, the Senior Tour got a game going, just in time to accommodate Messrs. Palmer and Nicklaus. There's an annual LPGA Skins Game too, and both the European and Australian Tours have gotten into the act.

LAUGHTER SATURDAY, BUT NEVER ON SUNDAY
On the first tee of a Skins Game, there's a carnival atmosphere. All four players are delighted to be there, and they're all equal—no one has won a skin, and no one's behind. Lighthearted banter and ribbing usually characterize the Saturday telecast. By midway in the back nine, however, one player has invariably taken the lead and one or two have been shut out. Grim faces prevail.

PICKUPS
Once a player fails to tie the low score on a hole, there's no need for him to putt out. Each year, there is at least one hole when a player puts the ball in his pocket before ever reaching the green, then stands by, praying the other guys will tie.

Practical Matters

FOR TICKET INFORMATION
OCC Sports
962 N. LaCienaga Boulevard
Los Angeles, CA 90069

Lincoln-Mercury Kapalua Invitational

KAPALUA RESORT
[PLANTATION COURSE]

Kapalua is about as close as a Tour pro can get to a working vacation. It's everything he's always wanted in a golf tournament—and less. Less hassle, less seriousness, less pressure.

It is here, and only here, that the pros get a chance to wear shorts in practice rounds, play goofy afternoon golf matches with their wives, and splash on the beach with their kids. There are no traffic jams, no press interviews to speak of, and virtually no autograph seekers to bug them. And they are ensconced at a place that has consistently earned *GOLF Magazine*'s Gold Medal as one of the finest golf resorts in the country.

Even the golf course is a refreshing change. Kapalua's Plantation Course was designed by Ben Crenshaw and Bill Coore, and the best word for it is big. Spread out on a hilly former pineapple field overlooking the sea, this is a course that favors Crenshaw's own game, with wide fairways (to accommodate tee shots that occasionally spray) and huge, undulating greens—a whopping 9000 square feet on average—that are easy to hit but tough to putt.

The Plantation also pays homage to Crenshaw's love for the links courses of Great Britain and Ireland. Most of the greens are unprotected by front bunkers and allow bounce-on approaches. This is a sensible design because the wind at Kapalua is virtually constant and usually strong. When the pros catch the 305-yard 14th hole downwind, there will be lots of sidewinding putts for eagles, and even the final hole—a par five of 663 yards—becomes reachable, since most of those yards are downhill and usually downwind. On Sunday, sponsoring Lincoln-Mercury offers a free car to the player who can strike his second shot closest to the pin. Just another perk for the pros in Paradise.

11th hole

What to Watch For . . .

PRIME TIME LIVE
Since Hawaii's time zone is six hours behind Eastern Standard Time, the players rise at the crack of dawn, and even the leading groups make the turn into the back nine by noon, allowing viewers on the East Coast to watch the finish live in prime time.

BUTTERFLIES
The Kapalua Resort is famous for the success with which it has marketed its symbol—the butterfly. It's everywhere—on golf apparel, napkins, towels, soap, ballmarkers—they've even named an exotic drink after it.

FREDDIE & DAVIS
Laid-back superstars like Fred Couples and Davis Love III swear they'd never miss this event, and in 1992 they proved it by flying nearly 10,000 miles directly after winning the World Cup in Spain. Love won Kapalua that year, and Freddie took the title in 1993 and 1994.

GOOD NEWS AT THE GATE
This is golf's best deal. Tournament spectators are welcome at no charge—assuming, of course, that you can get yourself to Maui.

RIDING
The sprawling Plantation Course features some long walks between greens and tees. At one point a deep canyon intervenes, so to keep play moving, the pros are shuttled across in golf cars.

ROLFING GOLFING
ABC-TV golf commentator Mark Rolfing got his start here, as an assistant golf professional in the Kapalua shop. He rose to become the Director of Golf and then a part owner of the resort. It was Rolfing who launched this tournament, and he continues to have a big hand in it. He also competes here each year as a pro, usually finishing last or thereabouts.

Practical Matters

FOR TICKET INFORMATION
Kapalua Resort
Kapalua, Maui, HI 96761

PGA Grand Slam of Golf

VARIOUS COURSES

Four players—no more, no fewer —constitute the field for the PGA Grand Slam of Golf. Basically a re-creation of the original format of the World Series of Golf, it as-sembles the winners of the year's four major championships in a 36-hole shootout. As such, this is the hardest tournament to qualify for in all of golf.

It began in 1979, not long after the World Series expanded its field to in-clude winners of tournaments around the world. That year the Grand Slam wasn't very grand, as the winners of the previous year's majors competed lackadaisically for 18 holes and barely any prize money. There was much jok-ing, and short putts were routinely conceded as Gary Player and Andy North tied for first and never bothered settling things with a playoff.

For over a decade, it remained a rather casual affair. In most of those years, one or more of the qualifiers failed to play, opting instead to reap the spoils of major victory through exhibitions and invitations to lucrative events in the Far East.

Then, in 1991, the PGA made two changes that turned the show around. First, they expanded the event to 36 holes over two days, and second—and by far more important—they put up a $1 million purse. Since then, the Grand Slam has had perfect attendance.

Above: 1994 Competitors– José Maria Olazabal, Ernie Els, Nick Price, and Greg Norman

Left: 10th hole at Palmer Course/PGA West

What to Watch For . . .

NOT–SO–SORE LOSERS
With a million dollars to be divided up, the winner gets $400,000, but even the fourth-place guy goes home with $150,000—that's more than first prize in some events.

ALTERNATES
If, as was the case with Nick Price in 1994, one player wins two major championships in the same year, the PGA of America desig-nates an alternate based upon performance in the year's major championships.

NO DEFENDERS
This is one of the few events where victory does not guarantee a return trip.

Practical Matters

FOR TICKET INFORMATION
PGA of America
100 Avenue of the Champions
Box 109601
Palm Beach Gardens, FL 33401-9601

Merrill-Lynch Shootout Championship

VARIOUS COURSES

One of the first signs that the PGA Tour proper has concluded and golf's "silly season" has begun is the playing of the Merrill Lynch Shootout Championship. A classic made-for-television event, it is taped in September, edited in a New York studio, and broadcast later in the fall.

The Shootout brings together 10 prominent players for a competition over nine holes. All 10 guys play the first hole together, and the player with the highest score is dropped from the field. At hole number two, the remaining nine tee off and again the high scorer is eliminated. This continues until two players come to the ninth hole to determine the winner.

If two or more players tie for high score on a hole, they go into a sudden-death playoff where a pitch shot, a chip, or a long putt is executed to eliminate the player farthest from the hole.

The Shootout Championship is the granddaddy of a series of lesser shootouts that take place at tournaments throughout the year. Devised as a way to pump up interest and crank the turnstiles during the early part of the week, they take place on Tuesday afternoons, with the top players in the field given first option to participate. With only a few thousand dollars up for grabs, these are basically yuck fests for both the players and gallery. A light-hearted announcer such as Gary McCord emcees the proceedings, and the pros are encouraged to needle each other and play to the gallery as well as the hole. It's a chance for the fans to see them as something other than the faceless clones they're constantly accused of being.

These weekly shootouts also take place on the Senior Tour, where in 1994 they became the subject of controversy when it was learned that the players were "purse splitting," agreeing in advance to share the prize money from the shootout, no matter who won. The offenders were fined and the chicanery has ended.

For the year-end Championship, the carnival atmosphere lasts only for the first few holes, as this time the money is serious—$130,000 for first place, $80,000 for second, $55,000 for third, $40,000 for fourth, and $35,000 for fifth, with the last five places decreasing in $1000 steps to $30,000 for 10th place. Thus, along about the seventh tee the smirks are replaced by jut-jawed determination.

What to Watch For . . .

STAR POWER

You'd think that the players who do well in the weekly shootouts could earn their way into the Championship, but that's not the case. This, remember, is purely a television event, so to boost ratings the first three spots go to the top three players on the current PGA Tour Official Money List, and the remaining seven spots are chosen by the sponsors. Outgoing types such as Fuzzy Zoeller and Peter Jacobsen tend to be selected, just to keep the banter lively.

SPOILERS

Don't be surprised if, in reading *USA Today* or your local newspaper, you learn who won the Shootout weeks before it appears on TV. Despite exhortations by the Tour and sponsors to keep the results quiet, the press loves to leak such things. However, even if this happens, it's a safe bet that, by the time the show is aired, you'll have forgotten the results.

CHIP BECK & DAVIS LOVE III

These two players have each won the Shootout Championship twice since 1989.

PACKAGING

Since this is a show, not a tournament, it's heavily edited by the time it hits your screen. Expect to see only the best shots and hear only the funniest lines by the players. And remember, the announcers' patter is mixed-in after the fact, so if you pay close attention to their tone and syntax as a player stands over a shot, you can usually predict whether he'll pull it off or miss it.

5th hole at the Mid Ocean Club, Bermuda

Practical Matters

FOR TICKET INFORMATION

Dana Communications
2 East Broad Street
Hopewell, NJ 08525

Andersen Consulting World Championship of Golf

GRAYHAWK GOLF CLUB
[TALON COURSE]

L ate in 1994, the PGA Tour announced this, the geographically broadest, chronologically longest, and financially richest tournament in the game. In a series of single-elimination matches held around the world, 32 top players from the PGA Tour, PGA European Tour, Japan PGA Tour, Australasian Tour, and FNB Tour of South Africa vie for the game's richest purse— *$3.65 million.*

This is the only tournament involving each of the world's major sanctioning professional tours. And although it is the world's youngest major event, it is also the longest-running tournament in history, since it extends over ten months of the year, from early March, when first-round matches are played at four sites around the globe, through the semifinal and final matches at the end of December. The venue selected for the first finals was the Talon Course at Grayhawk Golf Club, a David Graham/Gary Panks design in the high Sonoran Desert north of Scottsdale, Arizona. The site will shift from year to year, and presumably will move among the four tours.

If the title "World Champion" isn't sufficient enticement, surely the money will attract the top players. The ultimate champion gets $1 million, runner-up is worth $500,000, and even first-round losers get $20,000.

What to Watch For . . .

THE THREE SEASONS
Each Tour conducts a preliminary round of four matches in the spring, featuring eight select players. The four first-round winners then move into a second round of match play, held during the summer. One day after the second-round matches, the regional title is settled, as the two second-round winners go head-to-head for the championship. The four regional winners come together in December to determine the overall world champion.

TV GALORE
An unprecedented 52 hours of U.S. coverage and more than 300 hours of international coverage, on ESPN and ABC in the United States and on a variety of networks around the world.

7 PLUS 1
The top seven ranking players from each Tour qualify for the first round of match play, but the eighth player is chosen by the sponsors. The defending champion is exempt from qualifying the following year and is seeded number one in his bracket.

EARLY-WEEK VIEWING
All preliminary and regional matches are played on Mondays and Tuesdays except those in Japan, which take place on Friday and Saturday.

11th hole

Practical Matters

FOR TICKET INFORMATION
Andersen Consulting World Championship
1100 Spring Street
Suite 600
Atlanta, GA 30309

Acknowledgments

THIS BOOK HAS BEEN A HIGHLY COLLABORATIVE EFFORT. THE WORDS ARE MINE, but words are just one element of *Golfwatching,* which was designed from the beginning to be a highly visual, fast-paced book.

Three diversely talented artists have enlivened the pages with their work. The "Local Knowledge" tips were illustrated by renowned sports artist Jim McQueen, a staff illustrator for *GOLF Magazine* and a contributor to dozens of books on golf and other subjects. Each of the PGA Tour chapters features hole-by-hole diagrams by *GOLF Magazine* Art Director Ron Ramsey, as gifted an artist as he is a designer. And the whimsical cartoons that depict statistical facts are the inspired creations of Trevor Johnston, a member of the *Los Angeles Times* computer graphics department. I am extremely grateful to these men for their superb work.

Befitting the international scope of this book, the photographs are from all over the world. Most of the action photos came from PGA Tour staff photographers Sam Greenwood, Stan Badz, and Pete Fontaine, while the bulk of the scenic shots were taken by John Johnson. Mike Klemme and *GOLF Magazine* staff photographer Fred Vuich also made important contributions.

This is the only book that rates each of the PGA Tour events according to both course difficulty and overall prestige. Those ratings are the result of a pair of formulas developed by *GOLF Magazine* Senior Editor David Barrett, who also generated the special statistical items for the book. (All statistics are current through April of 1995.)

Countless tournament administrators contributed their time and knowledge, supplying everything from course yardage to green fees to pro shop phone numbers. PGA European Tour Commissioner Ken Schofield offered valuable insights on his most important events, as did Communications Director Mitchell Platts, while Japan's leading golf journalist, Sadao Iwata, was extremely helpful on the Japan PGA Tour events.

With up to a dozen or more visual and textual elements in each chapter, *Golfwatching* was an uncommonly difficult book to design, but the man who designed it, Larry Hasak, is an uncommonly talented designer. I am indebted to him for making everything come together so attractively.

Finally, for bringing the book expertly to press, I owe thanks to "the great triumvirate" at Harry N. Abrams, Inc.: Senior Vice President and Executive Editor Margaret L. Kaplan, Photo Editor John K. Crowley, and Production Vice President Shun Yamamoto.